# ANCESTRAL VOICES IN IRISH POLITICS

*To Jo, Lara, and Evelyn*

# ANCESTRAL VOICES IN IRISH POLITICS

*Judging Dillon and Parnell*

PAUL BEW

OXFORD
UNIVERSITY PRESS

## OXFORD
### UNIVERSITY PRESS

Great Clarendon Street, Oxford, OX2 6DP,
United Kingdom

Oxford University Press is a department of the University of Oxford.
It furthers the University's objective of excellence in research, scholarship,
and education by publishing worldwide. Oxford is a registered trade mark of
Oxford University Press in the UK and in certain other countries

Published in the United States of America by Oxford University Press
198 Madison Avenue, New York, NY 10016, United States of America

British Library Cataloguing in Publication Data
Data available

Library of Congress Control Number: 2023933548

ISBN 978–0–19–287370–5

DOI: 10.1093/oso/9780192873705.001.0001

Printed and bound in the UK by
Clays Ltd, Elcograf S.p.A.

# ACKNOWLEDGEMENTS

I feel a certain affinity for these two men. My mother, Mary Leahy, was educated at the same medical school in Dublin as Dillon and her family home in Charleville, Co. Cork, was called Avondale after Parnell's home in Wicklow—an act of homage from the Irish strong farmer class, the great victors of Parnell's revolution. I was myself a student at the same university as Parnell and was indeed, in 1996/7, Parnell Fellow at Magdalene College, Parnell's old college. I have spent the last fifteen years as an Irishman active in the Westminster Parliament, stopping from time to time to study Parnell's bust and the numerous paintings and drawings which evoke this era. This is precisely as long as Parnell spent in Westminster, though it is, of course, less than the thirty-six years spent by John Dillon. Parnell cast his eyes up from the chamber to his lover Mrs O'Shea; Dillon was to be embarrassed when his child cried out 'Daddy' from the family gallery.

But a sense of personal affinity is frankly not enough for the production of a serious history. My debts in the world of scholarship are profound: Roy Foster who has worked so brilliantly in his field is one such debt. I owe much to the late Perry Curtis, George Boyce, and Alan O'Day. For the coverage of British Liberalism I owe a great deal to Professor Jonathan Parry and Vernon Bogdanor. Above all, however, is the debt owed to Dr Patrick Maume of the Royal Irish Academy who has read the manuscript twice and is simply the greatest Irish research scholar of his generation. His advice has been of great importance to me. But of even greater importance is his example, his willingness to enter the minds of different varieties of Irishmen—whether radical republican or loyalist unionist, Catholic or Protestant—and write with sympathy and understanding in those hundreds of entries which are the glory of the Royal Irish Academy's *Dictionary of Irish Biography*.

In the case of this book, however, I have a new debt to pay. Professor Ged Martin, a Parnell scholar of note for many decades, has been publishing new material on Parnell in his *Martinalia* blog in recent years. He has brought out Parnell's profound concern with the development of Ireland's material and economic resources in a way that no other scholar has. I hope to have added some new elements to that analysis but the original insight is that of Professor Martin; even if I have not always accepted his interpretation at every point, I have been heavily influenced. I have argued for some years that Parnell had a more conservative element to his thought than his first classic biographer R. Barry O'Brien allowed. But this argument has to be linked to Professor Martin's thesis to create a full, rounded picture of Charles Stewart Parnell.

John Dillon, on the other hand, unquestionably was a radical liberal as well as an Irish nationalist. Here the interpretative gaps lie in the discussion of radical agrarianism and the remarkable link with British Liberalism to explain the full dimension of his conflict with Parnell throughout the 1880s. This book is an attempt to piece the relationships between the two great leaders at the centre of the interpretation of Anglo-Irish relations from 1878 to 1918. In this epoch Dillon, despite a great achievement in the field of educational reform, wrestled unsuccessfully with the issues posed by the legacy of the late Parnell.

# CONTENTS

# FOREWORD

Our Ministers labour under the delusion that the Treaty was won by physical force. What was the extent of our physical force? The capture of probably undefended police barracks and a fight, admittedly a good fight, against a motley army of Black and Tans. But did not Michael Collins himself admit that the Irish forces, so brilliantly led or helped by him, could not stand out more than two or three weeks longer had not the Truce been arranged? The last shot in the long battle for our Freedom was, no doubt, fired by Sinn Fein, but in truth the battle was already won by the Irish Party, led by Parnell [and] ... Dillon.

William O'Malley (MP for Connemara 1895–1918), 'John Dillon',
*Roscommon Messenger*, 13 August 1927.

Anyone who seeks to write Irish history in the twenty-first century has no choice but to work with the framework established by two decisive choices made by the people of Ireland in the twentieth century. Oddly enough, they were both in their way retrospective validations. The first was the decisive victory of Sinn Fein in the 1918 general election, which retrospectively validated the Easter Rising of 1916. This was a strong democratic statement in favour of an independent Ireland. The second retrospective validation was the referenda held, north and south, at the time of the Good Friday Agreement in 1998. This in turn was a strong democratic endorsement of the principle of consent in Northern Ireland; in other words, that Irish unity would require the consent of a majority of the people of Northern Ireland.

Of course, both the 1918 general election and the Good Friday Agreement had other cognate meanings some of which are the subject of legitimate debate—but the lead point of both popular decisions is undeniable. The 1918 general election was the final eclipse of the Union: the hope that Ireland and the rest of the UK might become 'one people', one imagined community. It was the defeat—always likely since the mid 1880s—of high Unionism. But the 1998 referenda were in their way equally decisive for mainstream Irish republican nationalism, which had always insisted that partition could have no democratic legitimacy.

It is no longer possible to consider the careers of major Irish political figures such as John Dillon and Charles Stewart Parnell without taking these realities into account. Both Dillon and Parnell lived within, respected, and felt the great mass of historical resentment which fuelled Irish nationalism. Both were fully aware of the elements which constituted the passions which fed into that movement. Dillon, for most of his political life, was more unrelenting than Parnell in conveying militant, aggressive messages. Both at a certain point, however, took steps to modify the tone.

In 1891 in Belfast, Parnell authored his famous conciliatory speech on the subject of Ulster Unionist opposition to Home Rule. John Hume utilized it in his dialogue with Sinn Fein—a key moment in the peace process which led to the Good Friday Agreement in 1998.[1] In 1914, at a key moment in the 'Ulster crisis', John Dillon told Tim Healy that 'our' record (that is, the Irish nationalist record) against coercion logically implied that it would be impossible to impose coercion on the Ulster Unionists. Both men, then, for all their flaws, were architects of the Irish political system as it exists today, even though they had exercised their principal influence before the foundation of an independent Irish state or, indeed, a devolved arrangement in Northern Ireland. They operated at almost all times under the pressure of constant political turbulence.

# 1

# Hereditary Patriotism

He [John Dillon] appears from his youth upwards to have imbibed a
hatred against the landlord system of Ireland, and now he feeds fat his
grudge.

Sir Richard Temple, *Letters and Character Sketches from the
House of Commons* (London, 1912), 177.

He [C. S. Parnell] did not desire the 'extinction of landlordism,' and
would probably have been a restraining and moderating force in an
Irish legislature.

James V. Bryce, *Studies in Contemporary Biography*
(London, 1903), 246.

Charles Stewart Parnell (1846–91) and John Dillon (1851–1921) entered
Irish politics in the same historical 'moment' of the mid 1870s: Irish
politics was defined by the marked failure of the insurrectionary Fenian
movement in 1867. But this failure had not destroyed the movement in
one important sense: its activists remained the most organized force in
Irish politics with a capacity to challenge both clerical elites and constitutional politicians whether of Liberal or moderate nationalist complexion. Both Parnell and Dillon in the eyes of the British press were
typical of the Irish tradition of political leadership which contained
'numerous examples of hereditary patriotism'.[1]

They both came from privileged, entitled Irish backgrounds, and
neither felt it necessary to be particularly diligent students—at
Magdalene College, Cambridge in Parnell's case[2] or the Royal College of
Surgeons in Dublin in John Dillon's.[3] Nevertheless, they were from very
different backgrounds. If we take as our frame of reference the last

*Ancestral Voices in Irish Politics: Judging Dillon and Parnell.* Paul Bew, Oxford University Press.
© Paul Bew 2023. DOI: 10.1093/oso/9780192873705.003.0001

decade of the eighteenth and first four decades of the nineteenth century there is no doubt that the Protestant Parnells are much better known than the Catholic Dillons. But matters begin to change in the 1840s when John Blake Dillon (John's father) became one of the more impressive leaders of the 1848 Young Ireland revolt in Ireland: he then reconstructed himself in exile as a successful lawyer in America. Finally, Dillon returned to Ireland to pursue a successful career as a Catholic Liberal MP, much admired by, for example, John Bright.

As for Parnell, the mainstream nationalist journal of the day, *The Freeman's Journal*, opined: 'His family's history is imprinted on the brightest page of Irish history.'[4] Parnell's great-grandfather, Sir John Parnell, was in the late eighteenth century the Irish Chancellor of the Exchequer. Parnell seems rather to overstate his great-grandfather's 'patriotism',[5] implying that Sir John's sympathies lay with the United Irish rebels of 1798. But, as Professor Roy Foster has shown, he was equivocal in his support of Catholics, capable of playing the Orange card and no exponent of 'high souled' patriotism. However, Sir John's sons definitely supported the cause of Catholic emancipation. In his 1815 book, *Parliamentary Portraits*,[6] Thomas Barnes acknowledged Henry Parnell's bravery in pushing the unpopular cause of Catholic emancipation in Westminster: 'it is impossible not to admire his cool perseverance in uttering what nobody seemed inclined to hear.' Sir Henry became a successful Whig technocrat politician serving in the Grey cabinet and becoming close to Thomas Telford, the great engineer. In 1841, he was created Baron Congleton but in 1842 he committed suicide. The grandfather of Charles Stewart Parnell was William Parnell. An even stronger advocate of Catholic emancipation, his books—definitely known to his grandson—advocated reform and Protestant–Catholic reconciliation.[7] Parnell's father, John, had an equally benign relationship with the local Catholic community in Wicklow, but he did not add to the lustre of the family name in such a distinctive way. He was in some ways rather more typical of the mainstream Anglo-Irish gentry of the period. 'Unlettered' and 'uncultured'[8] said Frank Hugh O'Donnell MP, a close colleague of Parnell in the 1870s, both of the Parnell family and the gentry more widely. The library at Avondale was well stocked but very few books seem to have been added in the 1850s, 1860s, or 1870s. In the *Contemporary Review* of 1882, Professor Mahaffy of Trinity College Dublin sadly recorded that the Irish gentry had no ambitions: beyond 'something with a rod or gun'.[9] W. J. O'Neill Daunt recorded that 'they—the gentry have not an idea beyond "this is a fine day," or "that is a good dog" or "will you have a drink?"'[10] Arthur Baumann was moved to think of Charles Lever's picaresque, rollicking novels of Irish gentry life when he contemplated John Parnell: 'Parnell's father lived like an Irish squire before the Lever traditions became extinct, in the open air and with an open house.'[11] John Parnell, a former captain of cricket at Eton, died in 1859. His son, John Howard Parnell, believed this was because he had ignored medical advice in his enthusiasm for cricket and could not resist playing in a big match between the Leinster and the Phoenix Clubs.[12]

This hardly compared with John Blake Dillon's career at this time—or, indeed, the Dillon family's steady rise out of the Catholic strong farming classes into the more entrepreneurial section of the Irish bourgeoisie just as the Parnells in the 1870s seem to have become, if not poorer, at least not much richer. John Dillon liked to say he was the grandson of an evicted tenant. As his father's biographer, Brendan Ó Cathaoir, put it, 'this colourful generalisation obscures the reality of considerable family resources even in the 18th century'. Luke Dillon, John's grandfather, held approximately 150 acres at Blenagh-bane, a substantial farm in Mayo. Brendan Ó Cathaoir argues that Luke Dillon gave up on an unattractive lease in exchange for a new and successful career as a merchant keeping a large shop in Ballaghaderreen, where he was also postmaster in 1834.[13] His seven children all had comfortable lives. In particular, his son John entered the Protestant academic citadel of Trinity College in 1834, registering as a son of Luke Dillon, *agricola defunctus*: a revealing phrase which reflects John Dillon's move into a new and broader world and suppresses the degree to which his family had accumulated money and property. It would not be quite correct to say that the Parnells were downwardly socially mobile as a perfect contrast to the way the

Dillons were upwardly socially mobile, but it is worth noting that John Parnell achieved little personal renown but John Blake Dillon's success at the American bar was noted across the Atlantic with respect:[14] this quite apart from John Blake Dillon's status as one of the unblemished revolutionaries of 1848. Perhaps it is worth noting also that John Dillon eventually lived in the beautiful house in North Great George Street, Dublin (the Irish Bloomsbury, it was said) which had once been the home of Sir John Parnell.[15] The Dillon family business in Ballaghaderreen, run by his cousin Mrs Deane, was not a small town business, rather a substantial province-wide business concern.[16] It survived until the 1980s.[17] In 1902, John Dillon formally became a director—although other Irish members such as Swift MacNeill believed Irish MPs should not be directors of businesses.[18] Or, put another way, by a fellow nationalist MP and once a 'staunch friend and supporter',[19] Jasper Tully, 'he is dug in as the head gombeen man of the West'.[20] It was a commonplace of a certain type of Irish social commentary to say that the landlord may have owned the land, but the 'gombeen man', as rural moneylender, owned the body of the tenant. The Parnells always seemed somehow more unstable—living on the edge perhaps: suicides, unhappy and broken marriages constituting a kind of family norm. John Dillon's descendants played a distinguished part in Irish political and academic life:[21] Parnell's grandson was reduced to visiting Avondale as a somewhat wistful and melancholy tourist.[22] His flamboyant sister Emily's 'wild child' refusal of Victorian norms for sexual behaviour was blunt: she died in broken-down poverty. The Parnells did not use the word 'madness' lightly, Parnell told William O'Brien.

The fractured nature of the Parnells as a family somehow created an openness to Catholic Ireland. Parnell was very close to Susan Gaffney, the long-time housekeeper at Avondale.[23] He fully accepted the local Irish peasant lore imbibed from her on the appropriate cures for various ailments and cuts; to the point of being actually dangerous in his credulity. His sister Anna loved to ride with the Comerford girls, the daughters of the local rich Catholic miller and, like Anna, excellent on a horse.[24] The Parnells were not a family who rubbed along together. Passionate sibling alliances—as with his sister Anna—could turn, if things went wrong, into frozen coldness.

At first sight, Parnell inherited his father's philistinism. James Bryce was correct to say of Parnell that he did not care for the things which men of his educational level usually cared for. In particular, he had no profound interest in literature, fictional or non-fictional. He wrote on 2 April 1886 to the *Freeman's Journal*, when invited to give his views on the 'Best Hundred Irish Books' that 'I do not feel that [my] opinion need be of much weight', and gave no personal choice, though others selected works by his grandfather and grand-uncle.[25] But he was fascinated by *Macbeth* and *Alice in Wonderland* and, contrary to T. P. O'Connor's suggestion,[26] he knew something of the works of Thomas Moore. He was intrigued by Dickens. O'Connor did note that Parnell read *The Engineer* avidly and his wife noted his affection for books on mechanics. Nobody, however, would ever say of Parnell, as was said of John Dillon: 'He is an excellent scholar, being equally at home among the classics of England, Spain and Italy. He has five languages apart from his mother tongue at easy command.'[27] William O'Brien says that when conversation in the Irish party turned to an abstract literary or cultural topic, Parnell preferred to discuss hunting (the Curraghmore hounds in Waterford) with Dick Power or the improvement of Irish harbours with James Gilhooley.[28] Tributes to Dillon's excellent and well-read library are legion if not universal[29]—by 1915 Herbert Vivian recorded that the piled-up books, including blue books (parliamentary enquiries) and press cuttings, reached the ceiling in Dillon's elegant Dublin home. But Parnell's most passionate interests beyond politics were in science and its practical applications: when Parnell appeared in the smoking room of the House of Commons in company with a stranger, 'as often as not', it was not a 'patriotic project' but the potential use of science which explained the new face.[30]

In this respect, he and Dillon had a connection. Dillon, like Parnell,[31] was considered to be a promising mathematician at university;[32] though Dillon later switched to medicine. It is worth noting that Dillon did, at least, share some of Parnell's interest in modern science. He certainly opposed Irish Catholic hostility to science, sometimes seen as Irish Protestant science. One of the bugbears of Irish Catholicism was the Irish scientist William Tyndall. As a medical student in Dublin at the Royal College of Surgeons, Dillon was, however, engaged by Tyndall's address, delivered before the British Association for the Advance of Science at Belfast in 1874. Tyndall had argued for a naturalistic view of human evolution, eschewing divine intervention. At this point, Tyndall seemed to lift up his head and address the religious leaders of Ireland: 'It is perfectly possible for you and me to purchase intellectual peace at the price of intellectual death.'[33] The young John Dillon agreed with Tyndall on this point. Dillon decided to raise his concerns about Catholic obscurantism with the recently formed Literary and Historical Society of the Catholic University. In his speech, he asked: 'What can it avail to keep a student in ignorance of such theories as those of Darwin, Huxley and Spenser when, on leaving University, he must find the intelligent atmosphere full of the opinions and writing of these men? Is it not likely that he will look with contempt on the teachers who made it part of their task to keep him in ignorance of much that is true and wonderful while they professed to offer every kind of knowledge?' Subsequently, Dillon felt compelled to write to the *Freeman's Journal* disclaiming any intention to attack the Catholic university—he was in fact a great admirer of its leading spirit, Dr Henry Newman[34]—but he had made his point.[35] Both men, therefore, had a positive interest in science. Parnell was unmoved by the conventional Irish Catholic dismissals of Tyndall.[36] He acknowledged the comfort the Catholic faith gave to Irish peasants: 'The Irish peasants' faith makes him a happier man under his thatch than any man of science can be.'[37] But he insisted that the only 'immortality a man had was through his children'.[38] Parnell became a great admirer of Tyndall's fellow Darwinist and Irish unionist colleague, the astronomer Sir Robert Ball.[39] Parnell, in essence, was, philosophically speaking, a cultural materialist; Dillon, while very interested in modern science, never broke with a specifically Catholic spirituality. This did not mean any refusal of intellectual debate. In the same spirit, Dillon's later wife, Elizabeth Dillon, was prepared to attend Huxley's famous 1893 Romanes lecture 'Evolution and Ethics' but found it no serious obstacle to her profound Catholic convictions.[40]

Parnell was, at first sight, an unlikely nationalist. He was said to have had an ancestor on William III's side at the Battle of the Boyne and not a drop of Celtic blood. He was a landlord, an officer in the Wicklow militia, a Wicklow High Sheriff, and a synodsman of the Church of Ireland. His mother added an inconsistent but definite streak of American Anglophobia but she was also anxious at times for the approval of the English establishment. The Parnells, important as they were, were not the dominant local family—that honour fell to Lord Fitzwilliam at Coollatin Park. C. S. Parnell was later to tell Henry Labouchere that his American mother found this social hierarchy unendurable.

> Although her husband was Deputy-Lieutenant, a High Sheriff and of the same stock as Lord Congleton, she felt, as she said, 'like a mean white' at county gatherings where there were Wentworths, Brabazons, Moncks, Howards and Wingfields. Her relative inferiority made residence at Avondale unendurable. It also led her to deny the alleged perfection of the British constitution, when her children were being taught by their father to revere it as a monument of ancient wisdom.[41]

With some pleasure, her son, even while he noted Lord Fitzwilliam's comfortable tenantry, did not join the Land League, observing that Fitzwilliam was somewhat miserly[42]—as it happens, a traditional theme of the Parnells.[43] But it is necessary to add a note on the finances of the Parnell family. It is now clear that even while a student at Cambridge he was constrained by a lack of funds.[44] There was no real improvement in the 1870s: Parnell family fortunes were in an unimpressive state and new means of making money had to be found. It is obviously correct to insist that Parnell was a landlord as he certainly was one. But nationalists knew that he was not a 'wealthy man', with an income of £1,500 a year in the late 1870s:[45] in part, this is why Parnell's willingness to lay out such money as he had for a political career rather impressed them.

Parnell was the object inevitably of much landlord hostility and he was reluctant to return it in kind. But this conclusion did not lead him to a simple acceptance of an unqualified social transformation. Parnell (however) appears to have believed that the socially *déclassé* and down-market nature of his Irish party was an obstacle in the way of Westminster granting Home Rule. He told Andrew Kettle, 'the men I would like to have won't come'; Kettle replied in agreement: 'England could not afford to delegate the governing powers of Ireland into the hands of any class other than that ruling England at that time.'[46] He devoted much attention to the way in which the land question related to the Home Rule cause; while he often criticized rather brutally the Irish landlord class for their short-sightedness, he was always on the lookout for settlements which gave them a soft landing in material terms. He believed that once the aggravation over rent was settled the landlords as individuals had an important role to play in Irish society. It was a theory which, regardless of its practicality, greatly reassured English politicians, in particular, Gladstone in the years after May 1882: it even reassured some leading Tories like Randolph Churchill. But he never believed in the possibility of a reinvigorated hegemonic Irish landlord class. He accepted fully that the vast global increase in the areas coming under cultivation combined with the transport revolution posed profound challenges for the weaker sectors of European agriculture, in particular in Ireland. He was also perceptive about the democratizing impact of electoral reform on late nineteenth-century Britain. These two developments, combined with the intrinsic ethno-religious divide in Ireland itself, implied the collapse of the old order. After all, Parnell's brother was in the business of sending iced peaches from Alabama to London. Parnell himself, with his passion for assaying minerals, always had an eye for possible business ventures linked to his estate. We should not think of Avondale as a rural idyll defined by Moore's poetry. In Parnell's youth, the Vale of Avoca had seen a deterioration of the local ecology:

'The purest of crystal' is sullied by water pumped from lead and copper mines. 'The brightest of green' has been effaced by the mounds of rubbish which the miners cast up.[47]

Parnell did not believe in the possibility of a bucolic prosperous Irish peasantry supporting his family by paying rent into a long-term stable future; this vision simply was not his imagined community for the future of his country. Whatever else might be said of Parnell, he did not have the mentality of a 'rent-seeker'.[48]

Parnell's imagined community of 'a new Ireland' was composed of a prosperous countryside of families with money in their pockets and incentives to improve new holdings, an Ireland governed through a local legislature empowered to encourage native industry[49]—a prosperous, industrious tenantry tilling land to the highest possible degree and on route to the ownership of their farms.[50] But in this imagined community, his 'own people' had a role to play. Parnell was an entrepreneur who happened also to have inherited a financially unsustainable landed estate. Once he is identified as a manufacturer and retailer of construction materials—sawn timber and stone for building—then his political trajectory makes entire sense. As Andrew Kettle says, he was keen to show visitors to Avondale his sawmills and his stone and other mineral materials on the estate. His primary motivation was to extend the legal rights and thereby the broader ambitions of his customers, actual and potential. In the traditional vocabulary of Irish history, this meant tenant right. For cultural and political reasons, this was closely woven with the demand for legislative independence—Home Rule. This did not imply a radical hostility to his own class. As Andrew Kettle, his loyal ally, put it: 'He was always very hopeless about the older landlords ever throwing in their lot with the people of Ireland but he expected that the young men would if the land question was settled by purchase.'[51]

Even though they shared political platforms together, Parnell and Dillon were hardwired in very different ways. It is important to record this, because their speeches were sometimes superficially identical in content—hostility to the British government and demand for an Irish legislature being at the heart of both men's rhetoric. But there is a definite sense in which Dillon's connection to the real suffering Ireland was a lot more obvious and telling than Parnell's. Dillon might have been a child of prosperous Catholic Ireland but he was, nonetheless, a child of Catholic Ireland with all its historic memory of defeat and oppression. John Dillon's roots in Catholic Ireland were undeniable. Frank Callanan has correctly noted that 'Dillon's nationalism was even at its most apparently populistic marked by a certain hauteur'.[52] One parliamentary colleague, T. P. Gill, noted that when Dillon spoke of the Irish as 'my people' he gave the phrase a certain patriarchal significance. When Parnell spoke of 'my people' it was more usually an invocation of a narrower group—the Parnell family or a connected social grouping—and noted as such.[53] Somehow this became dramatized around their respective physical appearances. Many sensed that Parnell was motivated by a displaced sense of family pride. 'Like most shy men with a frigid manner, Parnell was full of family pride.'[54] Parnell was widely seen as identifying with the Irish people because the English ruling class did not know the importance of the Parnells of Wicklow—'how could we?' asked Alfred Baumann. But Dillon was perceived as not making an act of *identification* but rather one of *representation*. There was always a mystery about Parnell's complex motivation. The *St James's Gazette* said in this context, 'who can say he knows Parnell?' It is important, of course, not to engage in nominative or ethnic determinism. Take the case of another John Dillon, also descended from a Luke Dillon, at the receiving end of agrarian crime. This John Dillon was awarded £600 compensation for the brutal murder of his father, Luke, on 17 November 1881,[55] at Logboy, Ballyhaunis, Co. Mayo. Luke Dillon had been an agent to John Nolan Farrell.[56] John Dillon, just like Charles Stewart Parnell, *chose* to interpret the Irish past in a particular way.

Both were exceptionally good looking. A society hostess described Parnell: 'Mr Parnell's appearance was striking, he carried himself well with dignified bearing and had charming manners. There was no mistaking him for anything but a gentleman.'[57] The right-wing Tory Arthur Baumann wrote of Parnell: 'I sat opposite Parnell in the House of Commons for six years from 1885 to 1891; Parnell's head was the handsomest I ever saw resembling somewhat Leonardo's imagination of Christ, with short yellow beard and brownish hair.' After his glowing tribute to Parnell's beauty, Baumann remarked sardonically: 'Most Madonnas were painted from wantons.'[58] But nobody really disputed that these were two very good-looking men. T. P. O'Connor recalled Dillon at the age of 30: 'Painters and sculptors and men of letters raved about the beauty of his face, and especially of his eyes. Henry Holloway, the great artist in mosaics, chose him for one of the saintly figures in a window he had to make for a church. George Meredith glows over his eyes in one of his letters.' Thomas Cox Meech wrote of Dillon: 'If an Irish artist had roamed the world for an Irish patriot he could not have found a more picturesque model.'[59] One Unionist writer felt it necessary to protest: 'We are not carried off our heads by the personal appearance of Mr Dillon. We failed to see that his head is large and finely moulded, his features are chiselled with deep and fine lines, his eye is as keen as his features.'[60] Tim Healy, of course, went further, Dillon had a face, he said, like a 'sick raven';[61] adding later that the Irish party only kept him to attend funerals.[62]

Parnell's clothes in later years were frequently ill-fitting and contributed at times to a drooping appearance. 'Generally he wore a brownish cutaway, with trousers of Irish homespun, baggy at the knees.'[63] 'His clothes might have been put on with a pitchfork' it was said. Dillon was usually more dapper; Members of Parliament noted his taste in trousers.[64] James Myles Hogge, the Edinburgh Liberal MP, described John Dillon thus: 'He was a fine Radical, the colour of whose trousers varied from brick red to sunset…They all knew when he was on the warpath by the degree of brilliance of his trousers. These trousers were a political barometer.'[65] Dillon, Parnell later declared, was as 'vain as a peacock'.[66] It was also widely said—without firm evidence—that Parnell considered Dillon's brain to be as large as that of a peacock. Who was more comfortable in his own skin—*bien dans sa peau*? Parnell was proud and prickly in business matters. The young George Bernard Shaw, working as a clerk in a land registry office in Dublin, found him 'deucedly disagreeable'.[67] His brother, John Howard Parnell, has described how in the USA he missed the opportunity for an excellent business deal through sheer arrogance.[68] But, as Parnell put it to William

O'Brien, life was insufferable without the company of a woman, 'be she good or bad', and in the last ten years of his life he had that woman. Dillon was the more obviously neurotic—suffering bouts of ill health, especially when prison terms loomed, yet living in the end a very long life. Parnell was often aloof and careless of the social comfort of others. Nonetheless, tales of Parnell's expansive geniality when he was in the mood are extensive; for Dillon such tales are more rare (though not absolutely non-existent) and the private character rather more consti-pated. William O'Malley, a parliamentary colleague, noted: 'He was really a shy man and because of this many thought him cold and proud.'[69] Serjeant Sullivan observed simply of Dillon that 'in his younger days no man had in him more quiet and good natured fun' but his 'sense of humour atrophied'.[70] Despite being the object of much female ardour, Dillon avoided close contact with women until his happy marriage to Elizabeth Dillon in his mid forties. Temperamentally, he claimed to be stoic, largely dependent on his own emotional resources. There is a striking moment in Elizabeth's diaries of a discussion of John Mitchel's intense political career. Dillon observed: 'Happiness we must remember, must always be *within* a man, and need not depend on his surroundings. Mitchel found Van Diemen's land unbearable, but I question whether I myself would not have spent a happier life had I been these last five years in Van Diemen's land rather than in all this struggle.'[71] Was he perhaps also thinking of his own self-imposed political exile in Colorado in 1883–5? An 'English statesman' who admired Dillon greatly admitted that Dillon was 'certainly not gay or effervescent'.[72] The *Derry Journal* noted: 'Dillon had not the magnetic personality or winning ways of other Irish politicians.'[73]

But while observers saw Parnell as Anglo-Saxon and in a sense dom-ineering, they saw John Dillon as Celtic and passionate. Parnell was per-ceived to be difficult to 'read'; Dillon, on the other hand, supposedly presented no such difficulties of interpretation. On their joint American tour in 1879/80, an American mentor of the audience put it this way: 'Parnell didn't impress me a bit. When I saw this sleek young dude, as well fed as you or I and a damn sight better groomed, I said to myself:

"The idea of sending out a man like that to tell us they are all starving!" But when the other man, poor Dillon came along, with hunger written on every line of his face, I said, "Ah! that's a different thing. There's the Irish famine right enough." '[74] But this was not just a matter of Dillon's more emaciated frame as compared to that of Parnell. The fact is that Dillon presented as, in some sense, not just as evocative of 'the Irish famine right enough' but the broader trend of Irish history.

It is important to recall the widespread historical view of the nineteenth century: that the original inhabitants of Ireland were supposed to be a fragment of the Celtic tribes expelled from Spain.[75] In fact, the view of the Irish as Milesians from Spain had been popularized by Geoffrey Keating in the seventeenth century. Here the Spanish looks of the Dillons, father and son, comes into play. It was commonplace to note that John Dillon's father also had a 'sombre, Spanish visage'.[76] Sir Charles Gavan Duffy said of John Blake Dillon: 'He was tall and strikingly handsome with eyes like a thoughtful woman's and the clear olive complexion and stately bearing of a Spanish noble.'[77]

In this respect, it was a matter of like father, like son, as Dillon inherited his father's appearance. It was not simply that he was considered to be good-looking, but good-looking in a particular way. William O'Brien observed in 1875: 'a tinge of Spanish colour about the handsome features'.[78] He was considered to be handsome in a Spanish way and therefore Irish way: 'Very tall, very thin, with a long, thin face, coal-black hair and eyes, he was another who looked rather like a Spanish than an Irish figure'.[79] The *Spectator* magazine, observing Dillon from London with a rather more caustic political eye, nonetheless repeated the Spanish theme with respect: 'he, whom we should define if we were summing up his character as a rather good Spaniard of much ability who happened to live in Ireland'.[80] Dillon as he reached his seventies naturally became rather more gaunt in appearance; even so, Lady Gregory noted in 1922, 'Dillon looks impressive in his old age—an El Greco type.'[81]

It is clear that Dillon has not attracted any new biographer in fifty years: in fact, more generally he has attracted little biographical interest.

While men such as Tim Healy, William O'Brien, Michael Davitt, and John Redmond all attracted biographies shortly after their deaths,[82] Dillon did not. It may reasonably be said that the quality of the F. S. L. Lyons biography published in 1968 deterred future biographers, but Lyons's similarly impressive and lengthy biography of Parnell did not have such a deterrent effect. The other Parnellite lieutenants like William O'Brien,[83] Michael Davitt,[84] John Redmond,[85] and T. M. Healy[86] have recently attracted numerous biographies and book-length studies—ten substantial volumes in all. The educated reader of Irish history could easily get the impression that John Dillon is not that interesting—an impression reinforced by a certain personal stiffness in temperament not to be found amongst his colleagues in the Parnellite leadership. But nobody at the time doubted John Dillon's political importance and intellectual ability; nobody doubted that he was possessed of a certain quality of intense integrity. The fact that Dillon enjoyed more long-term influence at the apex of Irish nationalism than Healy, Davitt, or O'Brien did not improve his reputation in recent years. In his impressive book, *The Irish Parliamentary Party at Westminster 1900–1918*,[87] Dr Conor Mulvagh has insisted on what he calls the 'dominance of Dillonism' within the party leadership. Redmond may have been the public face of this movement but Dillon was 'a Richelieu type of figure' behind the scenes. The fact that Dillon was so much a controlling force and advocate for a policy which after all failed—both in terms of Irish unity and as a model of self-government—merely increased modern disdain. In 2019, in a major work of scholarship, Dr James Doherty, in his *Irish Liberty and British Democracy*, describes Dillon's politics as 'calamitously shortsighted'.[88]

In particular, the Northern Irish 'Troubles' (1968–98) provoked a new way of looking at the key figures in the nationalist pantheon. Michael Davitt became more attractive because of his interest in social justice, John Redmond in the 1890s and William O'Brien in the 1900s because of their willingness to support certain types of compromise with those outside the Catholic nationalist camp. Tim Healy became more interesting precisely because he was seen as the key figure in the articulation of a narrowly Catholic nationalism. Dillon fell outside all these categories, hence his unjust neglect.

As Dr Philip Bull has noted, those who wrote about 'Irish land against the background of Northern Ireland' tended to be impressed by William O'Brien's conciliatory approach after 1902. They tended not to be impressed by Dillon's opposition to O'Brien:

> On the nationalist side, the champion of conciliation, William O'Brien, was attacked and progressively undermined by those in his party who could not stomach the idea of cooperation with their 'hereditary enemy', leading eventually to his resignation from leadership positions and the triumph of the anti-conciliationists.
>
> ...The philosophy that contributed to these outcomes was one based on the absolute right of majorities even in a society where majorities and minorities did not fluctuate with the changing fortunes of political parties but were largely fixed by birth. The developments in the land question between 1898 and 1903 had moved some small way towards 'unfixing' this demographic determinism, but consequent abandonment of any real commitment to a civic polity that allowed for minorities as well as majorities was bound to end in confrontation and violence.[89]

C. P. Scott observed of Dillon that 'on social subjects and in foreign politics he is a keen and active liberal'.[90] Thomas Cox Meech noted that Dillon was rather more liberal than most of his countrymen: but that in any conflict between Irish nationalism and liberalism, liberalism would always come second. The issue of the relationship between Catholicism, nationalism, and liberalism is at the heart of Irish history. In fact, it can be reasonably stated that while the political significance of the Catholic Church is now in retreat, the nationalism–liberalism connection remains as important as ever. John Dillon is the point man for the actual working out of this relationship; indeed his father, John Blake Dillon, also had a distinguished career wrestling between liberal ideals of nationalism, ideals of liberal reform, and the appropriate public activity of a serious Irish Catholic. John Dillon, however, unlike his father, was to be a key part of the leadership of nationalist Ireland for thirty years during which its most central objectives were fulfilled—and yet he was left devastated by the final victory. Such a paradox surely compels a historical re-examination—not just of the role of opponents who blocked and three times imprisoned Dillon, but of the internal elements of his political belief system.

There were several moments of severe tension in the Parnell–Dillon relationship in the 1880s, before its final collapse in the divorce crisis of 1890/1. In the mid 1870s, John Dillon and his brother William made themselves power brokers in Irish politics. They reserved the right to decide who was serious or merely an adventurer. They reserved the right (understandably) to judge Parnell's sincerity: more importantly, they reserved the right to control his access to a parliamentary seat. In November 1879, John Dillon also reserved the right to criticize Parnell's land war rhetoric from an ostensibly more moderate and realistic point of view. In August 1880, Dillon openly censured Parnell's waning enthusiasm for obstructive tactics in Parliament. In 1881, Dillon tried to push Parnell to take revolutionary risks—Parnell rejected them. In May 1882, Dillon made a speech in the House of Commons so militant in tone that it threatened to smash up the nascent coalition between Parnell and Gladstone. Dillon then retired from Irish politics and left for Colorado. Then, in late 1885, shortly after his return to Irish politics, he visibly and tactlessly rhetorically challenged a relatively moderate Parnell speech in Kildare on the land question. At the end of 1886, Dillon launched a new phase of agrarian militancy, the so-called Plan of Campaign. It became clear that this 'plan' did not have Parnell's sanction—even more to the point, that Parnell was now focused on a more complex and essentially more moderate approach to the Irish land question. In 1887, Dillon incautiously and incompetently raised the role of the neo-Fenian activist P. J. Sheridan in Parliament over four days: the very last thing Parnell would have wanted at that moment. Parnell's connection with P. J. Sheridan, an organizer of violence, made him particularly vulnerable. In 1890—months before the divorce crisis itself—Parnell's desire to redefine the Irish land question became more and more obvious—to the dismay of his party colleagues, John Dillon in the lead, who were perfectly happy with its existing definition. Even before the divorce crisis, Parnell's willingness to flirt with the Tories rather than the Liberals on the Irish land question was clear. Related to this redefinition of the land question—in particular an insistence that its dimension was typically exaggerated—there was an increasingly focused Parnellite intention to reduce the weight of moral obloquy traditionally resting upon the Irish landlord elites in the south and west and from the more popularly based Protestant democracy in the north/east. John Dillon was at the heart of those who set their faces against this project: the defeat and death of Parnell in the divorce crisis not only resolved the issue of his chairmanship of the Irish party, but also confirmed the inability of official nationalism to face up to the social complexity of actually existing Irish society.

Parnell and, after Parnell's death in 1891, Parnellism as a political credo inevitably defined the larger part of Dillon's career. Since the publication of the Lyons biography in 1977, there has been a growing awareness of the degree to which Parnell's political thinking contained significant conservative elements. In particular, it has become clear that, as Francis Hackett put it, 'Parnell was amenable to liberal considerations but utterly immune from liberal sympathies.'[91] Dillon, on the other hand, was in thrall to liberal sympathies except, of course, where they conflicted with the Irish nationalist movement's immediate needs.[92]

When a strain of social conservation became increasingly visible in Parnell's thought after 1882, Dillon was unimpressed. Dillon remained supportive of another world view. Passion on the land issue gave vigour to Irish nationalism. There should be no mitigation of agrarian militancy: such militancy forced the Tory government into illiberal acts of repression which disgraced Britain's constitutionalist self-image. This, in turn, promoted the case for Home Rule. Dillon never really broke with this guiding concept for the next two decades, though in the final crisis of his career he began to question some of the results of this strategy.

In the five decades since the publication of the magisterial biography by F. S. L. Lyons, interest in John Dillon has, in effect, fallen away. In so many respects, the work of Lyons was admirable. But it did contain defects: neither the full scale of Dillon's connections with liberalism nor Irish agrarian radicalism was explored. Dillon's friendship with Liberal insider figures—John Morley and Sir George Fottrell—is not analysed and his relationship with his great grass-roots militant ally, Laurence Ginnell MP, is not even mentioned.[93] The point is not so much about neglected personalities as it is about the nature of Dillon's relationship with agrarian and radical nationalism in Ireland alongside his relationship with British Liberalism. Above all, his difficult relationship with the greatest Irish leader of the nineteenth century, Charles Stewart Parnell, has not yet been fully explored.

# 2

# John Mitchel and his Legacy

It is now twelve years since I first entered political life. At that time very few people in Ireland—not one in ten—believed in the efficacy of parliamentary action. The Fenian rebellion was only recently over and the idea widely prevailed that revolution was the only means of securing justice to Ireland.

C. S. Parnell, *Hansard*, 13 February 1888, vol. 332, col. 346.

The advanced nationalist party exert less influence over the current of public events in Ireland, less influence in determining the opinion of the world, as to Ireland's wants and wishes than its numbers would entitle it to, if it took its proper share in public life and was organised for public action.

John Devoy, 11 December 1878, quoted in Lord Robert Montague, *Recent Events and a Clue to their Solution* (London, 1886), 423.

The decade of the 1880s was a revolutionary decade in British party politics: corrosive of traditional political alignment. It saw the rise of conservative unionism in British politics and a decisive weakening of the Liberal party. At the same time, it was clear that a substantial modification of the Act of Union—the dissolution of which Lord Macaulay had declared to be as likely as the restoration of the Anglo-Saxon heptarchy—had entered the realm of practical politics: in fact, the Home Rule crisis after 1912 was to provoke serious reconsideration of a form of English heptarchy. Even following the election of sixty-one Home Rule MPs in 1874 and the repudiation of Gladstonian reform unionism of 1868–74, this was a sea change in political life no one had expected. The Home Rule party led by Isaac Butt contained a solid majority of moderate conciliatory and cautious men. The mood

*Ancestral Voices in Irish Politics: Judging Dillon and Parnell.* Paul Bew, Oxford University Press.
© Paul Bew 2023. DOI: 10.1093/oso/9780192873705.003.0002

changed, however, following the last apparently unavailing fling against the British Empire by a dying Irish revolutionist, the former Young Irelander, John Mitchel.

Mitchel insisted that the Irish famine (1846–50) should be seen as a British genocide. G. R. Kitson Clark saw the Young Ireland movement as a perfect expression of the 'romantic element' in politics: 'with its encouragement to vehemence and self-dramatisation'. But Kitson Clark also notes the 'misery' of the Irish peasantry and 'the obduracy with which redress seemed to be refused…[so that] men might come to believe that violence was the only resort'.[1] Mitchel had been the greatest hero of the radical wing of the 1848 movement; jailed and sent into exile in Australia, he escaped and rebuilt his life in America as a strong supporter of slavery and ultimately the South in the US civil war. 'We deny that it is a crime or wrong or even a peccadillo to hold slaves, or buy slaves, to sell slaves, to keep slaves to their work by flogging or other needful coercion.'[2] Mitchel insisted in 1848 that Britain would never accept any form of Irish tenant right, and as the decades passed his view of the hostile and inflexible nature of British Liberalism as well as Toryism did not change.[3] He remained, however, a symbol of proud patriotic nationalism: during the winter of 1872–3, he published a series of articles in the *Irish American* designed to refute James Anthony Froude, a leading anti-Irish imperialist historian.[4] In October 1873, the decision was taken in Dublin to launch a national testimonial for Mitchel which aimed at raising £2,000. Mitchel's brother-in-law, John Martin MP, and other Home Rule MPs such as P. J. Smyth (who rescued Mitchel from Tasmania) and J. P. Ronayne and Father Thomas Burke OP, who like Mitchel had polemicized against Froude, were all signed up as treasurers of the fund. The two secretaries were William and John Dillon.[5] In the general election of February 1874, Mitchel had stood as the abstentionist independent nationalist candidate for Cork City against J. P. Ronayne, his recent benefactor. Seven years later Parnell publicly recalled Mitchel's defeat—'a tiny minority of the electors of Cork City'. Parnell was quite correct: the winner, Ronayne, won 1,917 votes but Nick Dan Murphy, also Home Rule, won 1,643 and the Tory candidates won 2,288 votes, while Mitchel won only 511. Mitchel's supporters had tried to form a bloc with the entrepreneur Joe Ronayne, who had strong Fenian historic associations. But, for Ronayne, there was a key difficulty: 'I had honestly joined the Home Rule Association and John Mitchel was opposed to it [Home Rule], and I would be a dishonourable man, if I went back on what I said.' There were briefly stories of threats against Ronayne but they evaporated. This opened the way for Nick Dan Murphy, a clientelistic politician, to win the second Cork seat. Murphy's victory was 'a triumph of Irish clanship'.[6] He was not really a political leader but he did belong, it was said, 'to a family widely and justly respected in Cork'.[7] It had run the brewery and produced a bishop. Mitchel stuck to his ideological guns—at the end of 1874 he gave a lecture in New York criticizing the Home Rule movement.[8] But this did not mean that he was not willing to put his name forward again for election, when Tipperary—where he was believed to have a particular level of popularity[9]—provided a by-election opportunity. Tipperary had after all returned in 1874 the imprisoned revolutionist O'Donovan Rossa, who was then disqualified. On 3 February 1875 in New York, Mitchel, apparently not impressed by the disestablishment of the Anglican Church in 1869, issued his manifesto: 'I am in favour of Home Rule—that is, the Sovereign Independence of Ireland.' He added, 'I shall seek the total overthrow of the Established Church; Universal Tenant Right, and abolition of ejectments; free Education—that is, denominational education for those who like it, secular education for those who like that, with the express organic provision of law, that no person shall be taxed for the education of another person's children.'[10] The sense of excitement Mitchel generated was quite remarkable.

*John Mitchel*

I

You're coming home to Ireland, John Mitchel brave and true,
A hundred thousand welcomes are waiting here for you;
A nation's voice is lifted—a nation's heart beats high—
To welcome back the patriot who for her cause would die.

Now march in grand procession,
Fair maids and stalwart men,
To welcome brave John Mitchel
To Ireland back again.

## II

The glorious news has reached us, John Mitchel's coming home,
God send him safe to Ireland, across the ocean foam;
The people are rejoicing throughout the Irish land,
To greet the noble exile and grasp him by the hand—
In every town and city,
In every vale and glen,
They welcome brave John Mitchel
To Ireland back again.

## III

Ah! well do we remember the year of 'Forty-Eight,
That dreadful year of famine, of woes and troubles great,
When you for loving Ireland by British laws were tried,
But still with soul undaunted their terrors you defied—
Ah, then your friends might murmur,
The time is coming when
We'll never see John Mitchel
In Ireland back again.

## IV

When to your foes defiance you flung upon that day,
A jury to convict you they packed without delay;
They bound you as a felon, but never could they bind
Your tyrant-hating spirit, your freedom-loving mind.
For fourteen years transported,
'Twas grief to Irishmen
To think they'd see John Mitchel
In Ireland ne'er again.

## V

They sent you o'er the ocean, away to distant lands,
But true men sought and found you with friendship's ready hands.
Fond friends and faithful comrades, whom gold could never buy,

Assisted you from bondage to freedom's land to fly.
In freedom's cause you struggled,
With voice and sword and pen,
And now you've come, John Mitchel,
To Ireland back again.

VI

You're coming back to Ireland, we soon shall see your face;
We'll put you forward proudly to represent our race;
For you're the same John Mitchel that left us long ago—
The faithful friend of Ireland, and England's fearless foe.
You have not changed or faltered,
You're now the same as then;
Oh! may you live, John Mitchel,
Till Ireland's free again.[11]

This poem—probably written by T. D. Sullivan for the *Nation*, which his family controlled—is revealing in itself: apparently a full-throated hymn of praise. In fact, the Sullivan family, whilst deeply patriotic, had reservations about Mitchel's politics, but, at this point, saw no reason to articulate them.

On 6 February 1875, even before Mitchel arrived in Ireland, the Dublin correspondent of *The Times* of London reported: 'The deadlock which has long prevailed in Irish political life is at last disturbed and the storm signals are up to tell us that a fierce gale is coming.'[12] Colonel White, the sitting Tipperary MP, had announced his retirement: John Martin, Home Rule MP, immediately declared that John Mitchel, his brother-in-law and fellow '48 man, would come to Ireland from the United States to canvass in person and seek the seat. In an open letter to Charles Kickham, the distinguished author and leader of old school Fenianism, Martin declared himself to be honestly attached to the Home Rule cause. But he had to admit that John Mitchel in a recent lecture had opined it was 'impracticable to induce England to consent to a just and honourable settlement of her national quarrel with Ireland'. Nonetheless, Martin called for Tipperary to 'elect John Mitchel unquestioned, unpledged and trust to him to what he may deem right and best for the cause of Ireland'.[13] On 13 February, the Disraeli cabinet discussed 'what shall be done, when Mitchel the escaped convict claims to take his seat for Tipperary'.[14] Mitchel was the focus of popular respect to such a degree that he was elected a Member of Parliament for Tipperary on 16 February 1875. The emotional impact was profound. Marching bands flooded the streets of Cork city, where Mitchel had been rejected at the polls a year before. In Tipperary, public sentiment was even more unambiguous. In Mullinahone, for example, 'every window in the town was brilliantly illuminated last night and the poor people who had no windows managed to fix candles at their doors.' The reporter for the *Irishman* noted: 'I noticed one window in particular, it belonged to a mechanic—a '48 patriot. There were fourteen candles placed on an open window in his workshop.'[15] Mullinahone had been the home of Charles J. Kickham, novelist and chairman of the Supreme Council of the Irish Republican Brotherhood (IRB), the 'President of the Irish Republic' for years before his death in 1882, who supported Mitchel.[16] Kickham had, after all, narrowly missed election in 1869 in Tipperary. On 18 February, Parliament, led by the Prime Minister, Benjamin Disraeli, following the advice of his law officers, formally rejected the legitimacy of Mitchel's election on the specific ground that Mitchel was an undischarged felon having escaped to America from Van Diemen's Land, his place of exile. But not everyone at Westminster agreed with Disraeli.

One indicator of the mood of British liberalism is to be found in the parliamentary intervention of the Bradford MP W. E. Forster, who had been much engaged on famine relief in Ireland in the 1840s, a humanitarian and strong opponent of slavery. Forster clearly felt that Mitchel should be welcomed in the UK Parliament if he chose to take up his seat. He urged Parliament not to get caught up in petty legalism—*was Mitchel still a felon or not?*—at the least, it should appoint a committee to look at that issue. After all, his sentence could no longer be fulfilled as transportation to Australia had been abolished. But Parliament should bear in mind the broader political question—given the degree of alienation in Ireland, was it wise for Westminster to intensify it by refusing elected

Irish members a right to sit? Forster noted: 'remembering the feelings which, unfortunately, were held by many of their fellow subjects, he should be exceedingly loth that any Irish constituency more or less reluctant to join in the British Imperial Parliament, should find that the Member they did send from that constituency should be refused admission on any but the most distinct and decided grounds'.[17]

Scholars have seen Mitchel's victory as a blow against the Home Rule movement led by Isaac Butt. In the obvious sense that Mitchel had no trace of Butt's moderation, this is accurate.[18] It is true that Mitchel made 'Home Rule' (redefined as sovereign independence) his main slogan[19] though his call for the release of Fenian suspects still in jail after the 1867 rising was commonplace enough. Mitchel was not strictly speaking an abstentionist in the sense that he noted the improvement in the quality of Irish representation with the implication that this was a good thing. Immediately, after the election, Mitchel reminded everyone that he had not committed to go to Westminster. But, he added, he promised he would never betray Tipperary 'whether I go to London or stay home'.[20] William O'Brien, the young nationalist journalist who was also part of Mitchel's campaign, interpreted this to mean that 'Mitchel might attend to deliver a tirade against British rule but that he would not remain in the U.K. parliament'.[21] For young men entering politics it must have seemed as if Irish politics was tilting to the left. Mitchel had, after all, made it clear that for him 'Home Rule' meant complete independence.

Westminster looked on in amazement. Technically, Mitchel could have been arrested on the grounds that he had escaped rather than having been pardoned. But even *The Times* noted: 'His arrest however strictly legal would have been looked upon as a harsh and vindictive measure, not called for by the exigencies of policy and unworthy of the generous spirit of the British constitution.'[22] Mitchel, arriving in Ireland the day after his victory, declared: 'He did not know whether he would go to Westminster but he would help them make laws for their country as well as England and Scotland.'[23] On 23 February, Mitchel, sitting beside John Dillon, gave an interview to the *Manchester Guardian*: asked to compare the Ireland of 1845 with that of 1875, he replied that Ireland was 'even more disaffected' and this was due to the increased education and intelligence of the people. A week later John Mitchel presented his case at the Theatre Royal in Cork. He noted: 'It seemed that although a felon, they could not bring him to punishment. If a felon it was the duty of the government to arrest him. If not a felon, he was now the legal representative of Tipperary.'[24] He added decisively: 'his election was an emphatic *pronunciamento* concerning the relations between England and Ireland. These relations were as unsatisfactory as they were 30 years ago.' In other words, they were as unsatisfactory as they were on the eve of the famine.

Mitchel, in fact, was not well enough to deliver the text he had written. It was delivered by a young ally, John Dillon. It included a strong defence of slavery, a cause dear to Mitchel's heart. In the flush of the election victory, Mitchel was lionized in Dublin by Lady Wilde (mother of Oscar and herself a Young Ireland poet) and Father Burke, the Dominican scourge of the great narrative historian[25] J. A. Froude,[26] widely read and frequently, but not always, 'anti-Irish' in tone. Then, suddenly feeling ill again, Mitchel went quickly to Newry, his hometown, and family. A second election returned the ailing Mitchel on 11 March 1875. The seat was contested by a Tory who got far less support than Mitchel but successfully claimed the seat on the grounds that Mitchel's supporters had deliberately thrown away their votes on a candidate whom they knew to be ineligible. The *Irishman* noted that Mitchel's total of votes was almost double that of earlier republican electoral forays by O'Donovan Rossa and Charles Kickham. While there were some hopes that his health was improving, these proved to be baseless. He died within a few days—the only person present at the end who was not a member of the Mitchel family was John Dillon. He was not a pall-bearer but listed as a chief mourner at the funeral in Dromolane. This was not surprising—Dillon had essentially managed Mitchel's campaign. He handled Mitchel's correspondence with key figures like Richard O'Shaughnessy, the Limerick Home Rule MP.[27] He campaigned with visceral passion. In Mitchel's absence, Dillon had been effectively the most important speaker on his behalf:

'The question at present was, whether Mr Mitchel or the old Jewish novel writer [Disraeli] should triumph. Mr Dillon went on to describe the nomination papers for Moore, Mitchel's Conservative opponent. "They were blue-blooded Cromwellians every one, whose very names propose them to be 'settlement gentry'." (hisses).'[28] Interestingly, Dillon embraced Mitchel's unceasing revolutionism against his late father's greater moderation—something no doubt made easier by the personal respect, if not political agreement, John Mitchel always showed to John Blake Dillon.

Later it was to be said that Dillon's support for Mitchel was marked by strategic self-interest. One of the Mitchel circle, Dillon's friend, T. P. O'Connor of Laffane (not to be confused with T. P. O'Connor later to be MP for Liverpool), argued before the second Mitchel election that Dillon should be put in his place, as Parliament would once again bar Mitchel. Dillon sat silently as the issue was debated. Only the angry interference of the Limerick Fenian John Daly—who in 1895 as a Fenian prisoner was also elected to Parliament—crushed the scheme.[29] Interestingly, support for John Mitchel's candidature had brought Parnell and John Dillon together in a political cause for the first time. John Dillon's brother, William Dillon, initially thought that Parnell's offer of financial support for Mitchel was purely opportunistic. Nevertheless he advised his brother that in the end he came to view Parnell's action as sincere.[30] The irony of the moment was heavy. Parnell and his mother were strong supporters of the North in the civil war.[31] The youthful Parnell even talked of joining the Northern army. John Dillon's family associations were also all with the northern side. But here were two young men at the start of their Irish nationalist political careers embracing an unrepentant pro-slavery politician. In the case of John Blake Dillon's son, this extended to reading out Mitchel's pro-slavery screed to an audience in the Theatre Royal in Cork.

Mainstream Irish nationalism had opposed slavery and mocked Gladstone, the great English moralistic liberal, for his ambiguous record on the matter.[32] Father Patrick Kavanagh was not alone among Mitchel's admirers in being shocked by his brutal defence of slavery on the grounds that black people had no souls.[33] Mitchel's defence of the Irish cause is intimately linked to his defence of slavery. Both reflect his contempt for British liberalism—'the British Providence' as self-serving hypocrisy. He saw the South as a civilization founded on agrarianism and armed citizenship as opposed to British commercial civilization— of which the 'North' in America was seen by Mitchel as a compliant extension. Not the least significant element of Mitchel's support for slavery was the hope that it contained the basis for conflict between the Royal Navy and the US Navy. Blacks were inferiors who needed to be forced or compelled towards a higher state of life: in this Mitchel followed some celebrated Victorian writers (including Carlyle and Froude), but they also tended to believe that the same principle applied in some form to the Irish. Mitchel, of course, rejected this point and attacked Froude,[34] but inevitably, given the broad tendency of Irish nationalism— following in particular O'Connell's benign influence—to oppose slavery, his stance remained a troubling irritant even to his most profound admirers. Irish nationalists believed their cause morally superior to antislavery. As Tim Healy put it in his famous Boston speech of 1881 'Begone Saxon', 'I say that the property of the Irish landlords deserved to be abolished more than the property of the slaveholders.'[35] Nonetheless, they supported the cause of antislavery.

Why then was John Dillon, like so many other Irish nationalists in the 1870s, a votary of the John Mitchel cult? John Mitchel, a child of the liberal Ulster Presbyterian clergy with roots in the United Irishmen of 1798, gravitated well beyond those shores to become the most ideologically important and unrelenting Irish nationalist of the nineteenth century. One of the defining features of the United Irish, and more broadly liberal Presbyterian traditions from which Mitchel, emerged was its hostility to slavery; yet Mitchel broke decisively with that tradition. Like Dillon's father, John Blake Dillon, Mitchel was a brave Young Ireland revolutionary in 1848.[36] Like John Blake Dillon, he endured years of exile: like John Blake Dillon he was elected as an MP for an Irish constituency in later years. But here the similarity ends. John Blake Dillon found a dignified berth in the ethos of respectable Catholic

Ireland in the 1860s and cooperated with British Liberalism.[37] Mitchel struck out on a more radical path in 1848 and never deviated. He insisted that the Irish Famine was a deliberate act of British state genocide. The high Tory journal[38] the *St James's Gazette*, clearly influenced by J. A. Froude, took a special interest in Ireland, frequently sponsoring anti-Irish discourses of one type or another. But even this journal was prepared—as was Froude—to concede ground on the famine issue: 'As to Mitchel's furious hatred of England; he himself attributes it to the policy pursued by the English government during the famine crisis in Ireland.' The *Gazette* admitted Mitchel's point: 'The government was "well warned of the huge coming calamity" and did "practically nothing".'[39] The resource of the empire proved 'unequal' to the sudden strain that was put upon it: 'it was absurd in its way as if a rich householder should find itself unable to provide food for a sick child'.[40] This image was to resurface at the very moment of Mitchel's election. John Bright, the great Liberal politician, gave a speech explaining the famine in terms of the response of Providence to Ireland's assault on the laws of political economy. The *Irishman* conjured up a child dying of hunger outside the door of Bright's banquet speech while Bright stuffed himself.[41] It is also worth noting that it is an admission that Froude himself was prepared to make: it is why he sought a reconciliation with Mitchel's friend, Father Burke. Mitchel attributed the famine failure to 'deliberate purpose': he did not throughout his life modify that view in any way. The *St James's Gazette* insisted, however: 'the truth is that behind what is called imperial policy there is nothing that can be called will or purpose, nothing that corresponds with the intelligence of an individual confronted by similar problems.'[42]

It is not possible to leave the discussion of English public policy quite where the *St James's Gazette* leaves it. There is after all the issue of the role of influential political economy doctrines preaching against interference with market forces. There is the alleged role of an English sense of threat—fostered in part from Mitchel's own violent language and hatred of English charity—emanating from a 'overpopulated' turbulent neighbouring island. There is the role also of 'compassion fatigue' in part generated by the reports in the London press of strong Irish farmers helping themselves to relief intended for the poor. Nonetheless, the acceptance of the scale of Westminster's failure is striking. Mitchel spoke of the 'savage wrath' felt by every Irishman in 1848: he saw it as his role to keep that sentiment alive, as did his epigones like the Dillon brothers. But acceptance of much of Mitchel's case on the famine did not lead to a wider acceptance of his broader views. The *St James's Gazette* argued against Mitchel's world view: 'During the last two decades [i.e. since 1868] England has been steadily destroying those Irish classes and interests which are loyal to her, and as steadily strengthening those which are hostile. How would Mitchel explain this on his theory of a selfish imperial purpose?'[43] These remarks are worthy of note. The progress of British reform in late nineteenth-century Ireland was clear enough—the disestablishment of the Anglican Irish Church in 1869 and the 1870 Irish Land Act are obvious indications of the direction of travel. The Land Act introduced some important protections for small tenants in practical terms; but, more importantly, symbolically it indicated a clear willingness by the UK Parliament to treat Irish land issues as a special case requiring possible reforms which were considered to be out of the question in England. The Gladstone government failed in 1873/4 to bring in a major university reform of benefit to Irish Catholics but it was not for the want of trying. This was why Justin McCarthy— later to be a key Parnellite MP and lieutenant—was amazed to find, on meeting John Mitchel in 1870, that Mitchel absolutely refused to accept there were *any* signs of British good intent towards Ireland.[44] To this extent, the *St James's Gazette* had a very strong case against Mitchel's view of Anglo-Irish relations, even as it conceded Westminster's effective failure during the Famine. The British 'official mind', as expressed by the mature Sir Robert Peel and Lord John Russell, or, more loosely, vaguely defined political common sense, had decided on a policy of co-option of the Catholic middle class of Ireland rather than a policy of confrontation. Liberals were usually more ardent in pursuit of that policy than Conservatives but there was little real challenge to it, except, of course, large-scale apathy. The *St James's Gazette* was well aware of the views of J. A. Froude as an alternative, but this required a commitment to sustained authoritarian even dictatorial government. In July 1889, the *Gazette* itself published a sharp critique of Froude's advocacy of an 'enlightened despotism' for Ireland by a 'loyal Irishman'.[45]

Nonetheless, there is a serious point at issue here; the most activist nationalist elites in Ireland in the late 1870s might decide to act as if Mitchel's world view was true, but what if it was not? Mitchel's life and work legitimized hatred of England but also a political strategy: Parnell does not appear to have felt quite this concentrated hatred—preferring instead a rather more laconic mockery of English double standards—and certainly never internalized the implied political strategy: the need for a revolution to break the union. John Dillon remained close to the Mitchel vision in both senses in the early 1880s and even in later years found it difficult to break with its emotionalism.

The Dillon brothers arrogated to themselves the role of gatekeepers in Irish nationalist politics at this point. They made key decisions about advancement: they offered Parnell's prospective seat in Meath (for which he was nominated and eventually won) to Charles Gavan Duffy, but then insisted on terms which made it difficult for Gavan Duffy to complete the deal.[46] They assumed a right to judge and place others which inevitably created a degree of irritation. When Frank Hugh O'Donnell MP was making a name for himself as a leader alongside Parnell of the 'obstructive' revolt of Irish MPs in Parliament, Dillon wrote to the press denouncing him as a 'penniless adventurer'. But, as Tim Healy noted in a letter to his mother, everyone in this peer group of ambitious young men might be said to be an 'adventurer'[47] and most were penniless by the standards of the Dillon family. O'Donnell in later years tended to exaggerate Parnell's levels of broad social and political ignorance in this epoch—but he and his friends undoubtedly added intellectual heft to the project of obstruction. As Dillon publicly reached uncharitable judgements on others, he cannot have been surprised that others were willing to make uncharitable judgements on him. As a response to Dillon's cold words, Healy's friends entertained privately, and eventually publicly, the idea that Dillon's involvement in the dying John Mitchel's last campaign for a parliamentary seat in 1875 was based on a calculation that Mitchel would die before the election and Dillon would then be drafted into the vacancy.[48]

But if it was true that John Dillon had remained so close to Mitchel because he saw it as a route to an early parliamentary seat—as later alleged—Parnell beat him to the punch. In April 1875, Parnell, following the death of John Martin, took the Home Rule seat in Meath with a solid majority—but also without any noticeable enthusiasm, measured by electoral turnout, for his candidature. The *Drogheda Argus* concluded: 'After all there is something in bearing an honoured name and having family tradition to be proud of and sustain...He had contested the most extensive constituency in Ireland with one of the oldest and richest conservative families in it and he has proven his principles out of his pocket.'[49] The reference here is to the Grevilles, a powerful Meath family. A combination of the Irish people's 'long memories' of the traditions of the Parnell family and Parnell's relatively deep pockets had taken him into Parliament. It is said that his election cost him £2,000— if so that was more than his annual income in the late 1870s. Parnell's election address had included a rather exaggerated claim: 'My ancestor, Sir John Parnell, was the advocate in the old Irish Parliament of the removal of the disabilities which affected his Catholic fellow countrymen and in the evil days of corruption which destroyed the independence of Ireland, he lost a great office and refused a peerage to oppose the fatal measure of the Union.'[50] Sir John had not always stood firmly for the Catholic cause and rapidly reconciled himself to the union. But Parnell's grandfather and grand-uncle *had* stood firmly for Catholic emancipation when it was an unpopular cause in Westminster. Parnell took his seat in the House of Commons on 22 April. On that day, the Home Rule MP J. G. Biggar made a 3½-hour speech on an Irish Coercion bill. On 30 June–1 July 1876, Butt's Home Rule motion was defeated by 291 to 61. Was this the high-water mark of Isaac Butt's historic achievement? In 1876 and 1877, Parnell threw himself into the work of the 'active' Irish party in the House of Commons—the work, as it was known, of obstruction of parliamentary business. Despite the dismay of the party leader, Isaac Butt, Parnell and his handful of allies were determined to send out the message that Irish nationalism in Parliament was now a force of some vigour and mental toughness. Parnell was successful, even if he was dependent on others for many of the ideas and data in his speeches. It is worth adding, however, that as it became more refined, humane, and progressive in its chosen issues, obstruction gained significant admirers within the London intelligentsia. Of particular significance here was the campaign to abolish flogging in the Navy.

Sometime in late 1877 or early 1878, a Dillon note in his private papers shows that he supported 'A plan for bringing about the final crisis between England and Ireland, by withdrawing Irish representation, setting up a parliament in Dublin and obstructing the carrying out of English acts. Avoiding as much as possible an armed collision but setting on the people to resist carrying out English laws.'[51] This was the essence of the thinking of neo-Fenians like John Devoy, Michael Davitt, Patrick Egan, and John Dillon—but would it ever be acceptable to Parnell? Parnell may have felt he had enough on his mind.

There is a sense in this period of impatient young men pushing aside an older, respected, highly intellectual leadership—whether that be Isaac Butt in the case of constitutional politics or Charles Kickham in the world of revolutionary politics. Neither Butt nor Kickham could really answer the question: If we continue on your lines will there be a breakthrough of some sort or simply more years of stagnation for the cause? In the spring of 1877, Parnell made thirty-four speeches on the prison bill. On a visit to Scotland in the recess, he asked the local prison governor for access to his prison.[52] He was initially refused, in defiance of the concept that an Irish MP had the same status as other UK MPs; however, eventually he was admitted and questioned the governor calmly and effectively about the humanity of his regime.

The 'obstructives' made a real impression on Irish public opinion. On a typical night in mid April 1877, Parnell, Biggar, and O'Connor Power ensured that a one-hour discussion of the Mutiny bill was extended to five hours. Nevertheless, at the Council of the Home Rule Members of Parliament held in October, an uneasy peace prevailed.

Butt backed away from his cherished notion of conciliation of English opinion but Parnell also 'deliberately' refrained from putting his future policy or plans to the meeting.[53] But others were unambiguous—as Dr Clare Murphy has pointed out, there was clarity on the part of the 'neo Fenian' radicals. 'We must secure the control of the public voice of the country… We have abstained from interference in elections, except on particular occasions, such as those of O'Donovan Rossa and John Mitchel…and in these instances we demonstrated what we could do…Ireland can never be freed…by constitutional agitation in any form…but constitutional agitation is one means of advancing our cause and we should avail ourselves of it…*When all is ripe we can command our representatives to withdraw from the British parliament.*'[54] In an open letter to Charles Kickham, Matthew Harris, a key figure in the west of Ireland, wrote on 18 December 1877:

> I fully agree with Mr. Froude that liberty has to be achieved and retained by material power, and I have all my life repudiated the false and immoral doctrine that an enslaved people are not justified in appealing to the sword. But calling upon people to take up arms will not make them do so. Supposing we allow that the object aimed at is liberty, and that the most fitting means of gaining that object is war, still I maintain that even for such an object, and the creation of such means, public movements and every form of popular representation is of service in preparing for the final struggle, provided they be properly used.[55]

In September 1877, Parnell had the nerve to claim in Sheffield alongside his ally O'Connor Power that he (Parnell) had the deeper resolution in the employment of obstructive methods.[56] At the end of the year, Parnell decided to speak in a Fenian heartland in Mayo alongside allies of Matt Harris. Fenians gossiped about Parnell's potential. Parnell replied by sending signals of respect. He articulated for the first time what became a famous theme of his—no man had a right to set the boundary of a nation. But he also insisted, against Fenian orthodoxy, there was 'no one method' of achieving Irish self-government.[57] In early February 1878, a very impressive young Fenian, Michael Davitt, was released from jail to great fanfare in Dublin. Parnell, John Dillon,

Thomas Brennan, and Patrick Egan were on the fourteen-man reception committee along James Carey, Daniel Curley, and James Brady. These latter three gentlemen were later to be part of an assassin group known as the Invincibles.[58] (Dillon was to claim that he had never met the three men.) On a train from London to St Helens on 12 February 1878, Parnell discussed politely but indecisively Davitt's invitation to join the IRB—something it was easier to do because Parnell was well aware that many of the most 'active' men now regarded the IRB Supreme Council as inflexible ideologues who were living in the past.

While Parnell relentlessly embarrassed Butt in Parliament at every turn in 1877, John Dillon throughout 1878 rigorously supported Parnell in Dublin. Like some 'beautiful' and rather 'dyspeptic bird' Dillon 'swooped upon his victim' (Butt) and savaged him.[59] There was no 'community of interest' between England and Ireland, Dillon said, and therefore Irish Home Rulers could not support England in international affairs and conflicts. Butt gasped in disbelief—what was more likely to turn English opinion against Ireland? William Archer Redmond MP, father of John Redmond later to be the leader of the Irish party, protested against 'dictation' by Dillon at this point. Parnell offered more soothing language than Dillon, but the direction was the same.[60] Parnell had acted, however, to soften Dillon's language; as F. S. L. Lyons noted, it would not be the last time.[61]

Parnell continued the work of obstruction in London. The reaction of English MPs was increasingly splenetic. In May 1878, in the debate on the Committee of Supply dealing with salaries and expenses of public bodies, Parnell and his friends pushed the patience of the House to its limits. Thomas Cave, the MP for Barnstaple, felt he was being prevented from performing his duty to the country in the Committee of Supply. Suddenly, in frustration, he blurted that Parnell's election to the House had been 'a curse to the United Kingdom'.[62] It was a revealing moment and for some liberal advocates of the union a worrying one. When Cave described Parnell as a 'curse to the Kingdom, we can not be very indignant to find that Dungarvan, Meath or Cavan swears pretty roundly in reply', the *Spectator* noted.[63] From Parnell's point of view, all this anger was very satisfactory. In the wake of John Mitchel's victory, noting British fears, the *Irishman* had recalled the celebrated lines of Julius Caesar in Shakespeare: 'Let me have men about me that are fat; | Sleek-headed men and such as sleep o'nights: | Yond Cassius has a lean and hungry look; | He thinks too much: such men are dangerous.'[64] English MPs denied their sleep by Parnell, the slim Irish obstructionist, would have acclaimed the foresight of this editorial.

But if the British liberal intelligentsia was impressed by Parnell, we cannot be surprised that Irish American militants with Fenian connections were also impressed. The leading figure here was John Devoy, who in late December 1878 made Parnell an offer of an alliance of what was called 'New Departure' terms. The serious revolutionary cabals discussed only one issue: how to work with Parnell. Would he work with them and on what terms? He was obviously open to some form of engagement but what did he really have in mind? The *New Departure* offer was an attempt to resolve this question. John Devoy called for:

1. Abandonment of the federal demand and substitution of a general declaration in favour of self-government.
2. Vigorous agitation of the land question on the basis of a peasant proprietary, while accepting concessions tending to abolish arbitrary eviction.
3. Exclusion of all sectarian issues from the platform.
4. Party members to vote together on all Imperial and home questions, adopt an aggressive policy and energetically resist coercive legislation.
5. Advocacy on behalf of all struggling nationalities in the British Empire or elsewhere.

These principles require some elucidation. A demand for self-government allowed Fenians to pretend to themselves they had not dropped their demand for an Irish Republic. The problem with Butt's federalism was that it made the disappearance of 'the Republic' all too obvious and no amount of Home Rule party respect for Fenian self-sacrifice could cover that up. Hence, the neo-Fenian opposition to the federalist slogan. The segment on the land question is unambiguous in its explicit meaning: the land agitation was permitted to have only one end, peasant proprietorship. It was possible that a British government might offer some measure of land reform, but no one in 1878 thought it would offer peasant proprietorship. Few thought it would offer any meaningful reform. Therefore any campaign to that end must inevitably raise the issue of Irish self-government: either by a secession of MPs to a Dublin Parliament or an insurrection. John Dillon was already contemplating secession in his private notes in 1877. This assumption of a negative British response to a popular Irish agitation owes much to John Mitchel. This is why F. H. O'Donnell MP noted sharply: 'The Devoy New Departure simply revolved itself into very old John Mitchelism.'[65] Parnell remained friendly in the face of these currents but always sought to maintain a certain independence of political action. In November 1878, the *Nation* reported Parnell's cautious comment that 'unless they went for a revolution, he confessed he did not see how they were going to bring about a radical reform of the system of land tenure in the country. For his own part he was disposed to devote his energies to endeavouring to obtain a settlement on the basis laid down by Mr Butt's Fixity of Tenure Bill as introduced in 1876.'[66] In February 1879, he gave his views a conservative gloss; if you had the land question settled on a permanent basis you would remove the great reason that now exists to prevent the large and influential class of Irish landlords falling in with the demand for self-government.[67]

In a speech signalled by Davitt to Devoy before it was delivered, Parnell said at Glasgow that separatists and home rulers should work together. 'Home Rule was a compromise but if that was refused much longer', he hinted Ireland would have to 'stand on her rights'.[68] This speech, predictably, was picked up negatively by Conservatives in Parliament; Parnell's popularity was thus further enhanced. It is worth setting alongside a speech like this—carefully 'leaked' beforehand to Michael Davitt—the view of Parnell given by Justin McCarthy, the former Young Irelander turned London liberal journalist, soon to be an Irish nationalist MP. McCarthy, who spent a considerable amount of time with Parnell in London at this time, wrote:

> Parnell, it should be borne in mind, was always and above all things a constitutional and parliamentary politician, He had measured the whole situation with calm and keen scrutiny; he thoroughly recognised the immense power which England could bring to bear for crushing a rebellious movement, and he therefore never gave the slightest encouragement to any policy which could bring about such a result. But he felt convinced that, even while keeping strictly within the lines of the constitution, the Irish members could so completely delay and disarrange the whole business of the House of Commons as to make it worth the while of any Ministry to come to terms with them on the subject of the national claims.[69]

It is, of course, simply not true to say that the Glasgow speech, for example, never gave the 'slightest encouragement' to the insurrection strategy. But, on the other hand, McCarthy's careful assessment of a man he had got to know rather well rings true: 'above all things a constitutional and parliamentary politician'.

Parnell's activism had impressed the men who had been involved in the debacle of the insurrection of 1867. These cadres were keenly aware of their failure to mobilize the great majority of Irish farmers in 1867. In the mid 1870s, they began to believe that any possible road to national independence involved mobilizing the land hunger of the Irish peasantry. The failure to mobilize the peasantry had been the defining failure of 'the 1867 men'. On 6 April 1879, two impressive leaders of this group, John Devoy and the Ulster Protestant, Dr Carroll, met with Parnell in Dublin. Parnell had made it clear that he was not prepared to join the Fenian movement but it was also clear that he was not prepared to criticize it in public. But if there was uncertainty about Parnell's political identity there was no such uncertainty about John Dillon. A special branch report described him concisely: 'Student for the medical profession; not very industrious ... Trustworthy persons who know him will say he fully agrees with J. Devoy's principles and is really a cool Fenian.'[70] Allowance should be made for the fact that 'cool' here means being in the camp of those who looked to an Irish withdrawal from Parliament, rather than insurrection.

On 20 April 1879, the Fenians organized a meeting at Irishtown in Co. Mayo on the theme of the 'Land for the People'. The banner with this slogan was designed by Mrs Patrick Sheridan, the wife of the Tubbercurry hotelier and key republican militant, and Mrs Patrick Gordon, wife of P. J. Gordon, another republican militant.[71] This was the opening move in a saga during which both men stirred a cocktail, of anticlericalism but also religiosity, or violent crime and agrarianism, not to mention entrepreneurialism. It was an explosive cocktail which was destined to have a profound influence on Irish history. The attendance was said to be about 7,000. Michael Davitt insisted that Canon Geoffrey Bourke, a member of a prominent local Catholic gentry family, was the unpopular figure whose land dealings had provoked the meeting.[72] At the beginning of June 1879, Gordon and Sheridan held a meeting for the purpose of intimidating a moderate priest, Father Cavanagh of Knock. Three hundred men marched in military formation to Knock. Patrick Sheridan[73] declared to a crowd of 1,500: 'Father Cavanagh (PP) now endeavoured to stamp then as blackguards, he had done everything to brand them (cries of down with him—cut off his supplies). He should not trample on the people who hoped to benefit their country.'[74] A few days later, on 8 June 1879, Parnell decided to address a land meeting in Westport alongside Michael Davitt. His own speech reflected his core principles: the need for land reform to secure social cohesion in Ireland. But a colleague on the platform, Michael Malachi O'Sullivan, openly advocated a violent revolution. Parnell now had a decision to make. Did he run for cover? Or did he continue to work with men who were determined to put John Mitchel's principles into practice? The Catholic clergy made a conscious decision to get a grip on the new agitation at the next meeting in Claremorris in mid July. In an effort to regain control, no less than eleven priests sat on the platform. These included Davitt's enemy, Canon Geoffrey Bourke, a platform presence as well as a close relative of Colonel Walter Bourke, a platform speaker as well as a local landlord—both unpopular with the League. Michael Davitt and John Dillon addressed the meeting. In the chair sat Canon Ulick J. Bourke of St Jarlath's, Tuam. Father Bourke's message was clear: it was the duty of good Catholics to obey the law. He disliked talk of an alliance with the English democracy. The English, especially the democracy, had no proper religion. Michael Davitt, in his Lancashire accent, on the other hand spoke sympathetically of both Fenianism and communism. The good Canon stated bluntly this was unacceptable language.[75] But in a nearby public house, John Devoy told the local Fenians later that day they would control the new agitation.[76]

Then in August 1879 the Blessed Virgin appeared on the gable wall of the parish church in Knock in a vision to her suffering people. Father Cavanagh embraced the vision but so did the local farmers.[77] Attending Mass the following Sunday, Mrs P. J. Gordon instructed her daughter Delia, who was suffering from an earache, to extract a piece of gable wall and place it to her ear. The earache disappeared—though Father Cavanagh appears to have believed that Delia was cured from deafness. The first miracle cure was now in place; pilgrims started to arrive at Knock, helped in their journey by the cabs provided by P. J. Gordon.[78] The 'miracle' which might have been expected to enhance the power of the Church was simply taken over by the Land League militants in a display of dramatic social power and creative opportunism.

Meanwhile, at Westminster, the British liberal intelligentsia continued to be impressed by Parnell and his friends. They had put legitimate pressure on the UK Parliament and were a means to improve its performance. The *Economist* was to write in admiration: 'The Home Rulers have done all they can have hoped, and far more than they can have expected. How can a political party be censured for many amendments which are sufficiently like real improvements to be accepted by the government?'[79] Parnell would have been happy to read this, and it has been noted that he gave significant attention to his media profile.[80] It should not be forgotten that Parnell had a real choice to make. He could have continued to give the great bulk of his energy and time to work in Westminster, which was going rather well and likely to go better if the Tories fell from power as they did in the spring of 1880. One of his ablest colleagues, F. H. O'Donnell, felt sure that this was the right course. He may well have dismissed the views of those neo-Fenians like Malachi O'Sullivan and Matt Harris who looked to using the land struggle to spark a 'traditional' armed insurrection. But he knew that men like Davitt and Dillon—as Davitt had explicitly told him in February 1878—looked instead to an eventual withdrawal from Parliament as the cumulation of the Land League strategy. 'And what then?' he had asked Davitt. Parnell once famously said that he believed his neo-Fenian allies did not have any *arrière-pensée* and they had a focus solely on land reform: but he knew this not to be true. But he had his own *arrière-pensée*—which he never deviated from—that the new more democratic Parliament could be made to deliver substantial benefits to Ireland.

# 3

# The Revolution

You must judge a popular movement as a whole, you must judge it by the circumstances and what it led to.

Parnell at the Corn Exchange, *Spectator*, 24 July 1889.

Yet still it is a party, I prefer to keep it together and to purge it and strengthen it rather than attempt any disruption.

C. S. Parnell, *Dublin Weekly Nation*, 30 August 1879.

In the autumn of 1879, Parnell made his decision to embrace this new Land League movement. Moderate Home Rule MPs looked on aghast: did he not realize where the 'hard men' were leading him? Did he not realize that his new friends wanted to use the land question to force conclusions on the national question? For example, Parnell and Dillon were both present in Dublin in September 1879 as a self-appointed nationalist elite declared it would call a national convention of 300 in 1882 which would be a putative Irish Parliament. The idea here was to exploit the centenary of the Dungannon Convention, Henry Grattan's 1782 Constitution that a claim by any body of men, other than the King, Lords, and Commons of Ireland, to make laws to bind this kingdom, was unconstitutional, illegal, and a grievance.[1] Mitchell Henry, a moderate Home Rule MP, grimly noted: 'members of the Home Rule League—a self-constituted body at the best—have solemnly determined to convoke in Dublin a representative Convention which would sit and foreshadow an Irish Parliament'.[2] This seemed to be the politics of fantasy. Experienced politicians looked on in horror. Parnell liked to use the phrase 'cowardly common sense' to dismiss his critics but his

*Ancestral Voices in Irish Politics: Judging Dillon and Parnell.* Paul Bew, Oxford University Press.
© Paul Bew 2023. DOI: 10.1093/oso/9780192873705.003.0003

critics retained their scepticism. Common sense after all was common sense. The language of the land agitation became more and more strident and more subversive of clerical influence.

Despite all this, Parnell pressed on. On 21 October 1879, he attended the Irish National Land League conference in Dublin and accepted the leadership of this new movement: John Dillon and his brother William joined the sixty-man executive of the movement but neither were appointed to the leadership group of seven officers—four of whom were Fenians or ex-Fenians. This executive rapidly issued a document on 4 November declaring that a peasant proprietorship was the only way out of the current crisis. But how exactly—and at what speed—was this to be arranged? In Manchester in November, Parnell talked of a thirty-five-year purchase scheme on fair rents as the route to a peasant proprietorship. He reiterated his support for peaceful and constitutional methods.[3]

Nonetheless, Parnell's decision to accept the leadership of the new movement here was highly significant. As a later Liberal Prime Minister, H. H. Asquith—who was engaged as a young lawyer in these matters in the 1880s—put it in 1907: 'Ireland from 1879–82...was honeycombed with secret societies and violence, cattle-maiming and assassination undetected and unpunished stalked through the land.'[4] Between October 1880 and the end of March in 1882, there were twenty-five actual murders and 136 attempted agrarian murders in Ireland. By early 1882, the government had established 235 personal protection posts.[5] Parnell cannot have known in advance these precise figures, but he must have known that there would be significant loss of life and violence accompanying this new movement. He certainly knew that there was a revolutionary element in his coalition. He also knew that there were social and class tensions within the movement. In particular, he may have intuited that one key theme—that the distress initiated by the poor seasons of the late 1870s might provoke another Irish famine—provided serious ideological fuel for any new campaign, even if the actual distress was substantially palliated by relief funds and the most distressed areas were often not at the heart of the new agitation. How would more moderate and respectable agrarians traditionally involved in the Central Tenants Defence Association (CTDA) react? Andrew Kettle, a farmer and leading light of the CTDA, called a meeting of that body at the European Hotel in Dublin on 18 November 1879. It was a significant moment. The huge Killannin demonstration held that very week was under the auspices of the Killannin Defence Association not yet the Land League.[6] Kettle arranged for Co. Meath priest Father Tormey CC, who had sharp and painful memories of the Famine, to make a militant speech. Parnell made an attempt to shift the CTDA away from its traditional exclusive defence of fixity of tenure towards the more radical stance of peasant proprietorship. He was clear that he thought the two policies could be maintained alongside each other: 'I do not see how there should be any reason for antagonism between these planks.'[7] But significant parts of his audience—'very conservative, cautious, moral and law abiding'—were not reassured. Many of them knew that the neo-Fenians surrounding the Land League leadership advocated peasant proprietorship rather than fixity of tenure, because they felt that mobilizing farmers behind that demand would create the conditions for a nationalist revolution.

John Dillon rose to support Parnell: but, as Andrew Kettle later recalled, at this juncture Dillon's view as to the solution of the Irish question was relatively moderate.[8] His support for Parnell was less than wholehearted. Dillon added that in a poor county like Mayo, 'peasant proprietorship had popular support—but there were large districts in which circumstances did not seem to favour peasant proprietorship; and surely Mr Parnell did not mean to say that they were to throw away all their energies upon that'. What this speech reveals is that Dillon looked to a strategy which would lead to Irish MPs withdrawing from Westminster; he did not see the demand for peasant proprietorship as an essential part of that project. In fact, at this point John Dillon felt that a coherent moderate reformist position on the land question was more likely to create the best possible context for a convention on the national question in 1882. Dillon insisted that the existing demand for fixity of tenure be not abandoned, but 'both should run in parallel lines and there should be no antagonism behind them'. Parnell cried out 'Hear, Hear'. Dillon replied that Parnell had confined himself to peasant proprietary 'and had deserted the other portions of the country'. Dillon's meaning here was clear: he accepted that peasant proprietorship had popular support in one poor western county, Mayo, but he did not accept it had the same level of popular support elsewhere. Parnell cried again: 'Oh, no you misunderstand.' Dillon replied again that it was the 'poorer portion' of the country 'where opinion was tending to peasant proprietary'. He added: 'they must remember that if they wished to obtain the cooperation of the North (an object which he thought they should never lose sight of) they must keep up the fixity of tenure platform, for he did not think the circumstances of the North were likely to be so pressed by the present depression as to bring on forced sales of property'.[9]

This is a remarkable display of caution by Dillon; oddly enough it may have reassured the stronger farmers who allowed the CTDA to be absorbed within the Land League over the next few days and weeks. In 1878, Dillon was pushing Parnell to challenge moderate nationalist opinion at the Dublin meetings; but on the land issue as such, Dillon in 1879 chose to moderate Parnell. On 19 November, the Tory government decided to arrest three leading activists who had spoken at the Gurteen meeting on 5 November—Michael Davitt, James Daly, and James Bryce Killen. They were charged with seditious libel. John Dillon—who had also spoken at Gurteen—was left alone: his speech at the European Hotel on 18 November would anyway have made it difficult for the government to treat him as a violent extremist. The arrests electrified Dublin politics. Parnell and Dillon roused the protest crowd at the Rotunda.[10] Parnell argued that the Tory government had defeated Afghans and Zulus but they would not 'place us on the same level as these savages'. (A voice cried out: 'They will find us more formidable enemies.') These references are to the Anglo-Zulu war (1879) and the second Afghan war (1878–80), and may be seen as part of the crystallization of an already popular Irish nationalist hostility to the British Empire.[11] Parnell's words are representative in that they reflect the heavily freighted nationalist response to these events. Zulus and Afghans were portrayed simultaneously as heroic exemplars for Irish resistance and as uncivilized savages—with the clear implication that the civilized Irish race would be more effective in resisting British power.[12]

Parnell did not have to wait long to make a further necessary show of anti-government defiance. On 22 November, there was a planned eviction of the Fenian Anthony Dempsey on Loonamore mountain in Mayo on the Blosse-Lynch estate. The popular force led by Parnell and Dillon mobilized dramatically in the locality and humiliated the police force whose safe departure from the scene depended on the good offices of Parnell. On all sides it was agreed that Parnell had displayed great leadership and bravery.[13] The next day he and Dillon addressed a crowd of 15,000 at Swinford—some of them acting in military formation. Dillon at Swinford wittily noted that the Tory Prime Minister had called on the Sultan of Turkey to make reforms in Asia Minor; he hoped to persuade America to call on the British Prime Minister to make reforms in Ireland.[14] But the state had one good resource—time. On 10 December, the state forces quietly evicted the Dempsey family. At this point the Land League paid the rent and costs of Anthony Dempsey.

All this pointed to the need for the Land League to have stronger financial resources. Davitt wrote to J. J. O'Kelly: 'What we want is money—money—money. Without it this movement must fail—with it success is almost certain.'[15] It also pointed to the need for the movement to create new forms of struggle, which also required money. The Mayo lawyer and Land League activist J. J. Louden told the League leadership that the 1870 Land Act contained neglected clauses to protect small farmers against evicting landlords; all it required was for the League to be able to finance the process of legal argument in the courts. But even with the CTDA element, the Land League had little money. The obvious move was to send Parnell and Dillon to the United States to gather cash. Irish farmers were adjured to keep a firm grip on their homesteads; they did not need to be told to keep a firm grip on their savings. The new movement needed the support of an Irish America which now had reached that important and positive stage in American society: in which its struggle for self-respect and a place in the sun implied an improvement in the perception of the home country—but also a vindication of its national story.

Even in the late 1870s, there was a decided myopia in the English political elite as to the existence of this world and to the passions which motivated it. In 1877, on a brief visit to Dublin, Gladstone publicly discussed the famine—'painful and mournful to the highest degree'. It was, he said, by 'severe dispensation of providence' in the 1840s that 'instead of eight millions of population you now have less than five and a half millions'. Furthermore, in Gladstone's view, 'the sufferings have been suffered—the ties have been snapped—the ocean has been crossed'.[16] But this, very precisely, was not the view of Irish America. There was no such easy Gladstonian closure on this issue to be had. Irish America did not view the famine as merely a severe dispensation of providence—the failure of the potato crop on which so many Irish depended for their main basic diet—but as a deliberate act of British policy. John Mitchel's polemical works—by far the most widely read works of Irish history in the nineteenth century—insisted that the famine was above all a product of a British genocidal mindset. Irish America, more particularly its activists, brooded on dark fantasies. This went beyond support for a bombing campaign in England—a campaign which enjoyed some success in the 1880s. There was even the construction of a dream of a reverse genocide: Patrick Ford, the hugely influential editor of the New York *Irish World*, wrote of a plan by which fifty Irishmen on a windy night set fire to London in fifty different places and generated a furnace of flames which left millions dead. 'Our Irish skirmishers would be well disguised. Language, skin colour, dress, general manners, are all in favour of the Irish.'[17] Of course, there were senior Irish politicians who condemned this article—pointing out how it had dreadful implications for the London Irish.

Parnell and Dillon were sent out to evangelize in this new and excitable world. 'I met plenty of Irishmen and women in America', said Parnell, 'who had lived through the famine, and who had seen the roadsides filled with the men, women and children starved to death.'[18] Both

Parnell and Dillon felt it right to move their rhetoric to the left—they did not just embrace peasant proprietorship but the specific cause of the poorest farmers in the west. This implied a wider land redistribution, possibly moving poor western cottiers on to better land in the Irish midlands. Dillon insisted on his first arrival in New York that he did not want the larger farmers to join the Land League.[19] This was a huge move from his cautious position in favour of the 3Fs (fixity of tenure, fair rent, and free sale) in November. He apparently believed that the larger farmers lacked a strong sense of group solidarity. Parnell's message was similar: 'Divide the good land and there will be 40 acres for every farmer.'[20]

In America, while they never stepped formally outside the bounds of a parliamentary strategy, both Parnell and Dillon adopted for the first time extreme radical positions on the land question. This was an especially dramatic move on the part of Dillon, who had been so cautious at the Dublin CTDA Conference in November. The point here is that the granular detail of the contemporary Irish land question as it actually existed in Ireland was swept aside in favour of a broad-sweep analysis of the Famine—and how to undo its effects—which made sense in Irish America. Both appeared to demand not just the abolition of Irish landlordism, but the wholesale reconstruction of the Irish rural economy in the interest of the most disadvantaged group of Irish farmers—the poor cottiers in the west. In his speech to Congress, Parnell did not flinch from stressing this theme. The invitation to address Congress was an honour of substance previously given only to two other foreigners, the Marquis de Lafayette in 1825 and the Hungarian patriot, Lajos Kossuth, in 1851:[21] to those who recalled 'official' American reluctance to acknowledge the Home Rule party in the mid 1870s it was a decided victory.

There was, of course, some emotive language in America: Parnell stated at Brooklyn, on 15 January 1880: 'You have to act upon English public opinion in some extraordinary manner in order to obtain any attention to Irish questions. We are, therefore, obliged to make the situation a very hot one indeed. It is impossible to suppose that the great cause can be won without shedding a drop of blood.'[22] At Newark, a few days later, Parnell, alongside Dillon, declared before a crowd of two thousand that a recent land case in Galway had infuriated him: 'I am no advocate of force but this was enough to stir the hearts of the most patient.'[23]

For Parnell the American experience had been intense. His brother John Howard Parnell's memoir insists that it had a profound impact. John Howard Parnell saw the tour as marking (for Charles) a pleasant contrast with 'Charley's' previous visit to America as an unknown.[24] His speech to the House of Representatives may have been sparsely attended but he had spoken to enthusiastic crowds in sixty-two cities and gained a new understanding of the importance of Irish America. That said, he pointedly never returned to America and was capable of making disparaging remarks about the experience.[25] Although Irish America took pride in the two distinguished-looking gentlemen— Parnell and Dillon—who represented their cause, no intimate bond was formed between the two men. Parnell's sister, Fanny, was infuriated by Dillon's disorganized, sloppy personal habits, as indeed were others. Dillon was also psychologically incapable of acting as private secretary for Parnell and Tim Healy had to be drafted in for the purpose. Healy, so anxious to escape relative poverty as an office clerk, was willing to help Parnell as a functionary; Dillon seems to have felt it was beneath his dignity. Yet in strictly political terms, the American trip was more important to Dillon than Parnell. His meetings with successful Irish Americans like John Boyle O'Reilly in Boston appear to have intensified his nationalist zeal and self-confidence: the level of caution, so characteristic of his speech at the CTDA in late 1879, simply disappeared.

Upon returning to Ireland in order to fight the general election of 1880, Parnell naturally moved to place his supporters in winnable seats. Parnell was a veritable force of nature. He told the American press he expected substantial Home Rule gains. He was firm enough: 'Do you suppose I will be dictated to?' he told Father Langan in Leitrim.[26] But there were rather more important Catholic clerics, in particular, the renowned John MacHale, Archbishop of Tuam. At the end of March, Parnell made a personal trip to the west to consult with the archbishop. But he did not accept even then the clergy's desired local candidate, Colonel Walter Bourke;[27] a relation of the unpopular Canon Geoffrey Bourke.[28] In New Ross, he was attacked by Papal Brigade veteran Chevalier O'Clery's supporters; but the town's merchants, led by William Murphy, gave him a guard of honour on the way back to the train station.[29] O'Clery lost out in the end to Parnell, as did Nick Dan Murphy in Cork, signalling the end of two great localist patronage networks. Parnell privately told candidates to be resolute on the land question, to talk of peasant proprietorship, not the 3Fs.[30] There was, however, one interesting moment when in Roscommon he visibly hesitated before effectively replacing an impressive old-school Home Rule figure, the O'Conor Don, with his loyal ex-Fenian friend James J. O'Kelly. John Dillon claimed that the O'Conor Don was a 'repressive' landlord; but Parnell does not seem to have believed this[31] even though he had been aware since November of the O'Conor Don's unpopularity with many local home rulers.[32] Parnell was rapidly elected as leader of the expanded Irish party at Westminster: a party which now had a key handful of his younger and able allies in place—for example, T. P. O'Connor, Thomas Sexton, Tim Healy, and John Dillon, elected for Tipperary.

Parnell now stood at the centre of a political storm. In the United States, he had never abandoned the concept of reform achieved through Parliament, for all his apparently social revolutionary rhetoric. But he knew perfectly well that his 'new departure' allies—Michael Davitt in the lead—looked to a moment when Parliament's denial of Irish land hunger pushed the country into support for Irish withdrawal from Westminster or even an armed uprising. Thomas Brennan was quite explicit in his public support for the John Mitchel approach. In March, Brennan told a Dublin crowd: 'they must not cease to wonder why men's souls were so fired in 1848.'[33] The allusion was not missed: 'Mitchel' a voice cried out. Then there was the legacy of socially radical language in the USA, moving beyond peasant proprietorship to land redistribution. The *Freeman's Journal*, the main nationalist organ, made it clear that it regarded such purposes as completely lacking in realism.'[34] In supporting the *Freeman's* analysis, F. H. O'Donnell, the Dungarvan MP, argued that there was an obvious delusion at the heart of the new agitation. If it was accepted, as it was, on many a platform, that the poor farmers of the west needed not just rent reductions and land ownership but more land, how were they to get it? There were 'good lands in the centre of Ireland'. But the inhabitants would 'crack the skulls of any would be migrants from the over-crowded west who dared to occupy lands coveted by local patriotism and cupidity'.[35] O'Donnell's remarks have the merit of demonstrating the difficulty of the position of Parnell and Dillon: they had both adopted an ultra-radical agrarian position in the USA, but was it sustainable on home turf? In particular, was it customizable in the face of a new reformist British government? More generally, the 1880 election returned Gladstone to power.

Gladstone's new Irish Chief Secretary, the Bradford MP William Edward Forster, was *un homme d'état*, unlike his more lightweight Tory predecessor James Lowther. A muscular Liberal, he had, nonetheless, thrown himself as a young man into the work of famine relief in Ireland. Full of goodwill towards Ireland, he broke down in tears when he received a letter from an Irish Catholic priest acknowledging his work in famine relief. Forster had, in fact, gone so far as to offer protective shelter to John Blake Dillon, one of the Young Ireland revolutionaries.[36] The goodwill was not reciprocated by the Irish parliamentary party or at any rate its Parnellite wing. J. G. Biggar, Parnell's lieutenant, liked to say that Forster had been merely motivated by a sadistic desire to observe human suffering. On the other hand, the young Irish Quaker lad who accompanied him was Alfred Webb, in later adult life to be a Parnellite MP.[37] If Forster hoped that he would gradually win more Irish affection and respect, he was to be disappointed. But Forster's career, given his high level of ability combined with basic human decency, reveals a more profound problem of the governance of Ireland in this epoch: as Conor Cruise O'Brien noted, in precisely this context, the self-defeating nature of the attempts to combine liberal democracy and colonialism, or perhaps, more precisely, the attempt to combine liberal democracy alongside the effects of Catholic Ireland's unhappy experience under the Union. It is notable that Forster, a determined reformist on the land issue and a determined upholder of social harmony, was never surprised when his initiatives ran into trouble, whether they were reformist or repressive. He had always anticipated the difficulty—that, for example, the state trials of the collective Land League leadership at the end of 1880/1 would be a failure—but felt that his duty and sense of appropriate behaviour required that he took a particular course of action however likely to be ill fated.

On his return to the heady world of Dublin nationalist intrigue, Parnell's political behaviour in April/May 1880 was quite extraordinary. He began by trying to persuade the Land League revolutionary cadres on the eve of a major Land League conference in Dublin that it should adopt the moderate programme of the Irish party—the 3Fs rather than the Land League's actual and existing programme of peasant proprietorship. The conference itself was full of fiery rhetoric but also obvious tensions between the leaders of the small farmers who had launched the movement in 1879 and the larger farmers who were now contemplating a takeover of it. Parnell, 'good naturedly' said Michael Davitt, accepted the veto of the revolutionary men on the 3Fs. When Parnell made up his mind on a point like this, he was decisive. He then within a few days in mid May tried to persuade the Irish party as its newly elected chairman to accept the policy of the Land League—even though only a few days before he had revealed a preference for the party policy rather than that of the League. It is little wonder that the party moderates saw him as an inexperienced young man who was being manipulated by hardened revolutionaries. He tried to offer a conservative gloss: the 3Fs would ensure continued class warfare in Ireland. The only way to ensure the unity of all social classes in the cause of Home Rule was peasant proprietorship. Some did see this as 'moderate' and 'reasonable'; others saw it only as a rationalizing fantasy of a naïve but ambitious man. But for all the cynicism provoked by Parnell's meditations on social harmony leading to Irish unity, it did provoke one genuinely reassuring thought; Parnell did not believe in using peasant proprietorship as an instrument of a revolutionary campaign to leave Westminster and set up a Dublin Parliament. His prospectus, unwise or not, was clearly long term and gradual.

He added as his distinctive gloss to this reasoning:

> The Land League had been charged with setting class against class. He took it as no given way of perpetuating the system which England had introduced into this country, *viz.* of setting class against class, could be desired than Mr Butt's proposal (hear, hear) for he believed that they would never obtain the national rights of the country until they united all classes in support of their rights.[38]

The *Freeman's Journal* felt it necessary to fall into line. The journal had been disturbed by the apparently uncontrolled land redistribution ethos of the Land League. Parnell's very radical article in the *North American Review*, actually written by his sister, had been worrying. But they were firmly told to accept the new discipline. 'Michael Davitt', Edmund Dwyer Gray told Frank Hugh O'Donnell, 'threatened me if that my paper continued to oppose the League he would have a hundred copies of it publicly burned on a hundred platforms and would start a new paper with the American money. I could not afford to ruin my family. I surrendered.'[39] Such were the brutal realities of Dublin political life in the spring of 1880.

Parnell did, however, move to soften his tone when he got to the other side of the Irish Sea. In June 1880, he spoke at St James's Hall in London. He asked the question: what were the legislative prospects for Irish farmers? Reasonably, he answered it himself. It would depend on the 'future progress of Liberal institutions in England' and the progress and attitude of the Irish party. Modestly, he declared that the party contained older men who knew more than he did on the land question. The implication seemed to be that these greybeards, usually more moderate than Parnell himself, had an important role to play.[40]

John Dillon was not, however, part of this softening of tone as his radicalization continued. T. P. O'Connor captured Dillon at this moment: 'He differed from many of the members of the Party, and especially from me and also from Parnell, in his view of the demands of the situation. He looked to the revolution in Ireland as certain to be ultimately victorious, and he was against all compromise that might interfere with its, as he thought, certain triumph.'[41] Chairing the Land League executive in Dublin in July, Dillon repeated the theme of American financial support for the movement, but it is worth noting that not every Home Rule supporter in the provincial press felt that the American money he claimed to control would be enough. At the same meeting, Thomas Brennan claimed there were 130 branches of the Land League in existence but noted that there were none in, for example, the county of Limerick.[42] Brennan insisted that the League had to be 'very careful' lest its money find its way into 'landlords' pockets'; but how was the League to get a hold amongst rich farmers in Limerick unless it was prepared to take such a risk? Patrick Egan spent some time at this meeting attacking Thomas Burke, a senior RC Dublin Castle official undersecretary, for the 'treatment of one of his tenants'.

The well-known revolutionary cadres had not lost their tongues. M. M. O'Sullivan spoke for the 'sword' at Rainsborough: 'Let us look to America today. What is that it has gained it [independence]?...Any person that tells you the contrary tells you a lie.'[43] O'Sullivan, of course, belonged to the group of Fenians—unlike Davitt, Egan, or Brennan—who explicitly believed in the strategy of an armed insurrection. On 1 August 1880, P. J. Sheridan urged the people to 'assert their rights, and if they did not get them through their members of Parliament, he would ask them to ring out their voices from the muzzles of *Minie* rifles'.[44]

On 3 August, however, the House of Lords played into Dillon's hands. A majority of even Liberal peers rejected the modest Compensation for Disturbance bill, and this, combined with the establishment of the Land Commission, gave real impetus to the League's struggle to expand outside Connaught.[45] The design of the bill had included only counties thus far involved in agitation—a perfect signal, as Parnell pointed out, for those left out to get involved. Dillon now threw himself into the campaign. Thus began what became known as Mr Dillon's 'young men' speeches. On 15 August, Dillon said:

What I was going to say to you is this. If the people desire to put down landlordism the only road to this is to have an organisation in the country, that every farmer shall belong to a branch of the Land League that exists throughout the country, that all the young men shall be prepared to march to the meetings, and in proper order too ... We in Parliament can see that Irishmen have a right to be out after eight o'clock or all night if they like.[46]

He added:

These organisers shall report to the branch of the Land League how many men they can march to the meeting, and they shall be able to march to these meetings like a regiment of soldiers. There will be more effect in two hundred young men marching to a meeting under the command of their leaders than twenty speeches.[47]

When the Chief Secretary, Forster, denounced this 'wicked' and 'cowardly' rhetoric before excited multitudes, Dillon repeated it in exactly the same terms in Parliament.[48] Parnell made it publicly clear that such rhetoric made him uneasy.[49] Forster 'had read with horror the cruel manner in which cattle had been maimed in Ireland as a punishment to their owners, and yet he found the hon. Member making statements instead of reprobating such barbarous conduct; which was contrary to the nature of the Irishman'.[50] In response, Parnell was to develop a new art form: a rhetorical trope whereby he supported Dillon's words while also simultaneously disavowing them. The method was an interesting one. Parnell understood British animal lovers would be shocked by Dillon's remarks and, indeed, they were appalled. They were unacceptable to Parnell himself. But, of course, there was room for a further translation. Dillon, it could be suggested, was merely noting the peasant superstition that animals on evicted land did not fare well. Parnell concurred with 'every word' of Dillon and the 'advice that he gave; but at the same time, he thought his hon. friend was wrong in using that expression about cattle which were put upon the land of an evicted tenant, because it might be interpreted as a concurrence with the maiming of cattle'.[51]

F. H. O'Donnell allowed himself to hope that Parnell had returned to the path of moderation. 'Has Mr Parnell abandoned the revolutionary programme of some months ago? Has he returned to the principle which made Ulster prosperous which can confer prosperity on Leinster, Munster and Connaught?' O'Donnell was here making reference to the concept of the 'Ulster custom', a form of tenant right practised in the north-east; it was clearly a rather less revolutionary slogan than that 'land for the people'. O'Donnell put Parnell's dalliance with revolution down to the fact that he was a 'patriotic Irishman, warm-hearted and clearly moved beneath his placid exterior, [when he] witnessed the never ending wretchedness of the hapless cultivators of the west'.[52]

By August 1880, Parnell had begun his affair with Katharine O'Shea—he was visibly keen to leave long parliamentary debates earlier than his colleagues would have liked. Stephen Gwynn wrote: 'Parnell and Mrs O'Shea fell in love at first sight and loved each other for so long as life lasted; for good or bad, let them have the credit of it.'[53] She later recalled at the launch of her memoir: 'Parnell as a lover was the most *parfait gentil knight* always most gentle, tender and considerate, but even here was sternly compelling, fiercely jealous uncompromising and passionate, brooking nothing that stood between us. Until I met him I could not dream that such happiness could exist in real life.'[54] Neither could Parnell believe it: his passion for Katharine exceeded his old passion for obstruction. She tended also to be a conservative political influence. Tim Healy recalled that Parnell 'half-jokingly' threatened to interrupt a Dillon speech with a call to 'divide' as he wanted to force a division and get away.[55] In fact, it was more than a private 'half' joke: Dillon was so angry that he responded by publicly criticizing his leader's willingness to curtail obstructive tactics on the Irish constabulary supply legislation.[56] Parnell may also have been enjoying his new status as a party leader in the House. One shrewd observer noted:

Mr Parnell is by birth and education a gentleman, and this cannot but tell to some extent, especially when he finds himself regarded by Ministers and ex-Ministers in the light of a responsible Parliamentary leader, and treated as such. Moreover since Mr Dillon has acquired notoriety in the House as chief among English haters and would-be conspirators,

Mr Parnell has clearly been anxious to establish his own chieftainship, on the ground of political ability and parliamentary Interests.

Whilst he [Parnell] is distinguished by Lord Hartington as the acknowledged leader of the Irish party, the Member for Tipperary, with his popular name and his dangerous faculty for 'out-Parnelling Parnell' in the matter of decrying landlords and denouncing the English government, sinks into his proper place as the violent young recruit who risks the prospects of the Party by his ill-judged zeal in the good cause.[57]

Florence Arnold-Forster catches an interesting moment. It is true that Parnell would have noticed with concern the unambiguously revolutionary and violent speeches given by Malachy O'Sullivan—with whom he had shared a platform in 1879 where O'Sullivan had been equally aggressive—and P. J. Sheridan. On the other hand, there were signs that English resolve was cracking. The fiasco of the Compensation for Disturbance bill seemed to suggest a polity quite unable to meet its historic mission in Ireland—a polity capable of sending the unwise signal 'we refuse for now all reform but if you want reform, please agitate and organize even more'. At the end of the month, J. A. Froude, often seen as the most unionist of historians, commented in despair: 'the question has arisen whether the experiment of an English Government in Ireland has not lasted long enough, for no Government which Ireland could herself establish could really be worse than that impotent mockery with which the English connection has provided it.'[58] This can only have stung Forster because Forster was an admirer of the historian, who had supported his educational reforms in the 1870s. Indeed, Forster had presided over the dinner in honour of Froude held in London in March 1875.[59]

The militant campaign continued. There was a clear hint of Fenian revolt in the air. In later years, talking to his son, Dillon claimed that the leaders of the 'New Departure' happily counted the numbers of those who had given up Fenianism in favour of the Parnellite party.[60] But there is no sign of such an attitude in his public rhetoric at the time. John Dillon was particularly keen to stress the unity of Fenian and Land League purposes:

It has been asserted, men of Tipperary, that the Nationalists of Ireland are hostile to the movement to set free the tenant farmers of Ireland and make them freemen in the land of their birth. (Cheers.) We come here to-day to a town where no movement can shew its head that is hostile to the Nationalists of Ireland; and I say that when the Irish Land League has assembled in Tipperary a meeting so large as this, that the man who will, in the face of this meeting, tell me that the Irish Nationalists are against the Land League is nothing better than a common liar. (Cheers.) No, neither are the Irish Nationalists hostile to the Land League, nor is the Land League hostile to the Nationalists.'[61]

In December 1880, Dillon declared: 'They knew that the greatest power in the country was a power that told the people that parliamentary representation was a sham. They all knew that if they wanted to decide on a Land Bill, they must go up to Sackville Street [the Land League headquarters], and ask the Land League before they could decide upon a plan of action. That might not be a very acceptable truth, but it is the truth.'[62] But it was Parnell's language that had the greatest effect. It fascinated and disturbed the framers of public opinion in Ireland.

At Ennis on 19 September, Parnell dismissed the Liberal government appointment of the Bessborough Commission to analyse the Irish land question. Its composition ensured a moderate reformist report. He agreed with John Dillon, who had criticized the Commission. 'The measure of the Land Bill of next session will be the measure of your activity and energy this winter. (Cheers.) It will be the measure of your determination not to pay unjust rents...to keep a firm grip on your homesteads.' Parnell replied to a cry of 'shoot him': 'He wanted to point out a very much better way, a more Christian and charitable way, which would give the lost man the opportunity of repenting. They must shun him on the roadside, shun him everywhere, and even in the place of worship.' This is the idea, soon to be termed boycotting, which was to achieve notoriety quickly. Parnell asked: 'What would the government think if they told the people some day or other not to pay any rent until the question was settled?' Of course, there was a related, rather complex question—what would the people think? Parnell moved rapidly on. They had not asked the people to do that yet. There might be an available fair and just settlement for all parties: 'If the five hundred thousand tenant farmers of Ireland struck against the ten thousand landlords he would like to see where they would get police and soldiers enough to make them pay. (Loud cheers.).'[63] At New Ross a week later, Parnell pointed out that his audience of farmers from Waterford, Wexford, Kildare, and Carlow had been left out of the Compensation for Disturbance bill because they had not joined the League. They soon did. On 12 October at Longford, addressing a crowd of ten thousand, Parnell said on the subject of radical and moderate views on the settlement of the land question, the Land League had not decided where it stood—though, he noted, it stood for a peasant proprietorship rather than a 'fair rent' solution. He defended work in Parliament but only if the Irish members displayed an 'unrelenting, persevering, troublesome opposition to every government until they do justice to Ireland'.[64]

Parnell had shaved off his beard to please his new lover and was, at first, not recognized by his supporters, but when finally convinced that this was the real Parnell the old enthusiasm returned. At Galway on 24 October, Parnell emphasized his national as opposed to agrarian motivation. He would not 'have taken off his coat' if he had not thought it would lead to independence. When Matt Harris at the dinner that night spoke of shooting landlords like partridges in the season, Parnell said to T. P. O'Connor, his dinner companion, 'leg it'[65]—so as not to be a collusive party to this verbal atrocity. Harris then 'explained' that he had simply meant that he would no longer repeat his youthful peaceful endeavours alongside Tom Steele, O'Connell's great 'pacificator'.[66] At Limerick in early November Parnell told the crowd that the Irish party was doing well. But he had a word of warning: 'If the Irish members failed in their effort then he for one would not consent to remain for an indefinite time in the English parliament but should consider it his duty to return to his countrymen and consult with them as to the course they might take. It was with the people to say what other way, what other methods should be adopted.'[67] Parnell cannot have been surprised when on 2 November the government announced it would take action against him and others, including P. J. Gordon, for conspiracy. The government was well aware that any state trial would strengthen Parnell but it felt it had no alternative but to go through the motions. Inevitably when the case came to court in January 1881 it collapsed due to jury disagreement.

Parnell's speech at Ballybricken, Waterford early in December— given after a three weeks' absence in the company of Katharine—was in certain respects strongly militant. He chided Waterford for being 'very late' to join the Land League. It would be better for Ireland if the 'Whig-radical government', as he called it, was 'broken to pieces'. He spoke aggressively of the need to 'break' the power of the landlord class: 'teach them to throw in their lot with the rest of the country'. He flirted (for the last time) with a radical scheme to redistribute land in Leinster and Munster to the poor families of Connaught. But he insisted that he was working within the 'lines of the constitution': he refused to plunge the country into the 'horrors of civil war'. Irish legislative independence was to be achieved 'openly and above board' and 'not by any subterfuge'.[68] This was an obvious rebuke to the strategy of neo-Fenianism. Professor Roy Foster has pointed up the paradox: that on this visit to Waterford he hunted with the very Tory Marquis of Waterford's hounds.[69] 'Who would believe that Charles Stewart Parnell, whose teachings had set the whole country ablaze, would be found following in the chase with the Marquis of Waterford and a host of other landed proprietors? Yet it is true,' declared the *Waterford Standard* with some amazement.[70] But the Chief was 'a hunting man' who rode 'straight'[71] and could not resist the chase. Parnell borrowed a horse from his chief whip, Richard Power MP, who regularly hunted with the 'Curraghmores'. At the hunt *rendez-vous* at Ballinamona, Lord Waterford and Parnell divided the honours of the demonstration with which they were greeted.[72] Such a genial moment of rapprochement was an illusion; by the following autumn, popular pressure forced Lord Waterford to confine his hunting activities to England.[73] It is perhaps not surprising, as Dr Margaret O'Callaghan has pointed out, that Lady Waterford was left with a deeply cynical view of the Irish character.[74]

By Saturday, 11 December 1880, the British media had decided, however, that Parnell was 'aiming at nothing less than revolution and could not have expressed himself in plainer terms than he used last Sunday' in Waterford.[75] Perhaps a little unsettled, Parnell on the day after this report, Sunday, 12 December, reached out to the London correspondent of the Viennese newspaper,[76] *Neue Freie Presse*: 'the speech was but a *pronunciamento* for the Home Rule members in connection with their parliamentary duties and his discourse was not of a revolutionary character.' The English press carried stories of a Fenian plot to seize arms at the Sunderland armoury. P. J. Gordon's rhetoric was read out at the state trial. He had noted allies in the Catholic Church—Archbishop Croke of Cashel would help them 'croak' the landlords.[77] At Shrule in June 1880, Gordon had said: 'We have no intention of cutting the throats of our friends but I don't care if half the throats of our enemies were cut before morning.'[78]

This was the unhelpful context in which Parnell tried to explain himself in Parliament. He spoke in the wake of an 'extremely spirited speech'—in the view of the Dublin press—by John Dillon. Parnell explained that his speeches required careful analysis: he was not seeking to use the land agitation for the purpose of violently destroying British power in Ireland, as was so widely believed. 'He admitted that sentences which had been read from the time of his speeches were capable of that construction.' He had simply advocated peasant proprietorship and, if that came about, there would be no class in Ireland interested in the maintenance of the union. The new Ireland would, however, be reconciled to the Empire. At that point they would then 'in a rational and peaceable way, without any violent revolution, in my opinion without a jingle of arms, but by the union of all the classes in Ireland achieve legislative independence'.[79] Parnell added: 'It would be criminal to plunge the Irish people into an unequal struggle.'

Parnell's speech in Parliament produced no serious response in the ranks of Conservative or Liberal MPs. It is not difficult to see why. Parnell suggested that Irish MPs were being pressed by public opinion to withdraw from Westminster. He also threatened—without any actual later effect—that the first arrest under coercion would lead to an Irish withdrawal from Parliament. Nevertheless, the *Spectator* a few days later wrote: 'Nothing irritates a quick-witted race (the Irish) like being governed by a slow-witted one... stronger and more stupid.'[80] Parnell might well have been tempted to agree with such an observation, but he was not given to overconfidence—despite the superficial appearance of a new-found national unity. He was also aware that his movement had an Achilles heel. The League had developed a new form of strategy to attract the strong farmers of the south and east of the country. These farmers could not benefit from the legal rights given to small western farmers under the 1870 Land Act, key benefits of which were reserved for smallholders. But there were other legal methods, subsidized by Irish America, such as an organized resistance to rent payment until the 'last moment' which often involved also the payment of the legal costs of the landlord. By the end of March 1881, it was clear that the Irish landlords had found a way to fight back. They established in January a Property Defence Association (the 'emergency men') under Norris Goddard. The PDA had been able to force through, albeit with the support of the Royal Irish Constabulary (RIC), sheriffs' sales of stock or interest on a significant scale. Suddenly, Irish tenants had to face the realistic prospect of loss if they continued to support the Land League. Anna Parnell has described the principal mobilizing tactic of the Land League in this era: 'It issued private instructions to its branches enjoining the payment of rent to use its own expression, at the last, promising to defray all the legal costs incurred by the delay, which they directed to make as long as possible, by interposing every obstruction they could to the collection of the money they owed to the landlords. This practice was dignified by the phrase "paying rent at the point of the bayonet".'[81]

On 24 January 1881, the government, unimpressed by Parnell's 'moderation', introduced coercion—the Protection of Person and Property bill in the House of Commons. It was essentially an instrument which allowed for mass internment of 'suspects' and was finally enacted on 2 March; in response, on 27/28 January 1881, in meetings in the House of Commons and later at the Westminster Palace Hotel,

Parnell considered but *rejected* a plan to withdraw the Irish party from the House of Commons, set up a national convention in Dublin, and launch a no rent campaign. On 28 January 1881 also, there was an important and significant clash in Parliament between Parnell and Gladstone. Gladstone quoted Parnell's advocacy of boycotting: 'You must shun him at the fair and marketplace and even in the house of worship…by sending him to a moral Coventry.' Gladstone asked: 'What was the crime this leper had committed? It was the crime of taking a farm from which a man had been evicted.' At this point Parnell interrupted to say that his words had been 'unjustly evicted'. Gladstone refused to accept this point, but later at a private meeting with Parnell he appears to have accepted Parnell's version.[82] Three days later, Thomas Sexton began his impressive critique of coercion in Parliament: Sexton insisted that in the sixteen counties where the Land League held meetings the average of crime was less than in the counties where there had been no meetings: two-thirds of all crime was in the zone of distress in the west.[83] Surely the implication was that distress rather than the League was to blame for crime? Sexton's speech was a remarkable example of the use of official statistics in politics. All his figures were correct. The League in many parts of Ireland was essentially the old Farmers Association under new leadership but in the west, nonetheless, it was to a very significant degree responsible for crime which was frequently organized by League militants.

On 3 February 1881, Michael Davitt's ticket of leave, as a Fenian prisoner on early release, was revoked and he was imprisoned once again in Portland prison in Dorset. Dillon was outraged and appeared to be on the verge of violence in the Chamber. It looked as if the House was to be scandalized by a scene of physical force: but just as this seemed inevitable, Mr Dillon rose, and after bowing to the chair left the Chamber in the company of the Serjeant at Arms.[84] 'The epidemic of rage now seized Parnell, who also lost his head for the first—and I believe the last—time in his parliamentary career, and under its influence insisted upon moving that Gladstone be not heard.'[85] Parnell too was suspended, as were many other Irish party members. Parnell then dropped out of public sight with Mrs O'Shea—'Why did Mr Parnell run away?' asked the London correspondent of the *Fife Herald*.[86] There was a rumour that he had gone to Frankfurt.[87] A few days later the Irish leadership met in Paris and Parnell refused the various revolutionary strategies on offer. He refused to go to America. He refused to withdraw from Parliament. He advocated instead 'a junction between English democracy and Irish nationalism'.[88] Parnell offered a way out and read from a prepared text. Andrew Kettle records: 'There was a pause or delay in running over the pages of the paper and in one of these intervals Dillon whispered to me saying: "It was Kitty wrote that. Parnell never wrote a line of it."'[89] The new and convenient idea was to deepen agitation amongst the English working class.

Parnell's new manifesto met with scorn in the London press. The *Spectator* spoke for many when it said: 'He utterly misunderstands the temper of British democracy. It is not in the least cosmopolitan.'[90] The British democracy, it was said, was simply not engaged on the Irish issue. But such clunky ponderous comment missed the point— Parnell's apparent embrace of a campaign connecting with the British democracy was simply an appropriate escape route from the dangers of an unsustainable—in his view—revolutionary policy. As he made explicitly clear (with J. J. O'Keilly acting as translator) in an interview with Henri Rochefort in Paris, Fenianism could only achieve its objectives by 'a brutal revolution'. He [Parnell], on the other hand, sought only to compel 'England to do for Ireland what Austria did for Hungary'. He added: 'We do not profess any intention of separating and constituting a new state. These projects are too bold to be capable of resolution.'[91]

# 4

# Dillon versus Parnell

I should mention here that Messrs. Davitt and Brennan voiced the
extreme democracy, but John Dillon inspired the revolt of the general
population of Ireland.

> Laurence J. Kettle (ed.), *The Material for Victory:*
> *Being the Memoirs of Andrew Kettle*, 78.

Did not Mr. Dillon in the House of Commons say he would assassinate
anyone—no but any number of people—who evicted him from his
farm. These are the words in the *Times* in black and white. When a man
openly says such things he cannot blame anyone for looking on him as
a patron of assassination.

> Geraldine Penrose Fitzgerald to Cardinal Newman,
> July 1882. In Patrick Maume, 'An Irishwoman of
> Letters between Newman and Wagner: Geraldine
> Penrose Fitzgerald (1846–1939), her Literary,
> Religious and Political Career', *Proceedings of the Royal*
> *Irish Academy: Archaeology, Culture, History, Literature*,
> vol. 118c (2018), 312.

Parnell's Paris decision not to endorse the path of revolution disappointed John Dillon, even if it did not surprise him. He became the
leading figure in the internal nationalist opposition to Parnell. William
O'Brien later insisted at this moment that Dillon 'followed the discipline of a physical force man as uncompromising as John Mitchel'.[1]
Dillon was not afraid to express an openly violent line in Parliament
itself. He launched a defence of American Fenianism in general and
John Devoy in particular; he spoke in apparent support for Irish civil
war. 'For a moment quietness reigned', said the *Nation* report, 'and

*Ancestral Voices in Irish Politics: Judging Dillon and Parnell.* Paul Bew, Oxford University Press.
© Paul Bew 2023. DOI: 10.1093/oso/9780192873705.003.0004

something very like a shudder ran round the House as he stated that if he were a farmer about to be evicted he would open fire and shoot as many as he could of the evicting party.'[2] Some believed that this moment signalled a decisive parting of the ways between Parnell and Dillon. In the broader English media, not just the private discourse of nationalism, Dillon was described as an 'unclaimable fanatic whose political opinions are derived from the writings of John Mitchel'. Dillon had administered the 'coup de grâce' to Parnell: 'There is no prospect they will again present a united front.'[3] Others were more impressed by Parnell's refusal to criticize Dillon. They noted his 'Hear, hear' when John Redmond appealed to Ireland's right to win independence by force in the previous night's debate. The Tory and Unionist *Belfast Newsletter* parliamentary reporter observed: 'Parnell's speech was intentionally spiteful. He ingeniously defended Fenianism, defended Mr Devoy, defended Mr Dillon, defended himself from the charge of cowardice.' Parnell also successfully mocked William Harcourt, the Home Secretary, whose tone veered uneasily on Irish matters from fear to contempt, for 'manipulating' Dillon's words. 'The House laughed, Mr Gladstone laughed, the Home Secretary laughed; but in truth it was a one-sided laugh. Mr Parnell was deliciously cool, as he invariably is, and treated Sir William Harcourt as mere detail—as one of those very low organisms that irritate only to ensure their destruction.'[4]

But, in fact, a careful study of Parnell's speech suggests a more complex reading. He criticized Harcourt's tone because it was more crudely anti-Irish than either Forster or John Bright, the Chancellor of the Duchy of Lancaster. Parnell recalled—hyperbolically—the effect of the Fenian executions in Ireland and suggested that Harcourt's effort was worse. Parnell was here making reference to the execution of Allen, Larkin, and O'Brien, who killed a police sergeant in Manchester in 1867 during an attempted rescue bid; the executions were privately supported by Gladstone but privately opposed by Disraeli. Parnell defended John Dillon as a high-souled patriot who had got carried away on a tide of emotion. He 'regretted exceedingly' the language employed by him— 'I will not for one moment tolerate such language.'[5] It was probably

Dillon's invocation of the desirability of Irish civil war which provoked this rebuke. He praised the Fenian movement's love of country and spirit of self-sacrifice: but he insisted that the project of armed insurrection was hopeless and, therefore, he had always avoided a connection with Fenianism.[6] Tim Healy was one of the few nationalists at this point who was willing to risk publicly defending Dillon wholeheartedly. The Speaker suspended him for his protests.

The Speaker's increasing effectiveness in controlling Irish protest in Westminster was a new factor. Some Irish farmers had begun to feel that their representatives might be able to paralyse the work of Parliament: increasingly it was clear that this was not the case. Sir George Young, the Liberal activist, academic, and expert in Irish agrarian matters, explained that this was part of the reason for his personal belief that 'in spite of Mr Dillon's fervent protestation, the power of the League to prevent payment is broken throughout the country'.[7] On the public platforms in Ireland Dillon was equally outspoken but here there was an underlying fear that the militancy of the farmers was insufficient for his purpose: 'with the people lay the power of destroying landlordism and if they failed they would never again get the chance'.[8] Birr, for example, one of Dillon's haunts, oscillated between moderation, then militancy, then moderation, in the period from February to March through to May 1881.[9] It sometimes appeared as if the most encouraging aspect of affairs for the League was not its own strength but the weakness on the other side: the March issue of the pro-landlord *Blackwood's Magazine* criticized the unwillingness of the Irish landlords to help the government uphold law and order. But was this criticism fair or accurate? What of the foundation of the Property Defence Association led by Norris Goddard in early 1881 which showed that the landlords were, at least, capable of some self-help?

On 7 April 1881, the Land Law (Ireland) bill was introduced in the House of Commons and enacted on 22 August. The British government was now showing its hand—the strategy was a combination of coercion and conciliation—but was the substantial conciliation offered by the 1881 Act likely to be sufficient? After all, it effectively offered the 3Fs (fair rent, free sale, and fixity of tenure), which had been Parnell's demands of the late 1870s. In April, Parnell addressed the largest ever Home Rule demonstration in the north of England at Newcastle upon Tyne. Between 8,000 and 9,000 men took part in the proceedings, the majority being Irishmen employed in shipbuilding, chemical manufacturing, mining, and other industrial pursuits. Although there was an overwhelming majority of Irish there were a significant number of English miners present. In so far as Parnell's appeal to the 'British democracy' had any meaning, this meeting fitted with that slogan. Parnell included a message for the English workers who were present: he implored 'the English working men not to allow anybody to set them against Ireland, or persuade them that the Irish people were an unruly people'.[10] Parnell announced his hostility to the emigration clauses of the Land bill as indicating contempt for the interests of small farmers: 'If then this bill was to be reality and not a sham, it must protect the interests of the small tenants equally with those of the large ones.' The emigration clauses should be dropped. Parnell added: 'Provision ought to be made by which tenants in arrears of the payment of rack rent should have those rack rents reduced to the fair, judicial rent which the bill proposed to fix (Hear, Hear).' It was impossible, Parnell stated, to sweep aside the poorer tenants in favour of the richer. In fact, the poorer tenants of the west had initiated the campaign in the first place. 'Only upon these conditions could the bill prove acceptable to the Irish people', Parnell said. He could not accept a measure which gave 'security' to the richer tenants while sweeping aside the poor man. Nobody who heard this speech could reasonably suggest that it was a revolutionary effort.

The Land Act certainly presented a problem for John Mitchel's doctrine. Mitchel in 1848 had dismissed—'never, never'—any possibility of such a reform.[11] While denouncing the Land Act, Dillon clearly feared that it might be effective. He declared in the Rotunda in Dublin on 12 April, 'no consideration would induce me to vote for this bill knowing as I do that I would be helping to rivet the collar of the master around the tenants.' On 14 April, *The Times* reported the internment of P. J. Gordon, a fellow traverser at the state trial alongside Parnell and

Dillon. Gordon defiantly called for a local landlord, Colonel Walter Bourke, to be 'blown to bits', as he left Claremorris station for Kilmainham. Gordon joined his old friend Sheridan in jail, but, by August 1881, Sheridan had cited his wife's illness (actually alcoholism) and was released. Dillon must have known that his own freedom was now at risk. In Donegal on 18 April, nonetheless, he described the Land bill as imposing an intensified form of slavery on the Irish tenantry. On 27 April, Dillon said that unless Parliament stopped all Irish evictions, 'the ensuing violence should be seen as the fault of the government'.[12] On 2 May, he delivered another aggressive speech at Grangemockler. He had developed menacing anecdote as a form of speech making. He spoke of a Tipperary story not yet in the newspapers. A priest had told an eviction party of police that behind the barricaded door there were several armed men ready to fire. The police had returned to barracks.[13] He was arrested but treated 'with every possible consideration', including first-class transport by rail arranged for him by Thomas Burke, the senior official in Dublin Castle: a grace from one member of the Irish Catholic elite to another; Burke was a grandnephew of Cardinal Wiseman. 'Instructions were given to the police to treat Mr Dillon with every consideration becoming a gentleman.'[14] Did Forster reflect at this moment on the irony that he once offered sanctuary to the Young Ireland revolutionary, John Blake Dillon, but was now locking up his son for challenging British rule in Ireland? It was immediately reported that Dillon was ill. Thousands, it was said, were watching nervously the health of the 'devoted' young member for Tipperary.[15] Interestingly, however, there was no talk of Dillon resigning his seat and forcing a by-election: even though the Press Association had reported that this idea had been seriously discussed in Paris.[16] The government feared that the 'rumour of split' between Parnell and Dillon would now end; Parnell would have to show complete solidarity with Dillon.[17]

But that did not happen. The next day, 3 May, a parliamentary explosion was expected; ministers like Harcourt sat nervously in their seats 'whiskers twitching'. 'But where was Mr Parnell?' asked the *Express*. He was in the Palace but declined for 'reasons best known to himself to come into the House'. The *Express* concluded: 'A great storm which was to have broken over the House of Commons and deluged that remarkable assembly, passed harmlessly overhead.'[18] On 3 May, the government heard that a journalist had been briefed by a member of the Irish party that 'Mr Dillon's arrest was no matter of surprise to anyone…it was evident that the only reason the Government had left him at large so long was that he might divide the party'.[19] By 10 May, Parnell was happy to return to the more non-political issue of Dillon's health: 'I now ask the Irish Chief Secretary and Lieutenant of Ireland if the government intends to keep John Dillon in prison till he dies.'[20] Michael Davitt later recalled that at the moment of Dillon's arrest 'his influence was second only to that of Parnell's at this time while he was much more in sympathy with the extreme policy upheld by Brennan and his advanced lieutenants who still ruled the organisation on new departure lines and principles'.[21] The poet 'Rollicker' in the *Derry Journal* cried out: 'Let us stand from shore to shore | And show the foe | Who strikes the blow | We have millions more.'[22] But did they?

During Dillon's incarceration, the big problem for the Land League was maintaining the internal solidarity of its support base. In this task, Dillon had the support of Parnell's sister, Anna. With coercion looming in late January 1881 the Land League executive took the decision to appoint Anna Parnell as the effective head of a Ladies' Land League.[23] On 31 January 1881, she presided alongside Kate Moloney as treasurer, Jennie O Toole (later the author Jenny Wyse-Power), and Dillon's cousin Anne Deane as president—the exceptional businesswoman who, in effect, funded John Dillon's career. Davitt was strongly in favour of the Ladies' concept: Dillon and Parnell less so. Anna Parnell possessed, as the *Manchester Guardian* obituary later said: 'a fund of febrile energy which found no outlet till the days of the Land League'. If her sister Fanny was the 'best writer in the family', Anna was the 'best speaker': in the course of 1881 she spoke at Leeds[24] and Kanturk[25] in March, Derry[26] and Bohola in May, Tullow in June,[27] and Clara, Co. Offaly, also in June[28]—where her audience was larger than that of her brother at the same venue.

At the end of May 1881, Anna Parnell went to Mayo to reassure the small farmers of the west that the rich farmers of Meath, Limerick, and Cork were now prepared to fight 'your battles for you, it is not all left on your shoulders now'.[29] But was she sure? She noted the collapse of the rent resistance of Colonel Tottenham's (MP for Leitrim) tenants in Wexford in June 1881,[30] and, even more dramatically, senior Land Leaguer Andrew Kettle's surrender in North Dublin the same month with the full 'decorum of the law' preserved.[31] As late as July 1881, Anna Parnell publicly supported Land League methods, including rent at the point of a bayonet. 'I can only suppose,' she wrote later, 'that I was wilfully shutting my eyes to the evidence before me, and refusing to see because I did not want to see.'[32]

As the League spread across the country, it was clear that areas where larger farmers dominated were quite prepared to join the Land League alongside the smallholders of the west. But it was also clear that they felt they had a lot to lose. They were exceptionally reluctant to be evicted just to be part of a process exercising pressure on the British government and the landlord class. They were prepared to engage in protracted legalistic conflicts. In particular, they were prepared to do so if the lawyers involved were paid, as they were, with Irish American dollars. But the provisions of the law which might be exploited for the benefit of farmers were mainly limited to the rights of smallholders.[33] In short, Ireland's middle and strong farmers already had a substantial effective property in their farms and the Land Act was clearly intended to enhance that property. This was the crux of Dillon's problem—how did he hold the bulk of the Irish farmers to a revolutionary line in such a context? On 12 July, Dillon wrote frankly to O'Brien about the differences within the Land League executive on this very question. The militant wing of the executive—Dillon, Egan, Brennan, and Davitt—were in serious disagreement with Parnell and the parliamentary section of the executive. 'I am not quite clear as to what course I shall take when I am set at liberty. But I am quite clear that I can not allow the people to suppose that the course adopted by the Parliamentary Party towards the Land Bill is satisfactory...It is not unlikely that I shall retire from politics.'[34] O'Brien later said that John Dillon was now 'at the heart of the semi-revolt of the "Kilmainham" Party in 1881 against Parnell for even his very qualified dependence upon the Westminster parliament'.[35] O'Brien added: 'Mr Dillon was simply influenced by that lack of imaginative insight, which is the principal element of greatness wanting in his character, and which led him habitually to view any new line of action, in the constantly shifting circumstances of the Irish movement, with a suspiciousness, an indecision, a certain revolutionary Toryism of mind, which fails to perceive that old "methods" can not always continue to be the most effective ones.'[36]

The government in August decided to release John Dillon on health grounds. While these distinctive health issues were real enough, it is hard to believe that there was not also a subliminal political calculation. This existed alongside a fear that the government appeared weak and indecisive. Florence Arnold-Forster, the Chief Secretary's adopted daughter, noted in her diary: 'Some talk about Mr Dillon. What will he do? Come back and receive an oration from his compatriots in the House? Will he deny that it is on account of his health he is let out and maintain that he is quite well? He himself will hardly do this, but the other Parnellites will be quite capable of maintaining that the Chief Sec. and the government have been frightened into releasing him.' She added: 'Each man who has sent a threatening letter will think that it was just his letter which did it.'[37] Dillon was released on 6 August. He publicly associated himself with the Davitt/Devoy tradition, which was still hoping that the land question could be linked with a nationalist upheaval. Dillon was well aware, however, that Parnell did not intend such a revolutionary course; in consequence, he announced his decision to resign from politics 'for many months'. His temporary resignation was tinged with a threat. 'Let us then resolve that for the future we will never trust any parliamentary party action and seek their inspiration at the hands of men who have come up fresh from the manhood and brain of Ireland.'[38] On 10 August, John Dillon warned the House of Commons of 'bloodshed' and 'massacre to come'.[39] On the other hand, many Parnellite MPs were contemplating work on the improvement of the Land Act with pleasure. On 18 August, Florence Arnold-Forster noted: 'the atmosphere even in the Parnell quarter of the House was very different from what it had been on the January afternoon when the Ch. Sec. introduced the Coercion Bill'.[40]

The intervention of Ireland's most popular senior nationalist clergyman was very helpful to the government. It was very unhelpful to Dillon. Archbishop Croke of Cashel declared:

> Speaking more generally I am decidedly of the opinion that the great bulk of our farming classes, and indeed, shopkeeping classes would be glad to see the present land bill passed substantially in law, especially if fair provision be made in it for leaseholders and tenants arrears, and still more so if the commissioners appointed to administer the act be such as to inspire confidence.[41]

Dillon was more and more despairing. At the end of August, he gave a speech full of double negatives in which he simultaneously denounced Parnellite policy and refused to disavow that same Parnellite policy. His original analysis, he stated, had been that the Land bill would 'take all the power out of the League'. After all, the 1881 Act had conceded 'free sale'—but the right of sale posed a major threat to the popular movement. For if tenants refused to pay their rents, they would be dispossessed and lose this valuable new right.[42] He added: 'The policy that he had adopted before his arrest was full of risk and danger. Still, it was a policy he believed in' but now 'that policy which he [had] urged [became] infinitely more difficult'. He was not prepared to say that it had made it impossible. He was not prepared at all to say that 'the policy put forward by Mr Parnell was not the best policy'.[43] Dillon added: 'I wish it to be distinctly understood that this bill will confer immense benefits to the Irish people.'[44] Gladstone understandably misinterpreted Dillon's stance—he saw it as the action of a principled nationalist who nonetheless did not think he had the right to prevent Irish farmers accessing the benefits of the Land Act. Dillon was, in fact, saying that he remained in principle a revolutionist but did not dare to condemn Parnell's non-revolutionary stance. This rather confused compliment from Gladstone, arch ogre of the movement, forced a reluctant Dillon back to Parnell's side. It was a classic misreading of Irish politics. But it serves to remind us how far Gladstone's disapproval at this point was fixated on Parnell to the exclusion of all others.

In September, Parnell had the problem of defining the Land League attitude to the new Land Act. He called a Land League convention. The 'Kilmainham party'—a group of malcontent suspects headed by Dillon—announced that if the Act were allowed to be tested it would break the power of the Land League within six months, and Dillon himself prepared to emigrate to live with his brother in Colorado if the Act was in any way tolerated. Parnell discussed with 'studied gentleness' the difficulty created by Mr Dillon—but he did not allow Dillon to determine his policy.[45] William O'Brien noted with some insight:

> Parnell's opening address was mostly listened to in a respectful but frigid silence. The sure and penetrating statesmanship with which he singled out the incurable error of the Act—that it proposed to reopen the Land question every fifteen years, and must consequently be a continual source of contention between landlords and tenants, 'and keep classes in Ireland divided so that we may thus be prevented from utilising our united strength for the purpose of recovering our lost rights of legislating for ourselves'—passed unnoticed at the time.[46]

Loud and prolonged cheering came only for remarks like the 'Land Act settled nothing' or 'our principal demand is that rent shall be abolished'. At a superficial glance, it seemed as if absolute rejectionism was triumphing. However, Parnell was holding two ideas in tension—one that the Act was in the long term unsatisfactory from an Irish nationalist point of view, the other that, nonetheless, the correct course was not at this moment to reject it but 'test' it. It is clear that William O'Brien admired Parnell's stance. O'Brien's comment requires some analysis. He is stating that Parnell's analysis was vindicated by the eventual passage of the Wyndham Act of 1903, which followed, intellectually speaking, Parnellite lines. But this abstract approach also had a more current application: Parnell's unity of the Irish social classes theme helped his case for exploiting the 1881 Act.

Had he embraced that Act without criticism it could have been disastrous; so an apparently purely abstract theoretical long-term mode
of thinking had direct practical effect on the moment, allowing for
the adoption of a more moderate course.

But the League's problems were not confined simply to the issue of
the Land Act, they also embraced the viability of its key mode of struggle: not the boycott of evicted land (which required more victims than
were willing to make themselves available) but rent at the point of a
bayonet. Lying in the background was the whole issue of Land League
strategy—designed to appeal to comfortable farmers. However, in July
and August 1881 it became clear that the League was running out of the
money necessary to sustain this policy. Parnell was perfectly aware of
this weakness in the League's armoury: if, at the end of the process, the
tenants paid at the 'point of the bayonet' while their legal costs were met
by the League, in Parnell's words, 'They might just as well have given in
first as last.'[47] Money sent to Ireland by Irish Americans would be
wasted. Thomas Sexton sent out a message that 'rent at the point of a
bayonet' was to be concluded as a policy, but there might be 'excep-
tions'. The absence of clarity was a recipe for further confusion. For
Sexton, at the centre of the League's financial affairs, 'rent at the point of
a bayonet' had become 'absurd, suicidal and destructive' but there could
be 'exceptional circumstances...'.[48]

The policy of testing the Act supported by Parnell was, of course,
also ambiguous. Was it, as the government feared, a policy secretly
designed to destroy the Act? Was it a genuine attempt at compromise?
Florence Arnold-Forster noted with some admiration: 'Mr Parnell was
placed in a rather delicate situation by his joint obligations towards the
Fenian and Socialist party in America, and the tenant farmers in this
country...the latter were known to have a lurking desire to derive practical benefit from the Act in spite of the abuse heaped upon its authors
by Mr Parnell and his associates...it must be said that this being the
case he conducted the proceedings with great diplomacy.'[49] Tributes to
political skill of opponents are often frothy and insubstantial—this was
not. It was of course private not public.

Parnell then set off on the process of selecting test cases for the Land Courts. Alas, this process rapidly mutated into farce. Recommended by the Mallow Land League, he turned up at the farm of Tim Foley. But, to general surprise, Foley's attitude to Parnell was decidedly surly, he 'displayed an inexplicable urbanity of manner descending almost to rudeness towards the Land League chief'. The 'inexplicable' was in fact quite 'explicable'.[50] Tim Foley was said locally to be a land grabber who had grabbed the land from his nephew, Jeremiah. Parnell became quite angry, recalling the sacrifices made by hard-working Irish Americans who financed the cause of selfish Irish farmers engaging in sham fights. The next day he sent emissaries to shut down the Mallow Land League.[51] He then proceeded to the Waterford Convention where he repeated his remarks about the Irish Americans who contributed so valiantly to the cause of ungrateful Irish farmers.

The operation of the Land Act requires some comment. Gladstone clearly felt that rents would not be largely reduced. He said on 22 July 1881: 'I shall be deeply disappointed with the operation of the Act if the property of the landlords does not come to be worth more than twenty years' purchase on the judicial rent.'[52] In fact, the administrative processes concerned in the implementation of the Act were chaotic and outcomes were far less satisfactory for the landlords. Parnell had a stronger intuition on this point than Gladstone.[53] W. O'Connor Morris shrewdly observed that those who wanted the Act to work might have borrowed Parnell's concept of 'having test cases' which would allow the establishment of principles. In fact, the commissioners were overwhelmed and not just by the volume of work but, more importantly, the political pressure from all sides. After all, had not Mr Justice O'Hagan laid it down that the object of the Act of 1881 was to allow tenants to live and thrive?[54] Harold Spender expressed the inevitable outcome perfectly when he spoke of the 'leaden, merciless pressure of the great Land Courts set up by Mr Gladstone's Act of 1881' gradually wearing 'down the dour and obstinate wills of the Irish landlords'.[55] In the first year, rents fixed by the Commission were 11.8 per cent above the poor law valuation: by the end of the year ending August 1887 they were 14.4 per cent below it.[56]

By mid October, Gladstone had completed his misunderstanding of Parnell by, in effect, ordering his arrest. The arrest caught the attention of the British public. It was the 'one topic of conversation in public circles in Accrington and the opinion was unanimously in favour. At Blackburn the news was received with satisfaction by all classes, except the Irish who are rather numerous here. In Birmingham general satisfaction was expressed except by members of the Reform League.'[57] In Dublin, of course, the mood was rather different, and contemptuous; John Dillon said to an intimate of the Forster family: 'This is a strong thing your friends have been doing.' Bartholomew Teeling answered, 'Well now, between you and me and the post don't you think that it was not a bit too soon?' On which Mr Dillon only laughed and then went his way to make a flaming speech at the Land League meeting.[58] On 13 October 1881, on the day of his arrest, Parnell wrote to Katharine O'Shea: 'Politically it is a fortunate thing for one that I have been arrested, as the movement is breaking fast, and all will be quiet in a few months, when I shall be released.'[59] Some months later, on 4 February, Parnell repeated his theme: 'At least I am very glad that the days of platform speeches have gone by and are not likely to return. I can not describe to you the disgust I always felt with those meetings, knowing as I did how hollow and wanting in solidity everything connected with the movement was.'[60]

Kilmainham prison was, as Parnell repeatedly said in later years, a humane confinement. It was also tedious, and the Gladstone family liked to say it cured Parnell of any desire for further extended spells in the company of Irish nationalists. Visitors referred to the 'gentleman's club' atmosphere but this is not quite right—it was more like a boarding school for nationalist adults. Good food was sent in by well-wishers. Some in particular, like Parnell himself, had a substantial study or 'apartment'; there was facility for exercise and some sport. But confinement is confinement: visitors noticed the wan appearance of inmates. James Bryce later noted: 'He [Parnell] never forgave either W. E. Forster or Mr Gladstone for having imprisoned him in 1881 ... the anecdote was told at the time that when he found himself in the prison yard at

Kilmainham, he said, in a sort of soliloquy: "I shall live yet to dance upon these two old men's graves."[61] Parnell said later to Davitt: 'You know he [Forster] put us in prison and we were obliged to strike back so as to deter others from returning to like methods again.'[62] 'Henri Le Caron', the British spy at the heart of Irish Fenianism, reported in December 1888 that the Leeds-born Irish American terrorist Luke Dillon had told him that Patrick Egan had told him that Parnell knew of, but did not approve of, a plan to attack Forster.[63] This is third-hand gossip. On the other hand, such notions were talked about in Kilmainham. Parnell later said: 'I never had the slightest notion that the life of the late Mr Forster was in danger, or that any conspiracy was on foot against him or any official in Ireland or elsewhere.'[64] This, at least, must be in doubt. Parnell himself talked of the need to 'strike back', a phrase he had himself used in a later discussion with Michael Davitt. The families of the Invincibles insisted it was hard to believe that Parnell knew nothing of their existence.

Once incarcerated, however, Parnell wanted to see the end of the active movement in the countryside; this was entirely separate from any emotions of revenge he may have entertained, or tacitly, if in all likelihood unenthusiastically, colluded in. He was, therefore, happy to adopt the ultra-leftist cause of the 'No Rent' manifesto. Dillon was reluctant to support 'no rent', in all probability distrusting Parnell's intentions, but in the end felt he had to acquiesce. Appearances can be deceptive in politics: Parnell, the moderate, adopted the revolutionary slogan 'No Rent' to divide the Irish tenant farming community and hasten the collapse of the Land League. Dillon, the revolutionary, distrusted the 'revolutionary slogan because he knew the time was not right for its successful application'.[65] It was observed later that the Parnellite manifesto was actually a means of exorcising the 'No Rent' fantasy from Irish politics by proving its unworkability. Of course, it read as a full-blooded call to arms. As William O'Brien put it, 'the country had been so long taught to regard a No Rent movement as practicable and irresistible, that, if it were not tested now under every possible circumstance of justification and of high and indignant National spirit to sustain it, the conclusion would be that a matchless opportunity had been lost'.[66] It was the means of testing a proposition to its destruction.

> Fellow countrymen, the hour to try your souls and redeem your pledges has arrived. The executive of the National Land League is forced to abandon its policy of testing the Land Act, and feels bound to advise the tenant farmers in Ireland from this day forth to pay no rents under any circumstances to their landlords until the government relinquishes the present system of terrorism, and restores the constitutional rights of the people.[67]

William O'Brien later explained Parnell's mindset: 'He did not believe' that the advice to the Irish tenants to endure evictions rather than pay their rents 'would be generally obeyed'. But he anticipated that it would be obeyed on 'a sufficient scale' to exercise upon the new Land Courts the 'same influence as the test cases', thus making the government of the country by Forster's ruthless coercive methods impossible.[68] Anna Parnell observed even more acutely:

> It enabled them to escape from the dilemma they had placed themselves in by promising to defray the cost incurred by paying 'rent at the point of the bayonet' without acknowledging they had made a mistake in assuming such a responsibility. They had sacrificed everything to keeping up the appearance of resistance to rent so long as they were at liberty and now they did not want to keep up that appearance any longer.'[69]

What this passage does not convey is that agrarian violence came to be separated somewhat from the rent struggle; it became a means of demonstrating to the government that it was wrong to coerce. At any rate, it soon became clear that the Land League was no longer prepared to pay the legal costs of a struggling tenantry. Before his arrest Parnell publicly alluded to this possibility—now it was a reality. At the end of October, the Press Association printed a message which it said came from the Kilmainham leadership:

> The only organisation any longer practicable is that the tenants should meet by estates when called upon to pay rent, and decide upon the common line of action recommended in the manifesto of the Executive. The time has now come for the Irish people to choose between the Government Law Courts and the principles of the League; but we can not do anything

for evicted tenants on those estates where their fellow tenants on the same estate are unmindful of those principles. We have therefore directed those in charge of the relief funds to refuse assistance to tenants on estates where the rest of the tenants have either applied to the courts to fix a rent or have paid their rent.[70]

Anna Parnell was furious. It was soon claimed that the message was a forgery but it was widely believed to be genuine at the time. It was clear evidence that the Land League as an organized fighting machine was over. If the tenantry wanted to organize their own resistance and cover the costs—that was another matter. But given that the government was tempting them with the fruits of the 1881 Act, it was unlikely that the bulk of the tenantry would be up for the fight. The 'No Rent' manifesto was as such a failure but, on the other hand, the alienation of Irish public opinion from the British government was still intact. Ideologically if not practically, the Land League carried the day. To the anger of Canon Dennehy of Kanturk, schoolchildren embraced the Land League alphabet. Canon Dennehy insisted the themes were anti-Christian in tone and set a bad example for children. Few nationalists supported him. They were quite happy to allow this displacement of the conflict which shifted its focus to the rhymes of children.

> A is the army that covers the ground
> B is the buckshot we are getting all round
> C is the crowbar of the cruellest famine
> D is our Davitt a right glorious name
> E is the English who robbed us of bread
> F is the famine they have left us instead
> G is for Gladstone whose life is a lie
> H is the Harvest we'll hold or we'll die
> I is the inspector who when drunk is bold
> J is the Jarvey who'll not drive him for gold
> K is Kilmainham, where our true men abide
> L is the Land League, our hope and our pride
> M is the magistrate who makes black of white
> N is 'No Rent' that will make our wrongs right
> O is the Old Ireland that yet shall be freed
> P is the Peelers who slaughter for greed

Q is the Queen whose use is not known
R is the Rifles who keep up the throne
S is the sheriff with woe in his train
T is the toil that others may gain
U is the Union that works bitter harm
V is the villain who grabs a farm
W is the warrant for death and chains
X is the Express, all lies and no brains
Y is Young Ireland spreading her light
Z is the zeal that will win the great fight [71]

For Parnell there were other encouraging signs. J. A. Froude allowed himself to say, 'in an independent Ireland the ablest and stronger elements will come to the fore and the baser elements be crushed'.[72] The sight of a famously imperialist and unionist intellectual contemplating an independent Ireland was exciting to some. Even more exciting was the controversy which followed the Land bill. This was the publication under official authority (HMSO) in a pamphlet form of a series of articles which appeared in the *Freeman's Journal* under the heading: 'How to become owner of your farm. Why Irish landlords should sell and Irish tenants should purchase and how they can do it under the Land Act of 1881.' At one level, the text presents itself as offering a middle way between militant 'No Rent' activists and aggressive Irish landlords, by calling for the exploitation of purchase claims of the 1881 Act. There was, however, a benign reference to the doctrine of Davitt that 'far seeing man' unfurled at Irishtown. The *Times* article says it is easy to understand why landlords should feel intimidated by such an article.[73] It soon emerged that the author of the most surprising section of the document—the very positive reference to Michael Davitt—was George Fottrell. Forster had taken the risk of appointing him at the Land Commission: Fottrell was a friend of Dillon and had sat beside him at the 1879 Home Rule meeting to establish the ground rules for the 1882 convention. By 9 February, Fottrell had resigned from the Land Commission but from Forster's point of view the damage was done— the government had been made to look absurd. It was, after all, imprisoning as a danger to social order a man (Davitt) its own official document described as 'far seeing'. But the fact that Fottrell had been appointed at all shows how far Forster was prepared to go to gain credibility for the Land Act. The *Times* coverage of the Fottrell affair gave succour to the League leadership. With great delight, Patrick Egan, the Land League treasurer holed up in Paris, wrote to the senior Irish American leader General Patrick Collins: 'I enclose this article which appeared in the *Times* of yesterday from their Dublin correspondent, who you are aware is [Dr Valentine Patton] the editor of the *Dublin Daily Express* the great Tory and landlord organ. It shows in unmistakable terms the hopeless condition to which we have brought Irish landlords.'[74] Of course, there was a price to be paid: Thomas Brennan, Egan's close friend, had been in jail since the early summer of 1881 and he was now said by his doctors to be displaying signs of heart disease.[75] But it was a price Egan felt was worth paying.

Dr Valentine Patton's unease was to be intensified by two Gladstone speeches in the House of Commons on 9 February and, a week later, on 16 February. Clever nationalist MPs like F. H. O'Donnell and Thomas Sexton correctly felt that the speech seems to accept the principle of Home Rule,[76] provided a plan could be advanced by which the local affairs could be separated from the 'Imperial Affairs of Ireland'. William O'Brien wrote in the Parnellite journal *United Ireland* on 4 March, that Gladstone is really 'making another bid for the favour of the Irish people and that bid is Home Rule'. *The Times*, increasingly the voice of English unionism, hated the speeches.[77] In the lobbies though, as Bryce noted, it became commonplace for ambitious young Liberal MPs to talk favourably of the Home Rule concept. Florence Arnold-Forster summed up the unionist unease in her diary on 19 February:

> It is much to be feared that in thinking of Mr. P. J. Smyth, Mr. Shaw, Mr. Morley, Mr. O'Connor Power, and a few other Irish politicians by whom perhaps reasonable propositions for the establishment of Irish local government would be met in the honest and friendly spirit in which they were put forward, Mr. Gladstone quite left out of mind the overpowering majority of Irish politicians, by whom any concession in this direction would be used as a leverage ground against our country.

However much there may be said theoretically in favour of giving a fair hearing to Home Rule demands it is hard to believe that in practice, and under present conditions such a way of dealing with the subject can do anything but harm; this is especially the conclusion one comes to after reading the Irish papers, and seeing the honest regret of such thoroughly Irish-minded papers as the *Irish Times* at a fresh incentive being given to agitation and the exultation of the *Freeman's Journal* over a concession which is evidently the result, it points out, not of the moderate tactics of past Home Rulers, but of the violent system of the present day.[78]

In the spring of 1882, John Dillon made a last major intervention on the Murroe estate of Lord Cloncurry. Cloncurry was an irresistible target: his lands were good, his tenants prosperous, and he preached the laws of political economy. The *Freeman's Journal* reported the sense of some that Cloncurry's land was good land and the tenants should pay good rents for it. The tenants had a rather different perspective. The *Freeman's Journal* reported on 6 March 1882: 'They believe that if they permit themselves to be evicted the farms will be waste...and that in the end the landlord will be willing to restore them on their own terms.' They were urged on by John Ryan, the local League secretary, a farmer but not a Cloncurry tenant. The local salaried Land League solicitor, McGough, well known to Parnell, appears to have believed the struggle was unwise but fails to have conveyed this to the vast majority of the tenantry. The most important local priest, Canon Wall, also seems to have favoured compromise—but, on the other hand, he was under the erroneous impression that Thomas Sexton of the Central Land League had promised to meet the costs (which in the end amounted to £3,000) if any successful legal action were taken by Lord Cloncurry. Canon Wall was also unwell at critical moments in the crisis.[79] This is where the ambiguity of Sexton's commentary in August created genuine uncertainty. On the one hand, a League commitment to the costs in a case like this was 'suicidal', he said, but, on the other hand, there was the possibility of an exception to the rule. At precisely this moment, John Dillon's advice was sought—he resisted all talk of compromise and urged continued struggle: in this he was supported by Anna Parnell.

Lord Cloncurry prevailed and the majority of the tenants were evicted. The Ladies' Land League built huts: Bartholomew Hickey, for example, was still living in one with his wife, children, and grandchildren at the end of 1883.[80] Dillon appears to have disregarded the Land League's own decision not to pay out for this type of conflict—with negative consequences.

Increasingly—as both the Gladstone family and Anna Parnell pointed out—it became clear the violence and rent resistance were becoming relatively separate issues. Anna Parnell declared in her memoir that she failed to understand this point at first and thus wasted the resources of her activists in the Ladies' Land League who were trying to encourage rent resistance. When the Forster regime in Dublin Castle signalled that an area was particularly violent, 'an unduly large proportion of our staff' was sent to such an area. 'The discovery we made as a result of this step was that these were precisely those which should have had least, instead of the most of our attention. As a rule there was simply no idea whatever in these districts of not paying rent.'[81] W. E. Gladstone on 24 March 1882 defined the Irish situation to Forster as the 'Land Act working briskly, resistance to process serving disappearing and rents increasingly and even generally though not universally paid'.[82] On 29 March 1882, Herbert Gladstone wrote in his diary that reinforcement of rent payment was achieved but crimes were committed as an 'act of revenge' against the government for coercion.[83] His father, W. E. Gladstone, wrote to Lord Spencer on 3 April 1882: 'Matters in Ireland do not improve so far as outrage is concerned though the Land Act works increasingly and rents are paid.'[84] Parnell felt otherwise. This was the perception which undermined Forster: why did he not see that coercion had defeated the social revolution and should now be dropped in order to remove the context and excuse for violence? Such narratives once started are difficult to stop—as Forster pointed out, crime began to fall in the weeks before his fall. But no one noticed or cared. Gladstone's circle muttered that it was time to sacrifice the 'old man' (Forster) for the good of the country. Ironically Parnell agreed with Forster. On 5 April 1882, he wrote: 'So far as I can judge, the number of outrages has diminished very materially during the past two or three weeks, and is likely to continue decreasing.'[85] But nothing can defeat a 'sophisticated' illusion whose time has come.

Parnell had new problems. On 24 March 1882, he declared: 'Mr Dillon's health was anything but in a strong state, especially the past few days.'[86] On 10 April 1882, Parnell took advantage of his temporary release, in connection with the death of his nephew, to begin the negotiations which led to the 'Kilmainham Treaty' with the government and his release from prison alongside John Dillon and J. J. O'Kelly on 2 May. The formal structure of the accommodation with the Gladstone government was clear enough. In return for an understanding that the arrears question would be dealt with and leaseholders admitted to the benefits of the Land Act, and a contingent understanding that coercion would be abandoned, Parnell agreed that the Land Act, thus altered, would be 'a practical settlement of the land question'.[87] The concern for the 'lease-holders', the 'flower' of the Irish tenantry, was striking because this was precisely the group Thomas Brennan had dismissed in his speech of April 1881.[88] On 28 April, restored to Kilmainham, Parnell told his visitor, O'Shea, that he was keeping his colleagues in Kilmainham in the dark, because he wanted to win over instigators of violence like P. J. Sheridan and Patrick Egan. In Parnell's creative phrase 'he desired to get the first run at them'.[89] Parnell was nervous about John Dillon's reaction, but O'Shea claimed in early May 1882 in a communication to Gladstone that Parnell has 'now got his hand upon Dillon'. Parnell went further when he argued that such a change would allow the 'Home Rule party to cooperate for the future with the Liberal party in forwarding liberal principles of general reform'.

Gladstone was delighted by this '*hors d'oeuvre*' and felt a debt of gratitude to Captain O'Shea, who had inserted himself into the negotiations. The Captain was so anxious that the deal be done that he decided to add a new Parnellite commitment. Early on 30 April, he told the Chief Secretary, Forster—who was, to say the least, unenthusiastic—about a deal: 'the conspiracy which has been used to set up boycotting and outrages will now be used to put them down and there will be reunion with the Liberal party'. O'Shea then added that Parnell hoped to make use of P. J. Sheridan, the well-known extremist League organizer, to stifle crime in the west of Ireland as he (Sheridan) was well acquainted with it.[90] In fact, Parnell, according to O'Shea, would undertake not only in a vague way to discourage outrage, but to persuade Mr Sheridan, the Land League organizer, to do the same.[91] If the government dealt with the arrears issue, Parnell would employ Sheridan to put down outrage. Impressed by all this talk, Gladstone decided to release Parnell on 2 May: Forster resigned. Parnell may still have had his fears about John Dillon's opposition but in early May he told O'Shea that he had his 'hands' on Dillon.

O'Shea's indiscreet remark to Forster in itself made the Parnell–Sheridan relationship a neuralgic issue for Parnell in later years. But when conveyed to Gladstone at the end of April, it had made Parnell's continued incarceration difficult to justify. But how to get him out of jail and keep face? Gladstone pondered the issue intently. Eventually the formula known as the 'Kilmainham Treaty' was produced. It was simply impossible to keep Parnell in jail, it was said, given his evident reasonableness. 'It was the vital turning point in Parnell's career', noted Michael Davitt. 'He had hitherto been in everything but name a revolutionary reformer and won many triumphs at the head of the most powerful organisation any Irish leader had at his back for a century. He now resolved to surrender the Land League and to enter the new stage of his political fortunes as an opportunist statesman.'[92] Davitt was absolutely right but Parnell was still the victor in early May 1882. John Adye Curran's judgement is hard to resist: 'For English administration it was peace at any price; for Parnell and his followers it was peace with honour, and the peace of victory.'[93] D. B. King wrote: 'One of the songs much used to express popular feeling was an adaptation of Moore's "Sound the Loud Timbrel" beginning, "Sound the loud timbrel over Ireland's blue sea | The Land League has triumphed, the suspects are free." '[94] The journal *The American* noted the personal element in the victory which was especially dear to the Irish heart. 'The Celts are full of personal loyalties and sympathies. No amount of general concessions to them as tenants could atone to them for the arrest of the leaders and the continuance of Mr Forster in office.'[95]

On 3 May, Forster's resignation reached the newspapers. More than any other factor, this helped an Irish audience believe that Parnell had somehow triumphed. But Parnell himself was concerned lest it be thought that he had 'sold out' in order to secure his release. He gave an interview on that day to the 'special correspondent' of the *Irish World*.[96] There had been no negotiations of any sort with the government. In fact, even on the morning of his release, he had no hint it was impending. The *Irish World* did not say who was the 'special correspondent' in this case. O'Neill Larkin, their regular Ireland correspondent, signed his articles in his own name. However, by the autumn, P. J. Sheridan was working for the *Irish World* in New York and, indeed, actually living in their offices. Was this 3 May article an early example of his work? He later boasted that he had met Parnell at this very moment and he had asked Parnell to swear a 'Fenian oath': to complicate the potential meaning of this phrase, there are also apparently surviving copies of the oath for the Irish National Invincibles in Sheridan's hand.[97] Did Parnell engage in such a piece of theatre—as Sheridan claimed, and some of his co-conspirators actually believed—in the admittedly 'incongruous' setting of Trinity College Dublin? There can be no clarity on this score. It is not in doubt that Sheridan's name was at the centre of the negotiations leading to Parnell's release. It is not in doubt that Parnell wished to send a message to the clique of which Sheridan was a key member that he was still a rock solid nationalist. He used the *Irish World* interview on 3 May to send such a message.

Even if we decide that Sheridan's claims about his meeting with Parnell are exaggerated or invented, the indisputable reality is quite remarkable enough. Parnell's back channel, Captain O'Shea, had offered Sheridan's name to Gladstone as someone who had helped initiate violence—as the authorities firmly believed—and who would now put it down. Even more remarkably, Gladstone excitedly accepted this offer, effectively dismissed his Irish Chief Secretary, and on 5 May asked for more releases of suspects to be made to help Sheridan in this particular work. Looking back on this moment of Parnellite supremacy, on 22 March 1883 Parnell gave an interview to the editor of the *Clarion*: 'The knife which killed Lord F. Cavendish nearly killed the Land League at the same blow. We were in a superb situation. My friends and I, as you are aware, had been thrown into prison; risings had taken place in Ireland; the Government saw that they were powerless to repress the disturbances; they came to us and asked us to intervene; they set us free. We said to them, "You must take such and such measures. The good provisions of the Act of 1881 must not be neutralized by the tribunals entrusted with their application." We were, so to say, the arbiters of the situation.'[98] Then came, as Parnell notes, the horror of the Phoenix Park murders of the new Chief Secretary Lord Frederick Cavendish and Thomas Burke his aide on 6 May. Parnell, presumably unaware that P. J. Sheridan was to be identified as one of the conspirators behind the murder, issued a celebrated manifesto:

TO THE PEOPLE OF IRELAND:

On the eve of what seemed a bright future for our country, that evil destiny which has apparently pursued us for centuries, has struck at our hopes another blow which cannot be exaggerated in its disastrous consequences. In this hour of sorrowful gloom we venture to give expression to our profoundest sympathy with the people of Ireland in the calamity that has befallen our cause through this horrible deed, and with those who determined at the last hour, that a policy of conciliation should supplant that of terrorism and national distrust. We earnestly hope that the attitude and action of the Irish people will show to the world that an assassination such as has startled us almost to the abandonment of hope of our country's future, is deeply and religiously abhorrent to their every feeling and instinct.

There was a moment of great public emotional confusion. Nevertheless the manifesto, as much as any such document could, worked with English public opinion. Later in the month, the *Economist* recalled how 'other Irish rebels like D'Arcy McGee and Sir [Charles] Gavan Duffy have not only been treated with but honoured by the Crown. It is certain also, that the English people...is essentially good natured...when the rebels are white.'[99] On 8 May 1882, Parnell even acknowledged that coercion of some sort was again inevitable after the Phoenix Park murders: 'I don't deny that it may be impossible for the government to resist and to feel themselves compelled to take some step or other in the direction indicated by the Prime Minister.'[100] But in Parliament in the 24–26 May coercion debate, John Dillon thrust himself on public attention again. F. H. O'Donnell noted: 'As for Dillon he was feared by Parnell more than words can tell for his gift of stating crudities in the crudest fashion.' O'Donnell added: 'Parnell was said to exclaim that "John Dillon never opened his mouth but he put his foot in it."' Parnell was often required to translate Dillon's words before an English audience. When Dillon declared that 'cattle did not thrive on evicted land', at the time when the news from Ireland was dominated by horrible mutilations of beasts, Parnell quickly intervened to say he had been merely referring to an Irish superstition that bad luck came to property placed on an evicted farm.[101] This was not totally reassuring; Geraldine Penrose Fitzgerald, sister of a prominent landlord and Unionist MP, wrote to Cardinal Newman of a case where tenants who did not support the League 'have had pins put in their cattle's food so the poor innocent animals died in torture'.[102]

Dillon's late May speech in Parliament was an exemplary statement of the essentials of the Irish nationalist worldview. He was already feeling the pressure of his unwise encouragement of the Murroe tenantry; he rather desperately raised their case in Parliament in the same week. Agrarian crime, he claimed, was inevitable as long as there were ongoing evictions. There was a long tradition of agrarian outrage in Ireland. Regrettably at the time of the famine, the people allowed themselves to be 'swept away' rather than resist—leading to the deaths of two million. He denounced O'Connor Power, the Mayo MP who, though once a Fenian, had started down a path of greater moderation. The government's own Compensation for Disturbance bill had implied the capacity of the Irish landlords to do wrong. These same landlords knew they had been defeated by the Land League agitation and were on the verge of surrendering and accepting a transition period of a mere five years' rent as compensation, but now the government's introduction of coercion had given them new hope and heart to carry on the fight.[103] Referring to the government's new attempt to fine localities for crimes, Dillon's use of the phrase 'blood tax' chilled the House: 'If it were true that there was an extensive system of terrorism, as the government believed, did it not occur to these men the Irish peasant won't prefer to pay the blood tax and to risk his life? The blood tax might make the Irish peasant sorry for the murder unless he obtained some advantage from it; but he failed to see how it would induce him to risk his own life in order to avoid the payment of a small sum.'

The dramatic and negative effect of Dillon's speech on the House is in a way surprising. Radical MPs who doubted the government's policy of coercion now spoke for a moment of supporting martial law. To be sure, Dillon's effort contained no acknowledgement of the emotional effect generated by the brutality of the Phoenix Park murders: an emotional effect which would still have been present in the Chamber. But, even so, his themes were hardly novel or unexpected. The reference to the Compensation for Disturbance bill was obviously fair. On the subject of eviction Gladstone had made a point of signalling the potential unfairness of eviction in Ireland and the role that this—understandably—played in generating outrage. But Dillon went further, in his words: 'He had never denounced outrage and never would until Parliament denounced evictions.'[104] The reason for Gladstone's upset is however clear. Forster had wanted to concede the full 3Fs of the Irish popular agrarian demand—fair rent, free sale of the farmers' interest, and fixity of tenure. But Gladstone had set his face against fixity of tenure—where in his view all power of evictions, no matter the gravity of the cause, was taken away.[105] On this point, many would have sympathized with Dillon but Gladstone most certainly did not. In effect, Dillon was inciting Gladstone to collude in a version of reality which in which he had eradicated all the social rights of one class (the landlords) as part of a contract relationship with another class (the tenants). In fact, this is exactly what Gladstone's conservative critics believed he had done, but Gladstone could not afford to admit it either to himself or others. He had to pretend that the distinction between just and unjust evictions was all-important and that his own remarks to the effect that evictions might be more morally heinous than violence applied only to unjust evictions. The point is, even the most casual glance at the Irish press revealed that many evictions were not unjust in the Gladstonian sense. Gladstone chose to insist that eviction, in certain cases, was an 'undoubted legal right'. Part of the reason for this lies in Gladstone's own complex process of rationalization and even self-deception as to the content of his own 1881 Land Act. He had always convinced himself that though he had conceded fair rent and free sale, he had not conceded the principle of fixity of tenure—to do so would flout the laws of liberal political economy. Dillon's speech thus touched on a sensitive point in the Gladstone psyche. His reply to Dillon was, he said, more in sorrow than anger but it certainly had the force of indignation behind it. Dillon, said Gladstone, on 24 May, was 'the apostle of a creed which is a creed of force, which is a creed of oppression, which is a creed of destruction of all liberty'.[106] Why would Gladstone say this? Because he passionately believed in the enforceability of legal contracts:

> But there may be evictions which are the last, the extreme, the inevitable remedy for the establishment of those legal rights on which the existence of society depends—against *the man who deliberately and insolently and wilfully denies them*, the *man who audaciously refuses to fulfil his contract*—the most equitable contract in the world—a contract under the judicial rents recently established, with money in his pocket, perhaps loaded with benefits from the man whom he defies. And in the case where the possessor of property, after exhausting every means of conciliation, is driven to make use of the powers of the law for the establishment of legal right, and perhaps to support himself and family, that man is placed by the deliberate declaration of the hon. Gentleman upon the footing of a perpetrator of outrage, and we are called upon to denounce evictions with the same sense, and even with the same unlimited scope, as we are allowed to denounce outrage.
>
> Eviction is the exercise of an undoubted legal right, which may be to the prejudice of your neighbour, which may involve the very highest moral responsibility, nay, even deep moral guilt upon the person exercising it. There may be outrages, all things considered—the persons and the facts— that may be less guilty in the sight of God than evictions.[107]

Gladstone wrote to Lord Spencer on 24 May 1882: 'Dillon in, I think, the worst Irish speech I ever heard, lifted the banners at once of illegality and revolt from Parnell.'[108] 'Parnell has thus far run quite true', Gladstone reported accurately to Spencer, but the Prime Minister then added a classic misreading of the moment: 'but it seems doubtful whether he [Parnell] can hold his ground. The Tories, and I am sorry to add Forster, have done much to increase his difficulties.'[109] In fact, the abuse directed by Forster and the Tories against the 'Kilmainham Treaty' served to validate it with Irish public opinion and increase the strength of Parnell's position. Parnell intervened—with one voice protecting Dillon and with another, in the same speech, marking his distance. The effect was markedly successful. A triumph of tone over content, perhaps, but nonetheless a triumph. In one respect, it is important to note that it built on Parnell's earlier assurance to Gladstone that he opposed only unjust eviction not all eviction. Parnell stated: 'I am bound to say that I think the impression which has been created, and the inferences that the Prime Minister drew in his speech from the remarks of my hon. Friend, were not warranted by the speech itself; although I think it is exceedingly natural that both the Prime Minister and the House generally should have drawn the inferences they did from many passages of that speech, and from its general nature and content.'[110] Florence Arnold-Forster noted: 'A remarkable speech by Mr Parnell this afternoon, with the object of explaining away Mr Dillon's defence of outrage and boycotting. If only Mr Parnell had spoken in this way in Ireland and at a time when his influence in diverting the cruel land agitation of 1880 might have had much effect, they would probably never have come to the point they have now.'[111] Lord Derby picked up on Gladstone's reference to Dillon's speech as 'heart breaking'. He noted acutely: 'The phrase is curious as indicating what the Premier's hopes must have been: for what Dillon said was only what everybody would have expected except that he expressed it in rather plainer terms than has been usual in Parliament.'[112] But Derby added later: 'Parnell last night made a speech in the House, in a tone new to him, apologising for Dillon but in a style which showed there was no great agreement between them: it is clear that he for his part is willing to act up to the understanding which the opposition have named the "Treaty of Kilmainham".[113] *The Manchester Evening News* noted that Parnell had replied with great skill to defuse the danger created by Dillon's 'shameful' speech.[114] The parliamentary correspondent of the *Irishman*, now owned by Parnell, insisted that there was no difference between Parnell and Dillon[115]—but Westminster public opinion simply refused to believe such a thing. Parnell, after all, refused to be embarrassed by the publication of his offer to cooperate with the Liberals in general measures of reform: 'I meant that the government having abandoned coercion, and having practically settled the land question, it should receive our help in passing the extension of the franchise and county government bills for some counties,' he told the *New York Herald*. The *New York Herald* asked Patrick Egan in Paris, was he sure that Parnell and Dillon still stood by the Land League revolution? Egan seemed to be uncertain but added that he, at least, had received a letter from Dillon to that effect.[116]

'The debate' on the Murroe tenantry which followed the next day was also interesting.[117] The case for Lord Cloncurry was a simple one: from 1870 to 1880 there had been rent rises and the tenants—who were admitted on all sides to be mostly 'comfortable' and well off—had paid promptly. In the spring of 1882, their disposition changed radically at the urging of the Land League, or more particularly John Dillon. Although none would guess this from the speeches of Sexton and Parnell, this was at Dillon's urging rather than Parnell's. Nor would anyone guess Dillon's specific role from his speech. The Murroe tenantry—who could have paid their rents—allowed their interests to be sold, probably expecting the League to come to their rescue with cash. The League had not rescued the tenants. As a result, two hundred and twenty persons were evicted. Cloncurry was willing to re-admit the tenantry but at the price that they give up their new advantages under the 1881 Land Act.

It was alleged in this debate that Parnell's speech at the Central Land League on September of 1881 had inspired the Murroe tenantry. But, in fact, that speech announced a change in policy—the end of the 'rent at the point of the bayonet' which had helped many strong farmers actively support the League. Parnell said: 'If we had gone on encouraging the tenants to buy in their interests at vast expense in the shape of law costs to the Land League it would certainly have failed.'[118] The decision to advance the Murroe struggle was made in February 1882 by John Dillon—with the support of Anna, but not C. S. Parnell—in confused circumstances where the tenants may well have hoped that 'rent at the point of a bayonet' was still partially operative when it was decidedly not in play. But Parnell's September speech did suggest that if the tenants kept the land vacant they would win and the worst outcome would be re-entry on the terms of the 1881 Land Act. It was this point which Lord Cloncurry took it on himself to refute and he did so successfully.

In early June, Parnell talked to Labouchere about his desire to set up a new 'tenant right association'. Fenianism, for Parnell, once a noble utopian ideal, was now simply a world of 'assassination' and 'outrage'.[119] In June, Parnell took the remarkable step of sending in to Gladstone a letter he [Parnell] had received from a senior Irish American nationalist, probably General Patrick Collins, the League leader in America, denouncing the extremism of Patrick Ford, editor of the *Irish World*— and other radicals like Davitt and Brennan.[120] Gladstone thanked Parnell for this enclosure but expressed his residual qualms about the recent murder of Colonel Bourke—which was considered by the Dublin Castle authorities to be the work of one (P. J. Gordon) who was known to Parnell and close to P. J. Sheridan. There is a grim logic to this murder. Colonel Bourke and Canon Geoffrey Bourke were close relations. The Bourke family was the target of the original Irishtown Land League meeting in 1879. Mrs Patrick Sheridan and Mrs P. J. Gordon had designed the banners for that meeting. Even so, in July 1879 a member of the murder victim's close family, Canon Geoffrey Bourke, had attended the Land League meeting on the platform in Claremorris. Colonel Burke's sister had been a key figure in the story of the Knock miracles, initiated and then financially promoted by P. J. Gordon, whose daughter had been the first miracle cure. The victim himself was the preferred Home

Rule candidate of the Mayo clergy in the general election of 1880. A year later, however, P. J. Gordon, at the moment of his arrest at Claremorris Station, called openly for Colonel Walter Bourke to be 'blown to pieces'.[121] Bourke was now an official 'target' for the Land League in 1882 and reluctantly accepted official protection soldiers—carrying, nonetheless, unloaded rifles. He was murdered with the assistance of a close employee—who chatted amiably with him on the day of the murder and who provided the assassins with the bullets. A local landlord, Captain Shawe-Taylor, who, in effect, witnessed the crime, gave rather restricted, fearful evidence when it came to trial.[122] In 1903, Captain Shawe-Taylor was to emerge as the leader of the conciliation movement in Irish politics.

On 6 July 1882 in Parliament, Dillon again defied Parnell's orders and spoke against the party line. He condemned Gladstone's effort to solve the arrears problem—part of the Kilmainham Deal—and allowed Arthur Balfour, a Scots landowner MP, to give him a lecture on political economy. Parnell responded through Mrs O'Shea to Gladstone: 'Dillon is curiously wilful at times, but his speech, though ill-judged was ineffective.'[123] But Dillon was not quite finished; in August 1882, he defended boycotting and claimed that such exclusive dealing as it advised was neither illegal nor productive of outrages.[124]

# 5

# 'What does Mr Parnell say?'

If men in America would constantly keep in mind that out of a population of 5,000,000 there are 1,500,000 Protestants who are against the
national movement to a man, and at least 500,000 Catholics equally
hostile they would come to understand that Irish politics need careful
handling.

*Devoy's Post/Bag*, 21 September 1882, vol. 2, p. 14,
J. J. O'Kelly to John Devoy.

This cold Protestant Englishman with his precision of speech, and
ungenial arrogance, and haughty inflexibility, this man like a cross
between the younger Pitt and Robespierre, but without the oratorical
power of either, rules Irish men like a true dictator.

'Mr Parnell's First Difficulty', *Spectator*, 14 November 1885.

In August 1882, Parnell set about the realignment of Irish politics.
Structurally, it became a more bureaucratic top-down movement.
Ideologically, and more importantly, the Parliament in London became
the focus of activity. More importantly, the philosophy of John Mitchel
was gently but openly rejected in favour of an explicitly parliamentary
strategy. John Dillon contemplated bitterly the fact that instead of
calling a convention in Dublin to articulate self-government—as
envisaged in the conference of 1879—there was a new unbreakable
dispensation: Westminster was to be the centre of the action. It was too
much for him. He announced his retirement from Irish politics and
departure to Colorado. The *Economist* noted: 'We do not affect to regret
the retirement of Mr Dillon from political life. He was unquestionably
the nearest approach both in temperament and in ideas, to a pure
Jacobin that the Irish revolutionary movement has produced.'[1]

*Ancestral Voices in Irish Politics: Judging Dillon and Parnell.* Paul Bew, Oxford University Press.
© Paul Bew 2023. DOI: 10.1093/oso/9780192873705.003.0005

Parnell no longer cared. At the banquet after receiving the freedom of Dublin on 16 August, he again defended the 'duty' of working in the House of Commons. Further land reform was likely to ensue, in his view. But, suggestively, Parnell proceeded to laud the prospects of Irish manufacturers, suggesting a form of voluntary protectionism by purchasing home-produced goods. With some frustration, he noted that the Irish people had 'very inadequate ideas to the improvement of their condition'. As the progress of popular reform was inevitable, he 'invited' those in 'higher stations of life' to join in his movement; though he noted that without them it would continue anyway.[2] It is worth noting here that the 'union of classes' which Parnell had declared as integral to the achievement of independence in January 1881 in Parliament was now not so integral. It was merely a desirable option—albeit a desirable option which continued to influence Parnell's interventions in Irish politics.

The *Spectator*, like the *Economist*, was perfectly happy with the new Parnell. Both journals assumed not just that the Kilmainham Treaty was being kept but that 'cooperation' with Liberals on general matters of reform was a meaningful part of that agreement. The *Spectator* stated: 'What does Mr Parnell say? He gives up the No Rent policy, one which Irish farmers will not accept; that he rejects Mr Davitt's proposal to seize lands for the benefit of the western poor; that he hopes by and large to change fixity of tenure into actual proprietorship through state aided purchase.'[3] Parnell had in this speech—so admired by the *Spectator*—finally broken with the Mitchel legacy: 'Some people have urged—the late Mr John Mitchel always urged—that the Irish members ought to withdraw in a body from the House and that the constituencies should refuse to send members. (Hear, Hear) Well I think there is a great deal in that contention, but I fear it is not a practicable one.'[4]

For the Liberal press, still infatuated with Gladstone, it was churlish of Forster not to go with this beneficial flow: a new more moderate Parnell was a great prize surely? But then came news from the police cells in Dublin. On 17 February, James Carey, one of the leading Invincible suspects arrested for the Phoenix Park murders, cracked; fearing that his fellow suspects would inform on him, he informed on them. On 19 February, the London *Times* report homed in on the ways in which the Invincibles had targeted Forster. This led to a flood of sympathy in Westminster for the former Irish Chief Secretary. Carey claimed that nineteen attempts had been made on Forster's life, each one marred by ill luck. But *The Times* also laid emphasis on the alleged role of P. J. Sheridan and Thomas Brennan, prominent Land Leaguers, in supporting the Invincibles.[5] From Parnell's point of view, Carey's account of the role of P. J. Sheridan as an instigator and financier of violence was the most dangerous. Parnell had authorized O'Shea to use Sheridan's name in his conversations with the government. It was a risky, morally ambiguous move in the first place—but it was even more so when Sheridan's name was linked not just to Land League violence but Invincible violence. Sheridan, according to Carey, was a major player: disguised as Father Murphy he (and his wife) delivered weapons and cash from Egan in Paris. Interestingly, however, *The Times* did not argue that Parnell had known Sheridan's full importance; it was, instead, stated that 'had Parnell known' he would have been even more confident in offering Sheridan's name to Gladstone. Sir John Gorst the next day in Parliament seemed prepared to follow this line: he was willing to believe that Mr Parnell 'was duped by this man Sheridan'.[6] This assumption of a certain distance between himself and Sheridan must have been a relief to Parnell.

On 22 February 1883, Forster launched his final parliamentary assault on Parnell. Basing himself on considerable research, Forster created a moment in which—as T. P. O'Connor put it—the 'blood of the House ran cold'[7] as incidents of murder connected to the League were read out. At one key moment, Forster read out a celebrated speech of Sheridan from August 1880:

> 'If we do not get these things [Irish rights] through our Members of Parliament, I would ask you then to ring out your voices from the muzzles of Minie rifles, as well as from many platforms.' Did the hon. Member approve of this? [Mr. PARNELL: Hear, hear!] Well, then, he did approve of what led to a great deal of violence. I do not myself believe he did; but he

was content that the League should be thus organized, and that his power should be thus increased.[8]

Forster concluded: 'It is not that he [Parnell] himself directly planned or perpetuated outrages on order, but that he either connived at them, or, when warned by facts and statements, he determined to remain in ignorance, that he took no trouble to test the truth of whether these outrages had been committed or not, but that he was willing to gain the advantage of them.' Parnell was encouraged by F. H. O'Donnell to make a defiant and brutal *ad hominem* attack on Forster, full of personal insult: Forster, for example, was compared unfavourably to James Carey, a contemptible informer.[9] Parnell's reply was not particularly effective—perhaps because, as he was to concede in later years, the last part of Forster's case was true. At first, the mood of Parliament was strongly in favour of Forster and then just as quickly that mood evaporated. The 'Kilmainham Treaty' had created a logic in which many Liberal MPs assumed that the future of the Irish question was to be defined by some compromise with Parnell. In such a context, Forster was inviting the contemplation of a rather more dismal vista.

Two of Parnell's associates, Thomas Brennan and P. J. Sheridan, were named in February 1883 at the trial of the Phoenix Park murderers as enablers of Invincible terrorism. P. J. Sheridan helpfully reappeared in a US interview in an effort to protect Parnell. Why, the press asked, had Parnell used Sheridan's name in early May 1882, during the negotiations leading to the 'Kilmainham Treaty'? Sheridan admitted a good knowledge of the west of Ireland. But he added also that Parnell was 'motivated by a kindly consideration towards myself' in view of the financial losses he had sustained in the struggle:[10] nothing to do with nefarious activities. Mainstream Liberals chose to be reassured by this sort of language. They did not want to ask difficult questions. Why did Parnell recommend someone widely believed to be an organizer of assassination to Gladstone? Why did Parnell think it wise to say 'Hear, hear' in the Chamber in response to Sheridan's most aggressive language? Sheridan's close friend P. J. Gordon was believed by the police to be the inspiration behind the murder of Colonel Bourke in June 1882. (Colonel

Bourke had brought his sickly sister to Knock for a 'miracle cure' but sadly she had died soon after. P. J. Gordon's daughter, Delia, had been the first successful miracle cure at Knock but, subsequently, Miss Bourke was the most celebrated of those who sought relief.) The Colonel's murder is a striking example of the intimacy which lies at the heart of much agrarian crime. The Liberals, however, did not want to listen to the complaints of Forster. They chose instead to believe with the *Economist* that the Irish 'consequently began to settle down and to seek to enjoy their gains and with their settlement Mr Parnell loses something of his hold'.[11] It was a fatal miscalculation. The opposite was the case—as Parnell was the perceived victor in the land war, he became stronger and stronger.

In April 1883, the decision was taken to raise a Parnell tribute—the phrase recalling the public financial appeals made for Daniel O'Connell. On 17 March 1883, Archbishop Croke of Thurles resolved to lead this appeal. It soon became clear that the Vatican—under English diplomatic pressure—was worried by the Catholic clergy's willingness to support this cause. The Propaganda *Fide* in Rome issued a critical circular. It was this—rather than the original appeal—which appears to have stirred Dillon to supportive action. In late May, he sent £5 to the Parnell fund. 'The only response to this blow [the Propaganda circular] is to make the Parnell Fund such a tremendous success that the Propaganda will realise how grievously it was deceived by those men under whose influence this circular was issued.'[12] This was hardly a focus on Parnell's specific services. Parnell, it was said, had lost materially by his services to the national cause. His family, it was said, had always supported the people. It was time for some recompense. J. R. Cox, the senior Invincible activist—according to police sources— became the Secretary of the Parnell testimonial fund.[13] The fund in the end raised £37,000 for Parnell—notably among the richer, and not the poorer, rural communities. Parnell was now, as was shrewdly noted, the 'hero of the bourgeoisie'. In the early summer of 1883, however, John Dillon, one of the Irish bourgeoisie's most substantial sons, bronzed and looking well—he had been recuperating in the South of

France—met a Scottish journalist in the Strand in London: Dillon assured the journalist he had 'no intention' to resume a parliamentary career;[14] indeed, he soon departed to spend time with his brother, William, in Colorado. Parnell, meanwhile, continued to make progress: the 1884 extensions of the franchise certainly strengthened his future parliamentary hand. But it is noticeable that the cooperation with the Liberal party did not go as smoothly as expected by many Liberals. In particular, Dublin Castle's alleged sanction of an apparent miscarriage of justice in the Maamtrasna case allowed for tactical alliances with Tories which became increasingly effective as the Liberal administration began to lose its way.[15]

To the surprise of some in London, Parnell now began to play the Tories off against the Liberals. Sometimes this went beyond the purely tactical; Irish nationalists, including Parnell himself, had always been prepared to flirt with the broad Tory critique of Liberalism and its alleged hypocrisies. In the 1883 to 1885 period, Parnell utilized William O'Brien and his journal *United Ireland*, which maintained an aggressive assault on Lord Spencer's regime in Dublin Castle: Gladstone stood firmly behind Spencer, but the Tories did not. In February, Parnell engaged in close conversation with the Tory Chief Whip; under what terms might he support a Tory government? The price, eventually conceded, was Tory support for an inquiry into the Maamtrasna murders case. This was the last straw for Spencer. When the Maamtrasna case—a particularly horrible multiple murder case, followed by miscarriages of justice—had arrived at Westminster, few in either British party were prepared to listen to the Irish party critique of the administration of justice in Ireland. When the Tories took it up as the price of taking office, Spencer was shocked. He had other reasons for his subsequent support for Home Rule—he always insisted that Irish economic and social conditions at home sat discordantly with the political and economic messages even the isolated parts of the west of Ireland received from the United States of America. But he was now prepared to give Gladstone support for Home Rule—support which Gladstone deemed to be a *sine qua non*. J. W. Croker, the conservative Irish unionist theorist, had always declared that one of the weaknesses of the union project lay in the way in which the British parties, for their own reasons, might 'bribe' the Irish MPs rather than hold out the prospect of long-term firm government. The Tory behaviour in 1885 was a classic example and an educational moment which Parnell exploited ruthlessly. Parnell became close to an ambitious Tory like Randolph Churchill and won his respect—to the dismay of the Ulster Tories.[16] Not even the exiled John Dillon could resist the opportunities for Irish nationalists at Westminster which were opening up. Weather-bronzed again and in a flannel shirt with a white sombrero, he told the Irish nationalist community of Lincoln, Nebraska, that he was returning to Irish politics in July 1885.[17]

Unbeknownst to Dillon, in March 1885 Gladstone was to say later, he had finally decided to embrace Home Rule. Lee Warner, the headmaster of Rugby, in 1890 asked Gladstone 'if he could identify in his mind the crucial moment at which he determined to adopt the [Home Rule] policy. I can see him now as he paused and thought then replied: "Yes, I had been reading a speech of William O'Brien's and I put it down and said to myself, what is there in this speech which I must get to realise before I throw it aside? And I saw then that never was and never could be any moral obligation on the Irish race in relation to the Act of Union." '[18] O'Brien's speech had been a strong one even by the standards in that era; the relationship of the Irish with England was 'simply the relation of civil war tempered by the scarcity of firearms'. But it included personal praise for Gladstone's 'personal character, intellect and tenderness for Ireland'. Gladstone may, therefore, have been suitably impressed in March 1885 and thus have given an accurate account to Warner. But it is worth noting that Gladstone heard the speech again when he attended O'Brien's special commission hearing in May 1889 and this conversation with Warner took place in 1890. It is also worth noting that in 1885 he was very critical of the Irish party tactics in Westminster which provided the immediate context of O'Brien's protest speech in the Phoenix Park.[19] It was possible, therefore, a slightly muddled Gladstone misled Warner but it is probable that Gladstone did not completely invent this 'recollection'.

At all events, Parnell's political influence was strengthening all the time. Regardless of Gladstone's private epiphany, in early summer 1885 (9 June) he formed a bloc with the Tories to throw out the Liberal government on 13 June 1885: noting the direction of events, John Dillon set sail for Ireland. On 4 July, he returned, after three years' absence, and 'henceforth refused to be beguiled back to his old attitude of critical suspicion of the parliamentary party'.[20] He sought out Parnell and asked for a safe seat. Not that everyone in the parliamentary party had forgotten Dillon's previous stance—T. P. O'Connor's picture of him in his *Parnell Movement*, published in early 1886, contained no praise of his political intelligence or rhetorical skills, as the *Times* reviewer noted.[21] All other nationalist MPs were hailed as absolutely superb but Dillon received a more low-key appraisal. Tim Healy was equally displeased: Healy could 'see nothing save harm "if a man so self-centred was again allowed to get a grip on the levers."' William O'Brien responded that 'Dillon's desertion of the party in 1882...should not be held against him'.[22] On 14 August 1885, the Land Purchase Act (1885), known as the Ashbourne Act, was passed by the Conservatives. It was the beginning of the effective triumph of the Parnellite approach to the land question. The context was set for an intense Parnellite–Conservative flirtation.

Dillon re-entered a world very different from the one he had left in 1882, when the Tories denounced Parnell in the most bitter of tones. By the middle of May 1885, a leading Tory, Randolph Churchill, had established a rapport with Parnell. He was certainly willing to drop coercion as an instrument of British policy in exchange for Parnellite support for a brief six-month spell of Conservative government at the far end of the 1880 Parliament. On 17 June 1885, Randolph Churchill told George Fottrell at the Carlton Club of his great admiration for Parnell. He also made it clear that he regarded Parnell as a Conservative.[23] This Tory/ Parnell deal enhanced Parnell's prestige in Ireland. As the *Spectator* put it on 20 June 1885: 'It is evident enough that the Irish peasantry will take the abandonment of all further legislation after the expiration of the Crimes Act as a tremendous victory for the Parnellite party, and as showing that whatever Mr Parnell chooses to resist in relation to Ireland he can really resist with effect.'[24] A month later the *Spectator* condemned 'Parnellite Toryism': 'The simple truth is that Parnell is now the Lord Lieutenant of Ireland and Lord Randolph Churchill the true Prime Minister of England.'[25] This condemnation had little effect. Henry Howarth, soon to become the Tory MP for Salford, supported the Churchill line. He called for 'a new departure more in harmony with the aspirations of the best men in Ireland'.[26] The Chief Secretary, Michael Hicks Beach, well known to be a critic of Irish landlordism, had a good personal relationship with Parnell. In another sign of Conservative interest in Parnell, the Lord Lieutenant Carnarvon met Parnell secretly in an empty house in Mayfair on 1 August. They had a serious and wide-ranging discussion including the issue of protection for Irish industries.[27] At Arklow, in late August 1885, Parnell said that 'without a freely elected National Assembly with power to control all the affairs of Ireland and with power to protect the struggling industries ... it is impossible for us to revive our native industries'.[28] The Liberal *Spectator* noted Parnell's personal selfish financial motive for supporting protection. 'In the Arklow speech, Parnell explained how he had persuaded the Dublin Corporation not to buy in the cheapest market their stone for the paving of Dublin streets, but to encourage native industry by buying from his own quarries stone dearer than the Welsh quarry-owners professed themselves willing to apply.'[29] The *Spectator* added sourly in an editorial: 'It is his good fortune to find the profession of patriotism, thoroughly genuine we are sincerely convinced, very profitable to him.' The *Spectator* denounced the whole project: 'First rent asunder by Home Rule, and then hermetically sealed from all by a policy of Protection, Ireland would, indeed, rue the blighting influence of Mr Parnell's ascendancy.'[30]

Yet there was another, specifically Irish way at looking at Parnell's business activities. In this perspective, he had created jobs and generated new skills. In February 1885, Parnell took a lease from Lord Carysfort and opened quarries at Big Rock, outside Arklow: interestingly, although he had been personally friendly with Lord Carysfort he thought (wrongly) that he might deny him a lease and negotiated through an intermediary.[31] By August 1885, Parnell was employing 140 men making Arklow paving sets. The Cambridge scientist, Dr James Dewar, insisted that Arklow stone was likely to be more durable than that of their Welsh competitors. This, in turn, helped to convince Dublin Corporation, aided by distinguished figures like Sir Charles Cameron, its (Unionist) public health officer, that this project was worthy of support. Whatever the *Spectator* thought about the matter, Parnell was perfectly sincere. In the last months of his life, he told his loyal friend, Dr Kenny MP, 'Well, the first thing I do, would be to put a protective duty on imports of British manufacturers.'[32] The problem lay not so much with Parnell's sincerity but rather the coherence of the policy. Would England happily accept agricultural goods tariff free while its own manufacturers were discriminated against in Ireland? Lord Salisbury was already tempted by a willingness to introduce tariffs. Parnell never seems to have seriously contemplated these problems—which came to a head in the Anglo-Irish economic war of the 1930s.

Shortly after giving the Arklow speech, Parnell met one of his close allies, Andrew Kettle. Kettle was a keen observer of Parnell. He questioned him closely on the matter; it should be recalled that several Australian colonies were protectionist:

> You were at Arklow yesterday, I said, opening the quarry and selling the stones to the [Dublin] Corporation, but what was the meaning of your strange speech on protection and Irish industries? Are you going to break with the Free Traders? 'Yes,' he said, 'we have a rather big project on hand.' He then explained the meeting with Lord Carnarvon and the project of Aristocratic Home Rule, with the colonial right to protect our industries against English manufacture. I seemed to be knocked dumb as I really was, by the unexpected news, and he went out to explain that it was not from a motive of justice or generosity that the Conservative party was making the proposals. Inspired chiefly by Lord Randolph Churchill, the classes in Britain were afraid that if the Irish democratic propaganda were to continue, in conjunction with the English radicals, class rule might be overturned altogether. So to save themselves, they are going to set up a class conservative government in Ireland, with the aid and consent of the Irish

democracy, having no connection with England but the link of the Crown and an Imperial Contribution to be regulated by circumstances.[33]

Kettle's response was striking:

> The world will be surprised and astounded when this becomes known, but you know what I always thought on this subject? England could not afford to delegate the governing powers of Ireland into the hands of any class other than that ruling England at the time. Here was I thinking that we would have to wait for home rule until the English radicals and the Irish democrats would become powerful enough to rule the Empire, and now it is coming from the top instead of the bottom. It is simply astounding but I fear it will not come to pass. You will not be able to get the Tories in a majority to do this. The Irish in Britain will not vote for them, and besides I fear that the Irish landlords, owing to their crimes in the past, are not destined to be placed so easily at the heads of the people's affairs in Ireland. But all the same, I am intensely interested, and I shall do the little I can to help you with the experiment.

Certainly Parnell was now heavily engaged in his Tory project. In a puckish and witty speech in Dublin, he conjured up some remarkable images. It is worth remembering that, as Parnell openly stated, the years 1882–5 had seen repeated dynamite outrages in London, and that even in Parliament ministers did not feel safe after a bomb was thrown into the Commons Chamber. Nevertheless, at the end of August 1885 he told a Dublin audience:

> Some of the more intelligent and reflective minds in the dynamite camp are reported to be eager to give Lord Salisbury 'fair trial' in his administration of Irish affairs, and there is a general feeling among such conspirators that policy of exasperation on their part would hopelessly destroy any chance which Ireland may have in the immediate future of securing a measure of self-government more or less in conformity with the principles of justice and common sense.[34]

Parnell's strategy was widely noted as an attempt to start a bidding war between Chamberlain and Randolph Churchill for eighty-five potential Parnellite votes in the next Parliament. But it was said neither Chamberlain nor Churchill might even be leader of their respective parties and both would 'wreck' their chances of leadership by a Parnell alliance. The Liberals declared that the voice of Parnell at Arklow was really the voice of Randolph Churchill, in an attempt to embarrass Churchill.[35] At Wicklow on 8 October, Parnell declared: 'I tell English Radicals or English Liberals it is useless for them to talk of their desire to do justice to Ireland when, with a spurt of selfishness they refuse to repair that most manifest of injustices, the destruction of our industries by England in the past.'[36] At the beginning of October 1885, the English press was mystified by Parnell's approach. *The Times* felt sure that the Parnell speech at Wicklow was delivered with the intent of openly killing Chamberlain's scheme for an Irish councils bill which would fall short of Home Rule. The Liberal press felt sure that he was still in the market for a deal with Mr Gladstone. The *Daily News* took a different stance, recalling an earlier judgement of the *Economist*: 'Is it possible that the voice which spoke through Parnell at Wicklow was as much Lord Randolph Churchill's as his own?'[37] But the voice which spoke through Parnell was Parnell himself. On 10 October, he renewed the call for protection in an interview with the *New York Herald* but expressed the view that the Liberals could well offer more to Ireland than the Conservatives. It was, however, a matter of supreme irritation to Michael Davitt that Parnell did not seem to understand that talk of protection was never likely to be acceptable to the 'free traders', the British Liberals and many Tories. It is clear that Davitt, at least, regarded Parnell's Tory flirtation as little short of absurd.

John Dillon also made no effort to engage with Parnell's new crypto-Tory theme. Instead, he sought to remind everyone of the wickedness of the Irish landlords. On 6 October 1885, he declared:

> I learned to hate them because I saw that they had this country by the throat. I learned to hate them because I saw that throughout all the long time since they were planted here by William [III] and by Cromwell, they never showed the faintest interest in the welfare of the country; and I learned to hate them because I know that wherever the name of Ireland is held up either in England or foreign countries to opprobrium and derision...you are almost sure to find an Irish landlord, or some stripling

who will become a landlord, in the very foremost of Ireland's foes. I learned to hate them because I read and saw with my own eyes that every effort in favour of Irish nationality was stamped and crushed out with all the savage brutality of a class who knew they were hated by the people, and who knew that that hatred was just.[38]

How did Parnell respond to this aggressive tone? He decided to speak at a meeting in Kildare: the meeting dramatized the awkwardness of his role as a Protestant leader of Irish nationalism. He chose to speak after a Mass and after the consecration of the new altar in the Church of Saint Brigid. Dr Kavanagh PP spoke of the growing pride of the Irish throughout the world—unfortunately, however, there was 'a nest of Orange vipers who have made the north the black spot on our island'. But it was noted that both leading English parties were 'vying with each other for our friendly support'.[39]

Parnell's key speech in Kildare on 11 October 1885 opened with an apparently ominous warning to the Irish landlords: 'the new democratic Parliament [elected after the third Reform Act of 1884] would not be so tender to the rights of landlords as the last was.' It must be recalled that most Irish landlords would not have regarded the outgoing Parliament as being particularly tender to their rights. But his message was to become more clear as the speech progressed—it was time for Irish landlords to cut a viable deal before it was too late. It was an important speech and stuck in the mind of the British political elites. Parnell made clear his new lack of enthusiasm for agrarian conflict: 'I have in no case during the last few years advised any combination among tenants against even rack-rents. Any combination that may exist in the country is a combination of an isolated character; it is confined to the tenants of individual estates...without any incitement from us—on the contrary, kept back by us.'[40] He urged Irish landlords to seize the opportunity: 'Let them not take the Land Purchase Act as an engine of intimidation, but take it as it was offered to them by the Irish party, who consented to pass it as a golden bridge to escape from an untenable position.' The concept that Irish landlords should be allowed a 'golden bridge' of escape was alien to many in Parnell's party—in particular, to John Dillon, who spoke later that day at Roscrea.[41] Dr Alan O'Day, the eminent Parnell scholar, observed incisively:

> A 'golden bridge' was scarcely to the taste of Parnell's main body of supporters and reflected his own intention. In fact, the militant tones of the earlier portions of the Kildare speech were merely a disguise for the moderate and somewhat unpalatable message he had to deliver. Moreover, he urged tenants 'where a fair offer was made to them...nothing would be got for themselves or the country by holding out against it'. Parnell in contrast to Dillon, set no precise terms for purchase but he provided a yardstick for calculating what a fair price might be in each circumstance.[42]

Parnell in Kildare spoke of a 'liberal number' of years' purchase. John Dillon appeared to think this was a 'loophole'[43] which would 'enable the tenant to do the landlord justice'. He spoke instead of two or three years' purchase as being realistic for below the usual price. Parnell was in the process of dialogue with landowners. Dillon declared sharply that two or three years' purchase would do—and that the man who offered more would be a 'curse to the country'.[44] Whereas Parnell had emphasized the benign *absence* of organized conflict in the countryside, Dillon, by contrast, stressed the 'power of combination'. This is why the *Spectator* said: 'We do not believe Mr Parnell at heart sympathises with the movement. Not to mention, that he is a landlord himself, and not a rich one, his mere intellect must tell him that there can be no commerce without contract, no order without law, no prosperity without payment of just debts.'[45]

A day later the Liberal former Chancellor of the Exchequer, Hugh Childers, in a major speech changed everything. The Liberals were now seen as making a decisive bid for Parnellite support. Childers had given Gladstone a clear signal as to the drift of his thinking. Gladstone had replied: 'I would disclaim giving any exhaustive list of imperial subjects and would not put my foot down as to Revenue but would keep plenty of elbow room to keep all Custom and Excise which might probably be found necessary. But considering the difficulty of placing confidence in the leader of the National party at the present, I would ask you to consider fully whether you should *bind* yourself at present to any details or go beyond general indications.'[46] Gladstone's final advice was to 'confine yourself to say a legislature for all questions not imperial'. Childers went beyond this 'confinement' and gave specific detail. He stated: 'With regard to the administration of Ireland, Mr Childers was prepared to leave Ireland to control her ordinary administration of justice, her public establishment, her police, her internal trade, her railways and public works, her poor and, above all, her education.'[47]

The reaction in Ireland was swift and delighted: 'John Dillon spent yesterday with me and we discussed the present position and prospects of politics in Ireland. I was amazed at hearing from him that when he and Parnell were in the train a few days ago on their way to [most likely from] the Cork Convention, Parnell read Childers' speech and turning round to Dillon said to him without a smile: "I really think that after all we shall find that we ought to deal with the Liberals. I fear that the Tories will not be able to do for us all we want."'[48] Even so, Parnell tried to maintain his relatively conservative line. 'We have never been able to resist an impression that he personally dislikes the agrarian revolt; that he sees how dangerous it must be to the very institution of property, and that if left to himself in an Irish parliament he would have agreed a judicial rent varying, like tithe, with the price of produce.'[49] Indeed, on 21 November Parnell issued a manifesto calling on the Irish in Great Britain to vote against the Liberal party in the coming election.

It is possible, however, that the Irish vote delivered a mere five seats overall to the Conservatives: much less than was expected or hoped for by Randolph Churchill, who soon adopted a hardline Unionist posture. When balloting ended on 9 December, the Liberals had won 335 seats, the Conservatives 249, the Irish party 86. On 17 December, Herbert Gladstone, the Prime Minister's son and political adviser, announced that his father had converted to Home Rule. Parnell was distracted temporarily by the need to placate Captain O'Shea by, in effect, granting him a Galway seat after he failed to win a seat at the general election despite Parnell's assistance. The Irish political class at its higher levels were well aware that this drama was caused by Parnell's relationship with O'Shea's wife. It was, however, effectively accepted because Parnell seemed to have brought Home Rule so close to victory.

On 26 November 1885, *The Times* published an evocative essay on 'Rent Collecting in Ireland'. A journalist accompanied a landlord as he went among his tenantry to collect his rents. There was much friendly chat with tenants, a request for help in getting a daughter a job in the post office, discussion of a local wake, etc. But at the end of the process, about one-third of the rent due was paid or agreed to be paid. Behind the affability, there was a visible decline in the status of the landlords. For different understandable reasons, both conservative[50] and nationalist historians[51] have tended to dismiss *The Times* in this epoch as a serious historical source; nevertheless there is much of substance in its pages.

On 8 December 1885, Parnell had told the *Boston Herald*: 'I expect the settlement of the Irish question to come from the Liberals.' Until late in the day he continued to hope against hope that the Liberals might accept protection. On 17 December 1885, Herbert Gladstone flew the 'Hawarden kite', indicating that his father, W. E. Gladstone, supported Home Rule. How would the Liberal elites react? Morley had stayed with Chamberlain at Highbury, Birmingham shortly after the election and they agreed *not* to follow the emergent Gladstone line on Home Rule. On reading a lengthy Gladstone document in the Reform Club in London, Morley changed his mind. Looking back, Morley had his doubts. 'J. M. [John Morley] has come to the conclusion, he says, that the machinations of December 1885 strike him as the most absolutely indefensible thing in Mr G's career. They drove him wild. There were, he adds, only two honest men in the whole affair, namely Hartington and Parnell.'[52] But, indefensible or not, the damage as far as Irish unionism was concerned, was done. The Dublin correspondent of *The Times* faced up to Parnellite power. It was a gloomy assessment:

> The year which has just passed away will be recorded in the history of Ireland as the most memorable since the Union. It is marked in dark, deep lines upon the nation's annals, but it has shed no lustre upon them; it has left no trace of its progress to which a reflecting mind can revert with satisfaction or with pride and hope. It came in gloom, depression and anxiety, and alarm. This year will be remembered as one in which the

flood-gates of revolution were opened, and the great Imperial institutions which were established centuries ago by the wisdom of English statesmen as part of one harmonious order were threatened with destruction. It was a year of disaster for the country.[53]

Parnell now entered discussions with senior Liberals as to the details of a Home Rule scheme. John Morley was to claim that Parnell displayed no constructive faculty 'during the Home Rule debate of 1885/6'. It is true that Parnell was casual in his attitude to certain constitutional questions, such as the retention or otherwise of Irish members at Westminster. Parnell's proposed constitution for Ireland was stark simplicity itself: 'An elected chamber with power to make enactment regarding all the domestic concerns of Ireland but without power to interfere in any Imperial matter.'[54] There were to be 300 members: 206 to be elected, 94 to be nominated. There were to be arrangements to preserve a proportionate Protestant representation. The police and judiciary were to be under the control of the new body. Parnell did display, however, a definite 'constructive' faculty, by offering his proposal to resolve the land issue simultaneously with the Home Rule issue.

On 6 January 1886, Mrs O'Shea passed on to Gladstone 'A communication the substance of which append, has been forward to me by the representatives of one of the chief landlord political associations in Ireland. It is thought that if this arrangement were carried out there would remain no large body of opinion amongst the landowning class against the concession of a large measure of autonomy for Ireland, as the Protestants other than the owners of land are not really opposed to such a concession.'[55] Parnell was now also willing to engage in private dialogue with those very moderate nationalist politicians like the veteran O'Connellite W. J. O'Neill Daunt and Edmund Dwyer Gray who had explicitly 'opposed him in the "New Departure" phase of his political life',[56] but who had thought deeply about the financing of land reform. Parnell successfully convinced Gladstone of the case for linking the Home Rule bill with a land bill offering good terms to the Irish landlords. Gladstone explained in early April that he acted because the 'landlords were our garrison; we planted them...we could not wash our hands of responsibilities for their doings...we were *particeps criminis*.[57] But all Parnell's efforts failed. The Liberals split and the Liberal unionists emerged as a crucial group led by Hartington and Chamberlain. The Home Rule bill was defeated: partly for a reason identified by Andrew Kettle: the *déclassé* nature of the Irish party.

The Royal Irish Constabulary in Dublin noted with some concern that twenty-one members of the newly elected Parnellite party were or had been Fenians.[58] The Liberal historian W. E. H. Lecky insisted that Fenianism was at the heart of the Home Rule movement.[59] But it was the social as well as the political composition of the party which caught the eye in London. *The Times* printed an analysis of twenty Irish members which contemptuously noted their relatively humble origins or place in society. J. Gilhooly (Cork West) was the draper son of a coastguardsman; T. Walsh (Cork North) was a working carpenter, Luke Hayden (South Leitrim) the son of a blacksmith, James Tuite (Westmeath) a watchmaker, William Leahy (South Kildare) a small farmer, while T. O'Hanlon of East Cavan was a grocer, and B. Kelly (South Donegal) was a grocer's assistant. Two MPs ran dancing saloons, Alexander Blaine of South Armagh was a Dublin tailor, and so on.[60] After the election of Blaine, Parnell had greeted Tim Healy, Blaine's patron: 'Healy, who the devil is this tailor you have brought in on us?' 'Who is that convict looking fellow?'[61] he asked when he first saw him. Blaine was certainly capable of social maladroitness in the Palace of Westminster: sitting opposite Sir Richard Temple he asked, concerning the famine in Hindustan, 'Were you a famine clerk out there?' Sir Richard had been the governor. This was, perhaps, an extreme example of a social gaffe, but the average Irish MP was a striking contrast to the status of the average English Member of Parliament; or indeed that of the Irish unionists.[62] It explains Andrew Kettle's remark that England would find it difficult to give self-government to the men Parnell was gathering about him and Parnell's acknowledgement of the truth of that comment.

It may be helpful to add further context to Kettle's remark. The debating skills of Irish MPs often attracted English admiration in the House of Commons, but Irish MPs were not exactly equal citizens at Westminster. In the era of Parnell and Dillon, most MPs dressed for dinner; but the Irish, being relatively poor, did not. Also, they almost always ate in the Westminster Parliament itself because the cost of dining was lower than in leading London restaurants. The Irishman's reliance on dining in the House was widely noted and was the subject of snobbish comment on the floor of the House. Even Parnell himself was subject to a certain disdain. Lord Salisbury, Tory Prime Minister with a seat in the Lords Chamber, never bothered to go to the other end of the Palace to catch a glimpse of Parnell, still less to hear him speak.[63] It is this social gulf which as much as any other factor explains why *The Times* was amazed by Gladstone's conversion to Home Rule, but the conversion was real enough.

On 8 April 1886, Gladstone introduced a parliamentary bill which offered Irish autonomy over domestic affairs. He linked it with a new Land bill. It was designed to enforce cooperation between the two Irelands—or at least between a predominantly Catholic rural bourgeoisie and a Southern Protestant propertied class. It held few attractions for Ulster Protestants. This reflected an underlying ideological assumption, as Gladstone stated explicitly many times—that not only was Parnell naturally *conservative* but so were the Irish and this would become clear once Home Rule was granted. Gladstone accused the opponents of Home Rule of thinking that the Irish possessed a double dose of original sin. His opponents, like Joe Chamberlain, the leader of a new Liberal Unionist bloc in conjunction with Hartington's Whigs, accused him of thinking that they had a double dose of original virtue. In UK parliamentary terms, Gladstone was never quite able to overcome this challenge and answer the question: Why trust Irish nationalists given his own relatively recent passionate denunciation of the bad faith of Parnell and his movement? In his major speech on 16 April 1886—which ran to thirty-one pages in the National Press Agency pamphlet printed for the Liberal Central Association—Gladstone further explained his thinking. He quoted James Anthony Froude, the historian, to prove the historic evils of the Irish land system. The resentment of the Irish people was entirely reasonable. Yet Gladstone admitted: 'I have the honour of knowing myself many Irish landlords who are an honour to the class to which they belong.'[64] The British state had a duty to extend its credit to finance an Irish land purchase scheme. Gladstone explained, exploiting his own reputation for sound finance, that it had the financial capacity to do so. But, he added: 'The aim and end of all our endeavours is not, in the first place, for its own sake, simply the contentment of the people in Ireland—it is the social order of the country.'[65] The Irish people would be contented as they acquired their land. 'But I am in hopes that many a nobleman and many a gentleman in Ireland will long continue to inhabit his mansion and his demesne in a new and a happier state of things; yes, I believe it may be possible that even the Irish Nationalists may desire that those marked out by leisure, wealth, and station for attention to public duties, and for the exercise of influence, may become, in no small degree, the natural, and effective, and safe leaders of the people.'[66] This speech of Gladstone's reveals an acceptance of the Parnellite world view: more than that, he was now infatuated with the Irish, telling an unimpressed Margot Asquith 'about the Irish character, its wit, charm, grace and intelligence'.[67] But it evaded key questions—in particular, questions about the future of the large Protestant democracy in the north-east corner of the island.

There were, of course, important discussions on the Ulster issue. Speaking in the House of Commons on 3 May 1893, Gladstone declared that:

> In 1886, in proposing the Irish Government Bill...we did state that if the inhabitants of the North-East corner of Ireland, forming a very small and limited portion indeed of the general community, were resolutely desirous of being exempted from the operation of that Act, we should be prepared to entertain a proposal to that effect, and I believe we made that declaration with the general concurrence of those who are termed the Nationalist party.

Gladstone in the 1886 debate did, in fact, list the partition option among a set of various 'schemes' that had been advanced on behalf of Ulster, none of which seemed to have enough merit, or support, to warrant inclusion in the Home Rule bill, which deserved 'careful and unprejudiced consideration'. On 4 May 1893, Gladstone explained to astonished nationalists that while he understood Parnell's dictum of 7 June 1886—'No, sir, we can not give up a single Irishman'—to be an earnest deprecation of such exclusion, he took him not to be opposed 'provided it were found to give concord to Ireland instead of the present painful disagreement'.[68]

One of the great Victorian intellectuals—and a keen progressive—Alfred Russel Wallace was amongst those liberals fully alive to the difficulties of the Ulster question. 'These counties have shown their wish to remain under direct English rule by returning almost exclusively Conservative members to the present Parliament: and the very same Liberal principles which compel us to grant self-government to the great bulk of the Irish people forbid us to force these northern districts into a union which is repulsive to them, and which would inevitably lead to extreme dissatisfaction and perhaps even to civil war.'[69] Gladstone simply could not persuade enough parliamentarians with a rhetoric that was subtle but also inadequate. In the early hours of 8 June, the Home Rule bill was defeated in its second reading by 341 to 311.

Parnell's first great biographer, R. Barry O'Brien, attributes to Parnell the belief that 'Gladstone had committed a tactical mistake in mixing up land purchase with the question of an Irish parliament'.[70] But it is clear that while he was forced to admit the failure of Gladstone's strategy, he, Parnell, played a major role in initiating it. This is a clear example of a point well made by Elizabeth Dillon—Barry O'Brien's broad intelligence is undoubted but he tended to exaggerate his 'insider' knowledge. It is clear also from Parnell's conversation with Davitt at this point that he was resolutely opposed to any further bouts of agrarian radicalism. He was prepared to consider expanding the Acts of 1881 and 1885 but he did not want to see an attack on the land system as a whole.

For some it had been a war of civilizations. As J. A. Froude wrote to an American friend in June: 'three centuries ago when Britain became Protestant, Ireland had remained Catholic.' Froude recalled the Catholic saying of the sixteenth century: 'He that would England win | With

Ireland must begin'. In Froude's view, if, with Ireland's help, spiritual liberty had been crushed in England, political liberty would also have been crushed. The Armada of 1588, the Rising of 1641, James II, 1798—these were the four great episodes of this conflict: Home Rule was merely 'the fifth act' of an old essentially unchanged drama. If Home Rule was passed, the final logic would be to ensure 'with our own bayonets' the subjection of Ulster.[71] In July 1886, speaking alongside Sir Lushington Phillips in Salcombe, Devon, J. A. Froude returned to a brutal message. 'Down to the time of Henry VIII they [the Irish] were nothing better than a set of savages.' They were living an 'old Red Indian sort of life', without English influence. Home Rule was 'not wanted and would do no good'.[72] John Dillon had eloquently addressed the Cambridge Union on 10 June: 'Let them trust the Irish people for once in their history, for England was strong enough not to be afraid if they then abused that privilege.'[73] His Cambridge audience had low expectations of an Irish MP, but, Vivian Herbert recalled, Dillon 'astounded everyone by his knowledge of Dante, philosophy, science and foreign affairs'. Dillon presented a picture of modern Ireland to be set against Froude's dismal vision.

In the face of his defeat in Parliament, Gladstone called a general election on 10 June. Balloting took place between 1 and 17 July. The scale of the swing against the government of 5.7 per cent revealed that the Liberal leader had failed to convince the country just as he had failed to convince Parliament. The Liberals won 191 seats while the Conservatives and Liberal Unionists returned with a total of 394. The Conservative government proclaimed its firm support for the Union but suggested—above all by the appointment of Michael Hicks Beach as Chief Secretary—an interest in social and economic reform in Ireland as well. There was also a hint of a more intimate relationship with the Catholic hierarchy.

Parnell remained, however, steadily optimistic in outlook. The Tories owed their arrival in government to Liberal unionism: Liberal unionism itself would have dissolved under scrutiny if the electoral campaign had been three weeks longer. He echoed John Morley—Irish nationalists had every reason now to be moderate because 'ours is a winning cause'. He had, he admitted, dallied with Conservative land purchase notions in 1885 but that was in an era when the Conservative leadership was sending out flexible signals on Irish policy. He made it clear that in his view the Gladstone Home Rule *cum* Land bill proposal of 1886—the settlement of the question of the purchase of land in Ireland, concurrently with that of the national question—was the most viable and safe form of settlement yet proposed.[74] He and Gladstone had been realistic about public money. He (Parnell) had placed the sum to be spent on the settlement of the land question at 100 million, Gladstone at 150 million—Gladstone interjected '113 million'. Parnell happily accepted this correction. These were serious policies of serious men but, in contrast, the Conservatives merely floated extravagant ideas of wasting the Treasury's money in Ireland. Parnell expected them to advocate a channel tunnel from Northern Ireland to Scotland or something else equally fatuous.

As the new Parliament met, Parnell was very determined to show the new Tory government that he remained a power in the land: 'determined to show the Tory government the full significance of his influence in Ireland'. The *Spectator* added: 'Mr Parnell enjoys nothing so much as in acting the spectre at the feast. If Shakespeare could but have given a hint that Banquo's ghost thoroughly enjoyed his part, he would have given some notion of the impression which Mr Parnell produces on the British parliament.'[75] Parnell, in this image like Banquo's ghost ('thy blood is cold' says Macbeth), subdues and frightens Parliament—'Let the earth hide thee', muttered English MPs to themselves.

# The Ambiguities of the Liberal Alliance

Mr. Dillon's Dublin Parliament must be free and independent if it chooses to wreak its vengeance upon Irish Protestants, landlords and officials—as Mr. Dillon has promised it will—the Imperial Parliament must not be in a position to prohibit such a course.

*Preston Herald*, 26 November 1887.

Oh! That some power the gift would give us to see ourselves as Parnell sees us. The surrender of the Gladstonians was so sudden and has been so complete as to embarrass and confuse the calculating chieftain of the nationalists.

*Sporting Gazette*, 10 September 1887.

Following Gladstone's defeat and resignation, Parnell opened the new session by stressing the reality of agricultural depression in Ireland. He proposed legislation designed to restrain eviction by increasing the power of the Land Commission or county court judges to assist in that function. The Liberals supported the legislation but on 20 September Parnell's Tenants Relief bill was defeated. John Dillon immediately made a most passionate speech in Parliament threatening a new land agitation in Ireland; at this point there was little public sign that Parnell was likely to oppose it.

In the autumn of 1886, Parnell appeared to signal a new attack on landlordism. He declared in Parliament: 'Not that the majority of Irish landlords are necessarily just, for the Act of 1881 showed amongst them as few just men as there were in Sodom and Gomorrah, for in almost every case where the conditions of the holdings were brought under the notice of the Land Commission a reduction was given.'[1] His lieutenants appear to have assumed that Parnell was happy to see a new wave of agitation on the land issue. A meeting at Loughrea directed against Lord Clanricarde on 31 October showed how dangerous such rhetoric could be. It also showed John Dillon's considerable personal bravery. The *Freeman's Journal* recorded:

> Just as the resolutions had been read, a scene of great excitement occurred. A number of horsemen forced their way in front of the police, thus cutting them off from a view of the platform. The crowd surged backwards, driving the horses with them. The police vainly tried, by changing their formation to hold their ground, but were slowly driven back. There was great shouting and noise. The chairman called to the mounted men to withdraw to one side. The crowd cried, 'Out with the police;' the horses plunged and their riders shouted. Then one or two faced about and made in on the police. Bayonets were fixed almost immediately, while half a dozen baton men sprang forward and belaboured the horses on the heads and noses, and there is no knowing what consequences might have followed *had not Mr Dillon appeared and diverted attention from the police, who, however, had a very uncomfortable position, being in the rear of horses hooves during the whole time of the meeting.*[2]

Despite his Sodom and Gomorrah rhetoric, Parnell did not intend to declare open season on the landlords of Ireland, but John Dillon certainly intended to do just that. Noticing that they were often heavily mortgaged, he initiated a challenge against hate figures such as Lords Cloncurry or Clanricarde. At Murroe he declared: 'I will tell you what we will do, we will carry on this battle for years if necessary and as long as we have an organisation in Dublin, as long as we have friends at our disposal, and as long as the people of Limerick and Cork show themselves to be men, so long shall we support the Murroe tenantry. (Cheers.) They had kept their pledge. They had supported the Murroe tenants on a liberal scale from Dublin. Now, the moment had come to finish off the campaign and bring Lord Cloncurry to his knees.'[3] It is obvious that in Dillon's book the Murroe conflict was unproblematic and defensible. Living in Colorado he may have missed the embarrassing court hearings of 1884. At any rate his remarks in November 1886 appear not to show the slightest self-doubt about his course of action. But it was soon to emerge that Parnell was not in agreement with Dillon on such matters.

On 1 December 1886, William O'Brien and John Dillon decided to escalate with the agrarian agitation known as the 'Plan of Campaign' suggested by Harrington and Healy. The ploy here was that dissatisfied tenants on particular estates were to combine to offer the landlords their notions of fair rent. If this was refused, they paid him nothing; instead they contributed the proposed sum to a fund which would be employed for the protection of tenants in the event of landlord retaliation.[4] The key principle of this new agitation was the lodgement of the accumulated rent on an estate or a common defence fund—both Harrington and O'Brien were determined that the successful winning of legal costs, as in 1881, should not be an objective open to the landlord. O'Brien claims that Dillon was rather slow to get the point.[5] Such a strategy suggests an acknowledgement that Irish Americans would not this time fund the agitation of Irish farmers.

The Plan of Campaign was always of less significance than the Land League crisis. One key element of the Land League was conspicuously absent—the presence of a serious neo-Fenian political leadership interested in turning the land issue into the means of forcing an Irish withdrawal from the UK Parliament. The leading neo-Fenians—men like Patrick Egan, Thomas Brennan, Frank Byrne, P. J. Sheridan—had fled to the USA in the wake of the Phoenix Park murders. Their 'front man', Charles Stewart Parnell, made himself unavailable as a leader or even a supporter. Michael Davitt, now a supporter of land nationalization, and Henry George—to John Dillon's great personal annoyance— refused to work in the Plan of Campaign.[6] The Plan operated on hundreds of Irish estates but with varying degrees of effectiveness. It did, however, intensify the signal to Irish landlords that they were on the 'wrong' side of history. The dozens of senior British liberals who came to Ireland in solidarity with the Plan drove home that point. It also pushed a young government lawyer, Edward Carson, decidedly to the right. While the government developed a counter strategy of some calculation and toughness after Balfour became Chief Secretary, there were inevitable disasters—the deaths at Mitchelstown for example, or the death, shortly after a prison spell, of the patriotic gentleman farmer

John Mandeville; not to mention the imprisonment of O'Brien, Dillon, and other MPs, including the British Liberal W. F. Conybeare. If any Irish landlord had been tempted to think that the Land League was simply a bad dream—now ended—the Plan convinced them otherwise.

As Dillon explained at this time his objective was to overthrow the system established by William III and Cromwell. On 5 December at Castlerea, Dillon decided to use language which could only be interpreted as meaning that a day of reckoning would come for policemen and others who helped with evictions when Ireland had a government of her own.[7] 'When we come out of the struggle, we will remember who the people's friends were and who were the people's enemies, and we will deal out our reward to one and punishment to the other.'[8] Dillon's threat at Castlerea was all too credible to some in Ireland. Gladstone's Home Rule bill had, for example, guaranteed an unchanged future for the Dublin Metropolitan Police for only two years.[9] The DMP had been at the heart of the fight against the Invincibles: why were they placed in so unsure a position? The judiciary was left in a rather more secure place. But it was widely assumed that the next iteration of Home Rule would include rather more by way of devolution of justice as well as policing powers. After all, what otherwise was the point of Home Rule?

Senior Liberals such as Gladstone and Morley were worried Dillon's language had raised precisely the type of fear which weakened British support for Home Rule. O'Brien insisted that both Gladstone and Parnell were more concerned about Dillon's language than about the Plan as such. If so, they had good reason. Thomas MacKnight pointed out to Earl Spencer that Dillon had given one of the few glimpses of what a nationalist government would do if it held power. Spencer, vital to Gladstone's project, visibly winced.[10] A message of concern from Gladstone was sent to Parnell on 6 December. Three days later Parnell met with O'Brien behind Greenwich Observatory in a dense fog— Parnell dismissed it as no worse than the fogs on the Wicklow Hills. Parnell insisted that Gladstone had noted with great unease Dillon's recent speech at Castlerea. Parnell recalled that Dillon had said every magistrate, police officer, or government official who was seen as an enemy of the people[11] would suffer when the Liberals came to power. William O'Brien accepted that this was a genuinely damaging speech but insisted—reasonably—that Liberal leadership was not in principle opposed to agrarian agitation in Ireland which created problems for the Tory government.[12] Parnell in response pointedly recalled one of the embarrassing failures of the original Land League campaign: he blamed Dillon for provoking the crisis in the Murroe tenantry in which the tenantry were, in effect, defeated. This was a perfectly fair point as Dillon had recently at Murroe recalled precisely the moment in 1882 when he did this.[13] 'The exploit of your Mr Dillon in the Land League years was to get the rich Limerick farmers on the Cloncurry estate to throw up their dairy farms, and they have been a millstone round our necks since.'[14] Parnell knew and had recently met with McGeogh, the Land League solicitor who handled the Murroe case.[15] The Liberal leadership in the meanwhile continued to complain privately about Dillon's rhetoric. But was O'Brien—rather than Parnell—right on the deeper point— that the Liberals did not want agrarian peace in Ireland, a peace which would have strengthened the Conservative government?

O'Brien's intuition as to the position of Gladstone and Gladstonian Liberalism more generally was, in fact, correct. There was no real Liberal opposition to a renewed bout of Irish land war. Gladstone on 8 December wrote to Morley: 'I am glad to find that the Dillon speech is likely to be neutralised. I hope effectively. It was really very bad. I am glad you wrote to him.' Morley had, indeed, written to Dillon. Dillon did not even tell O'Brien of the letter and quietly buried it. O'Brien notes that a formal withdrawal was out of the question but Dillon did promise to use more sensitive language in future.[16] On the other hand, Gladstone felt that Tory acquiescence in Randolph Churchill's fiery language in Belfast in 1886—'Ulster will fight and Ulster will be right'— in the wake of the collapse of his Parnell flirtation, invalidated their attempts to make others speak out against extreme nationalist rhetoric. 'But all I say and do must be kept apart from the slightest countenance direct or indirect to illegality. We too suffer under the power of the landlords but we can not accept this as a method of breaking it.'[17]

The balance of this analysis requires a little decoding: Gladstonian Liberalism, after all, did not suffer under the power of the Irish landlords in any sense. The suggestion that Irish landlords had such a power implies that they were, at the least, justified objects of Irish public militancy. On 9 December, Gladstone was keen to tell Lord Ripon, former Viceroy of India, that 'I gather that Dillon will do something towards explaining or withdrawing his most improper speech at Castlerea'. Dillon, in fact, never withdrew or explained his Castlerea speech:[18] as became embarrassingly clear in 1893. It did not matter. Elizabeth Dillon's diaries show that by 1888 Lord Ripon was part of John Dillon's support group.[19]

On 10 December 1886, Gladstone expanded his views to former Irish Chief Secretary, Henry Campbell-Bannerman: 'I see no objection whatever to the allowances you propose to make the Irish people and I should dwell strongly on two things (1) Ministers themselves reopened the question of rents, signified that in some cases they *could not* be paid, appointed a Commission to inquire in what cases and then left the law to take its course by evictions in the meantime (2) the deplorable scheme in the state of Ireland since the cup of hope was dashed away from the lips of the people.'[20] This is the core of the matter. He, the G.O.M., had offered a 'cup of hope' to the lips of the Irish people—he could not accept the idea that it could just be 'dashed away' without dreadful consequences. But if Ireland remained quiet where was the proof of these dreadful consequences? There was no need, of course, to endorse explicitly nationalist campaigns, though many Liberals did—but it would have been a serious upset if there had been no such militancy in Ireland. Of course, the Tory strategy was the reverse—a conviction that it would be possible to ride out the inevitable storms in the countryside. As this became ever more clearly Tory strategy, the Gladstone investment in, and therefore tacit support for, Irish agitation increased even if it was a love that dare not speak its full name.

In O'Brien's later version of these events, John Morley is subject to added scorn. Gladstone, on the other hand, is granted a deeper and wiser understanding of Irish affairs. It is Morley who had attempted to convince Parnell that the effect of the Plan of Campaign 'in

England...was wholly bad; it offends almost more than outrages'. Gladstone, on the other hand, was in a rather more ambiguous place: he refused to countenance the Plan of Campaign, but for him 'the question rather is how much disavowal'. O'Brien's reply to Parnell was effective in these respects. In the first place, Parnell had effectively opened the door himself to the Plan of Campaign by his rhetoric and speeches in the autumn of 1886. Secondly, Parnell did not grasp that there was substantial and solid support, much more than for the Land League, amongst the Catholic clergy at all levels for the Plan of Campaign. Thirdly, and this was the most important point of all, Parnell—thanks to the tone of Morley's communications—hugely overestimated the amount of mainstream Liberal disdain for the Plan of Campaign both at leadership level and amongst the generality of MPs and activists. Writing in 1926, O'Brien could not resist reminding his readers of the veritable flood of Liberal MPs and activists who came to Ireland in the late 1880s to offer their support for the Plan: even the most 'chicken hearted' of Liberal MPs went along with this process. Despite Gladstone's assurances to Ripon, Dillon never retracted or moderated his Castlerea remarks in any way: indeed, he repeated them at Ennis on 3 September 1887, a few days before Mitchelstown. Nor did it much matter. In 1893, when Joe Chamberlain raised Dillon's use of such language in Parliament, Dillon claimed to have spoken in the aftermath of the emotion generated by the police violence at Mitchelstown. Unfortunately, the Castlerea remarks were dated December 1886 and Mitchelstown did not take place until September 1887. When caught out on this point, Dillon's apology—to the effect that he had misremembered a similar speech to that of Castlerea after Mitchelstown—was lame and unconvincing,[21] except in the generalized sense in which he put it—that he was used to replying on behalf of an oppressed people. The real significance lies in the fact that Dillon had so effectively repressed his Castlerea remarks— rather than address them, as he promised John Morley—to the point where he did not even recognize them.

On 15 December, Dillon had collected about £7,000 to support the Plan; he headed towards the well-chosen Clanricarde estate.[22] The

Marquess of Clanricarde was almost a parody of the selfish hard-hearted Irish landlord, 'one of the strangest monsters in recorded history'.[23] His father—whose political career collapsed because of a sex scandal—gave a cottage on the estate to one of his Irish girlfriends. Clanricarde had the woman evicted. Clanricarde owned 57,000 acres in Galway; he resided in London in a luxurious Albany bachelor suite, and only once visited his estate in Ireland, but he was known to visit on a more sustained basis courtesans like the famous 'Skittles': 'the epitome of the absentee and miserly Irish landlord'.[24] On 29 June 1882, his agent, John Henry Blake, was murdered and Clanricarde's relations with his tenantry further deteriorated. But, as Clanricarde openly declared, the murder of his agent did not worry him. In August 1886, some tenants on his Woodford estate were evicted for non-payment of rent. Three months later Clanricarde's estate became—unsurprisingly—the site of the first struggle declared under the Plan of Campaign. His tenants marched into Portumna and told Clanricarde's new agent, Francis Joyce, they would only pay their rents on condition of a 40 per cent reduction and reinstatement of the evicted tenants: to the exasperation of successive Tory Chief Secretaries, Sir Michael Hicks Beach and Arthur Balfour, the Marquess maintained an aggressive stance, continuing to evict defaulters.[25]

The Plan was now under way—in the next three years it was adopted on just over 200 Irish estates ranging in size from less than 100 acres to 100,000.[26] It is clearly the case that while the Land League may have suffered defeat at the hands of Lord Cloncurry, the Plan of Campaign did not. The rents collected on his estates dropped in the 1885–9 period, 43 per cent below the 1870–5 figure.[27] The *Economist* felt sure John Dillon was, in effect, a big vote loser for the Liberals[28]—but was it right?

During the new 'land war', it was noted that William O'Brien's language was less aggressive than John Dillon's. The Irish Loyal and Patriotic Union liked to say that Dillon 'out Briened O'Brien' during the Plan of Campaign.[29] O'Brien's language was certainly militant as he imagined the moral solidarity of the tenantry. But Dillon added a personal element to his rhetoric which some found shocking. At Loughrea on 13 December 1886, he said: 'I am sure that Lord Clanricarde would rather be left without his rents than to be sent among the tenants of Woodford without police protection.'[30] 'What is the meaning of this?' asked the *Standard*. 'Every Englishman knows. It implies that Lord Clanricarde would stand a chance of being shot.'[31] John Dillon, who had been spotted on 3 December 1880 reading his copy of the *Pall Mall Gazette*, which supported his role at that moment, would not have enjoyed its verdict in November 1886: 'We regret that Mr Dillon should have allowed himself to indulge in language which, being interpreted according to the usages of the locality, means simply murder.'[32] Dillon certainly insisted that he was driving the process. There was no suggestion that he was responding to distress. There was talk of falling prices but more about angry initiative: 'I will show him men who can pay and won't pay, because I tell them not to pay.'[33] But was this open arrogance fatal? Certainly not with Irish public opinion. Dillon's cool bravery and willingness to face prosecution and jail won him widespread admiration. Alfred Webb, the Quaker nationalist MP, recalled: 'A street incident may illustrate the temper prevalent in Ireland at the time. As I passed some railings dangerous to climb upon I saw a little girl disporting herself. "Come down out of that," said a passing policeman. "Yah!" answered the little one, "Take me, do, I'd love to be in prison."'[34]

It should be remembered that nationalist families could find themselves on the wrong side of popular feeling. The Curtins in Kerry, for example, suffered when their house was raided for arms. Curtin senior resisted and was shot—some of the perpetrators were sent to jail. This made the Curtins decidedly unpopular. After Mass, their pew was smashed in front of their eyes. Both Parnell and Dillon, in effect, disapproved of efforts by the senior Quaker nationalist, Alfred Webb, to speak up for the Curtins. Parnell after all had spoken at Ennis in 1880 of shunning enemies of the League even in the place of worship. The Curtins had to leave their home for a new life. Webb noted drily: 'I considered it somewhat disingenuous of nationalist friends who so entirely disapproved of my visit to the Curtins, afterwards, at the Parnell Commission to instance my interference as evidence of the efforts put forward by members of the National League to stop boycotting.'[35]

Despite his solidarity with Dillon on this point, there really is no doubt that Parnell disliked the growing public visibility of Dillon. Parnell had no desire to return to agrarian radical platforms—in fact, he never did so. William O'Brien has declared that Parnell viewed Dillon with a 'settled distrust' from late 1886: this distrust seems to have intensified in the summer of 1887. Parnell appears to have insisted that Justin McCarthy should retain the post of vice chairman; he also appeared to criticize publicly Dillon's recent style of work in the House of Commons.[36] It was, however, easier for Irish politicians to support the Plan of Campaign in the Irish countryside as work in the House of Commons became more and more unrewarding, On 17 February 1887, the closure was firmly applied, by majorities of 210 and 215, and the Speaker three times interfered decisively (once against John Dillon) to stop individual members who tried to obstruct. Parnell was at the centre of this work, putting down a Home Rule motion, but he was defeated by a majority of 105.[37] The double use of the closure allowed the Queen's Speech to pass, despite a later amendment by the Parnellite MP and former leading Invincible, J. R. Cox, concerning distress among the working classes.

On 7 March 1887, *The Times* began a series, 'Parnellism and Crime' (also 10, 14 March, 18 April, 13 May, 1 December). On 18 April, the paper published a facsimile letter purported to show Parnell's approval of the assassination of T. H. Burke on 6 May 1882. As Tim Healy noted 'for the credit of English public life', several unionist organs, including, as it happened, the Belfast *Northern Whig*, felt it likely that the letter was not genuine.[38] This, of course, tended to increase the solidarity of Parnell and Dillon. On the day of the *Times* story, Sir Edward Russell met Dillon in Parliament: '"Has Mr Parnell come?" Mr Dillon said "No". "Is he coming?" said I: And he added "I'll tell you something which will surprise you. If Mr Parnell comes, and when he comes, not one of us, his Irish colleagues and followers, will mention to him what has appeared in this morning's *Times*."'[39] If anything Dillon was too cavalier. When Parnell did eventually arrive in Parliament, having completed some chemical experiments at home, he spoke with some dignity: 'I cannot understand how the conductors of a responsible, and what used to be a respectable, journal could have been so hoodwinked, so hoaxed, so bamboozled, and that is the most charitable interpretation which I can place on it, as to publish such a production as that as my signature. My writing—its whole character—is entirely different.'[40] But Gladstone's speech on the same day is even more revealing. He ignored the *Times* charge and stressed how the Tory government was not justified in applying coercion in Ireland: in particular, it was not justified by references to his own record. In 1887, Gladstone said rent resistance does not 'blossom' into crime, because the organization was so perfect. Gladstone insisted that was not the case in 1881—an increase in crime accompanied the spread of the Land League.[41] This was precisely the allegation elegantly refuted by Sexton in the 1881 coercion debate, but no matter. Parnell then retreated to Avondale and Dr Kenny insisted that he was not well. In early May, it was reported: 'Mr Parnell is still in Avondale, and his friends here know little of his movement.'[42] Behind the scenes Parnell was more agitated. Frank Hugh O'Donnell (as did John Howard Parnell) recalled Parnell's edgy mood in 1887/8: it was 'his alarm, his falsehoods, his fear of cross examination, his pitiful anxiety to have the "*Times* show its hand" – which first convinced me that he had guilty knowledge of infamies'.[43]

Dillon's decision at this point to intervene in the *Times* controversy was impulsive and ill-judged. He seized on the allegations about the role of P. J. Sheridan—given Parnell's special sensitivity with regard to that particular personality, this was very high risk. Parnell had many other dangerous connections. When he and Dillon had attended as part of the welcoming committee for Davitt in Dublin on his release, three of the fourteen-man committee were Invincibles. There were other links. Parnell was well aware of P. J. Gordon, a fellow 'traverser' at the state trial and still believed to be involved in murder and still an activist in Mayo. Patrick Egan, the Land League treasurer, and believed by the police to be the paymaster of the Invincibles, was also one. Frank Byrne, the secretary of the Home Rule league in Britain, was another—Frank Byrne's wife had brought the Phoenix Park murder weapons to London. Parnell knew Byrne well, sitting beside him at numerous Home Rule

League meetings in Britain, for example. But Byrne had worked hard for Isaac Butt; Patrick Egan had helped the Home Rule election campaigns of George Errington, later a British agent of influence in the Vatican, and Colonel King Harman, later a Tory minister. J. R. Cox, a senior Invincible according to the police, was secretary to the Parnell testimonial. Such connections in the broad church of Home Rule politics proved little as to Parnell's guilty knowledge in themselves, however much they infuriated Tories and Unionists. But Sheridan was a different matter: named by Parnell himself as a strategic and influential figure in the world of illegal violence and capable of gossiping with friends and journalists about his dealings with Parnell on the eve of the Phoenix Park murders. P. J. Sheridan was the very last man in the world whose name Parnell wished to see dropped into debate in the House of Commons over a number of days but that is precisely the outcome John Dillon arranged. Parnell will have noted a former Irish Chief Secretary, Sir George Trevelyan's claim that he would remain a private citizen rather than vote for a Parliament in which Sheridan was likely to be elected.[44]

On 22 April 1887, Dillon dealt with Sheridan's famous August 1880 speech and his reference to the use of Minié rifles. This was, Dillon said, clearly predicated on the failure of a parliamentary strategy; Sheridan was clearly speaking as a supporter of Parnellism and was 'understood' by his audience to be making a reference to physical force only if that strategy failed. Dillon stated that Sheridan had ceased to have any connection with Parnellism in the spring of 1881.[45] This was easily disproved by reference to public meetings. The correspondent of the *Yorkshire Post* reported on 10 May that Parnell was 'sulking' and had no faith in Dillon's parliamentary tactics. If so, Parnell certainly had good reason. Dillon damaged his own reputation here. It was easy for *The Times* to show that Dillon and Sheridan attended Parnellite meetings, including the Land League executive, together in October 1881.[46] *The Times* concluded: 'It is right and necessary that the world should know that "the Bayard of the League"—the knight without reproach—has given a relatively fictitious account of a series of important transactions in which he himself and several of his leading colleagues in the House were principal

actors.'[47] The limited riposte of the Irish party was to point out that
Colonel King-Harman, a government minister, had been linked to
Sheridan in the 1870s.[48] As *The Times* pointed out, Dillon's reputation
as the 'Bayard' of the League was damaged, though not with Liberals
like W. F. Conybeare who had explicitly prompted it. Indeed, Conybeare
was (alongside R. B. Cunningham Graham) to be one of two Liberal
MPs to suffer imprisonment for support of the Plan of Campaign.
John Dillon's failure to refute *The Times* may have encouraged the
government's decision to hold a Special Commission of inquiry into
the *Times* allegations in 1888. Margaret O'Callaghan has observed
icily: 'Dillon, however, choleric, dyspeptic and devoid of judgement—
relished the politics of unreality on which he began to lead in 1887.'[49]
But he escaped the consequences of sceptical scrutiny in Ireland
because of the overall direction of the struggle against the *Times* forgery
and Tory coercion.

In early June 1887, Michael Davitt spoke at the scene of the Bodyke
evictions in Co. Clare. The landlord, Colonel O'Callaghan, was seen by
Dublin Castle as dangerously inflexible.[50] But Davitt was 'disagreeably
surprised' by the lack of popular resistance. In an act of self-criticism,
he argued that he, Davitt, had become too moderate of late and invoked
the spirit of John Mitchel. Perhaps disconcerted on this point he allowed
himself to use aggressive language: 'The sun might one day shine upon
England's difficulty when they in Ireland and their countrymen in
America might have revenge upon their crimes in Ireland.' This remark
produced a degree of nervous shuffling on the platform, which included
the Liberal MP Sir Wilfrid Lawson and his friends—Lawson, though, had
a significant Irish vote in his Cumberland seat.[51] At any rate, Gladstone
did not rebuke Lawson. The G.O.M. was at that moment 'coruscating
through Wales, and stopping at every railway station to identify the
cause of Wales with the cause of Ireland'.[52]

In July, Parnell returned to the House with a major speech. Again it
deepened the solidarity with Gladstone. It offered precisely the rationale for Gladstone's policies in 1881/2 which the G.O.M. loved to hear.
Gladstone told Sir Edward Russell it was quite superb:[53]

You know not what the legislation of 1881 [achieved]. It was not the Coercion Act of 1881, it was not the Coercion Act of 1882, that broke down the Land League movement. It was the Land Act of 1881. I know well the truth of what I am saying. I watched from Kilmainham, 90,000 tenants going into the Land Court, and I say that had it not been for the Act of 1881 it would have been possible for us, even from our cells in Kilmainham to have pushed the Land League movement to any extreme goal we chose it to reach.[54]

This was typical of Parnell. He was quite prepared to play up to Gladstone when it suited. There was no point in not pleasing the old man if it came without a cost: especially when so many Tories seemed willing to give credit to the *Times* allegations. 'Does Lord Salisbury really believe them?' he asked one London society hostess. But the very fact that Parnell asked the question showed that he was still interested in the mindset of the Tory leadership.

# 7

# Friendship or Hatred?
## 1887–1891

### The Contradictions of John Dillon

I am driven to the conclusion that he really has a hatred of England.
He is reputed to be estimable in private life, and has, when quiescent,
a calm and refined, sometimes even a gentle aspect, but all that alters
very much when he is moved by political passion. In public speaking
he has become so used to violence that he no longer seems to be himself unless excited to invective.

> 'John Dillon 1886–1892', *Sir Richard Temple, Letters and Character*
> *Sketches from the House of Commons* (London, 1912), 176.

It had ever been his [Dillon's] aim to promote friendship between his
countrymen and their more powerful fellow citizens.

> *St James's Gazette*, 7 December 1889.

The perception that Bodyke marked a failure of popular mobiliza-
tion was answered by a huge demonstration on 3 September in
Ennis of some ten thousand. Dillon and O'Brien led the way but this
time the radical Liberal MP Philip Stanhope joined them. Stanhope's
wife, the Countess Tolstoi, added to the occasion: leading to sardonic
comments about absentee landlordism and oppressed serfs in the
Conservative press. Stanhope told the crowd, 'citizens of the British
Empire', that millions of British hearts were praying for them, but in
England there were those who suggested that if so, they were praying
that the Irish ignored Stanhope's rhetoric.[1] It is perhaps more revealing

*Ancestral Voices in Irish Politics: Judging Dillon and Parnell.* Paul Bew, Oxford University Press.
© Paul Bew 2023. DOI: 10.1093/oso/9780192873705.003.0007

that Thomas Cave Junior was present: he was the son of the Barnstable Liberal MP, Thomas Cave, whose abuse of Parnellite obstruction ten years before had been condemned by the *Spectator* as offensive and corrosive of the Union.[2] At the heart of this Ennis adventure was the local MP, J. R. Cox, the former Invincible who led the police on a merry dance by small changes to the precise venue. All passed just about peacefully on that day but disaster at some point was inevitable. There were two hundred police at Ennis, two companies of Leinsters, and a troop of the 3rd King's Own Hussars: there was an angry mood. It was remarkable that events did not get out of control. At Mitchelstown on 9 September 1887, the cavalry of the campaigners executed a similar manoeuvre to that of Loughrea. This time events did get out of control. Finding that they were losing what the *Leinster Leader* reporter called a 'fair' fight— with fists and sticks against batons—the RIC escalated the violence. The police opened fire on the crowd and three were killed and two wounded. All this was watched by Henry Labouchere, the Liberal MP, and by Sir John Brunner MP and the four young English ladies who had accompanied him on this trip. They were, not surprisingly, 'paralysed with fear'.[3] 'This was bad enough but worse might have followed if Dillon, with great personal courage, had not walked out across the now deserted square up to the barracks gate and urged the officer in charge to desist.'[4] John Dillon was the hero of the hour. His admirer and eventual wife, Elizabeth Mathew, watched on nervously as the parties of young English Liberal ladies who joined these trips seemed to be all too enthusiastic about the handsome John Dillon.[5]

Parnell was forced to come to Dillon's side in Parliament in September 1887: in fact, they were also supported by John Morley. Dillon insisted that the thirty Irish MPs likely to be arrested during the recess 'should not be treated as felons'. Morley supported Dillon by saying that in all foreign countries, treatment different from that of ordinary criminals was accorded to political prisoners. Parnell's speech was considered to be unusually vehement in his denunciation of the government. 'Mr. Forster treated his political opponents in a very different fashion; but the right hon. Gentleman is going to treat them as they treat garroters.'

He ended with a half-threat, half-warning of reprisals coming from men of violence in Ireland and America. These, he said, would be very injurious to the Irish cause.[6] But it is clear that Parnell and Dillon were still divergent on questions of strategy. There was no disguising the gap between Parnell and Dillon: Dillon cannot have been pleased when Parnell took a legal action against one of his own tenants—Matthew Kavanaugh—distracting from the 'extraordinary scene' connected with the Plan in the rest of the country.[7] In the Mitchelstown area, any-one suspected—no matter how vaguely—of lack of sympathy for the Plan was ferociously boycotted.[8] Parnell and Dillon watched on with different emotions. They held to an entirely different analysis of the political situation. Frank Lockwood, Parnell's lawyer, at the beginning of 1888, was clear about Parnell's private opinion:

> Mr. Parnell said he never approved of the Plan of Campaign and would always think it a blunder as, but for it, matters would have come to a crisis long ago and the moderate Tories represented by Hicks Beach would have retired disgusted from the coercion programme. Mr. Parnell hopes and trusts that his colleagues will give up any semblance of obstruction and let the government proceed as far as possible with the local government measures and split up by itself, as it assuredly will.[9]

This private opinion was all too visible. The *Liverpool Daily Post* noted that Parnell, displaying the 'skill of a tactician', felt that the Plan was unifying a governing coalition which might otherwise fall apart.[10] *The Times* noted Parnell's 'icy silence' concerning the 'treatment of political prisoners'.[11]

In reading such a comment, it has to be recalled that when Hicks Beach had retired from office due to his eyesight problems, the nation-alist press gloated that they had 'blinded' him. Parnell, on the other hand, who had a long history of parliamentary clashes with Hicks Beach going back to the heyday of obstruction in 1876,[12] still regarded him with favour. In mid February 1888, Parnell, striking a different note as against the autumn of the previous year, rather implied that the repression provoked by the Plan of Campaign was trivial; he com-pared it to the Land League days—'a blow from the paw of the British lion'—to the 'scratch of a cat'. When Forster acted decisively to repress the League, no Land League branch dared call a meeting—fearing government repressive actions. Parnell seemed to refer wistfully to Forster: 'Well, there was a man.'[13] His main charge against the Tory government was hypocrisy—had not senior Tories opened up a dialogue with him on the future of Ireland in 1885? The implication was clear enough: the Plan of Campaign heroes were not the heroes of the Land League era. On 20 April 1888—following intense British diplomacy behind the scenes—a Papal rescript was issued denouncing the Plan of Campaign and the campaign of boycotting as illegal and forbidding clergy to take any part in either. The willingness of many of those attending Mass in Ireland to walk out when this message was conveyed was an early sign that the rescript would fail. Both Dillon (on 7 May) and Parnell (on 8 May) made it clear that they were opposed to the rescript. Dillon was particularly bitter in his denunciation of Bishop O'Dwyer of Limerick: the two men were to be enemies for decades to come. Dillon declared that nationalists owed it to their Protestant fellow countrymen to resist such clerical dictation: ironically, of course, this was precisely a case when most Protestant Irishmen would have preferred Irish Catholics to follow the instructions of the Pope; the Irish Roman Catholic clergy remained heavily involved in the Plan. While Parnell supported Dillon on the rescript, he was clearly not supportive of the Plan, even at a moment when Dillon was facing the courts on account of his engagement in that campaign.

On 11 May, Parnell told the Eighty Club of prominent Liberals of his lack of enthusiasm for the Plan: 'I was so feeble…I was positively unable to take part in any public matter…If I had been in a position to advise about it, I candidly admit to you that I should have advised against it.'[14] Elizabeth Dillon noted in shock: 'Many of us there felt pained that Mr Parnell's declaration that he has never entirely approved of the Plan, even though he recognises the enormous good it has done—had to come on the eve of Mr Dillon's trial.'[15] On 13 May, Dillon was sentenced to six months' imprisonment without hard labour. The Plan leader, William O'Brien MP, wrote: 'For the first time and the last time in my life it must be owned I was really angry and lost not a moment in telling him [Parnell] so in London.'[16] Parnell responded in a slightly catty way: Dillon and O'Brien had not really suffered for the cause, they had brought any suffering on themselves. As Andrew Kettle reported, at this same minute Parnell had no faith in O'Brien or Dillon's leadership skills: 'He was low spirited, cross like, when renewing the outlook just then.'[17] At this juncture Parnell also ignored an invitation from John Morley to 'make the Irish people wake up a bit'.[18]

In June 1888, Dillon was incarcerated in Dundalk prison—more accurately the infirmary of Dundalk prison where attention was given to his precarious health. A serious public health warning from Parnell to the effect that Dillon was very poorly—so common a feature of life in 1881–2—was this time, however, not issued. Nonetheless, Dillon was widely said to be consumptive[19] and it was also claimed by W. S. Blunt that Balfour wanted to see him die in jail. At the end of June, Dillon's periods of exercise were extended.[20] In Wales, in particular, Dillon attracted public sympathy. The *Pall Mall Gazette* declared: 'It is impossible to make Englishmen understand the intensity of the sympathy with which the Welsh people regard Mr. John Dillon.'[21] The *Cardiff Times*[22] agreed. 'In Wales, John Dillon is the most popular man of the day. Ninety thousand in Wales signed a petition for Dillon's release.'[23] Dillon used the time to read Burke and Macaulay. William O'Brien was asked: 'How will Mr. Dillon's imprisonment affect the Plan of Campaign?' He replied: 'If Mr. Balfour had caged him a few months ago it would have been almost fatal to the agitation in which Mr. Dillon was the heart and soul.'[24] But now, he assessed, it would not be so serious in its implications.

Also in June 1888, Kegan Paul, Trench in London published Dr William Dillon's two-volume *Life of John Mitchel*.[25] There was much comment at the time to the effect that it was important that the book had a distinguished London publisher; even opponents of Irish nationalism regarded this as a positive development. Kegan Paul was actually a full member of Dillon's progressive English entourage—and a convert to Catholicism. John Dillon wrote the introduction for his brother's book: 'There is hardly a man now in the ranks of the Nationalist party in Ireland who can not recall how his blood was fired and his heart beat faster, when as a boy he read of the scene at Mitchel's trial; when, under Mitchel's guidance, he followed the fortunes of the great chieftains of Tir-Owen and read for the first time how O'Neill triumphed over the stranger at Yellow Ford, and left the fields round Armagh piled with the bodies of his foes.' But Mitchel's real historic importance lay elsewhere; what really mattered was his ability to sharpen the Irish capacity for anger rather than acquiescence in the 'British Providence'. John Dillon made the point with exceptional clarity: 'And, finally, Mitchel more probably than any other man, put into immortal language the deep and fierce anger which burned at the heart of every true Irishman at the utterable degradation and shame to which his race had been subjected.' John Dillon's introduction avoided completely the issue of Mitchel's ardent support for slavery. His brother, however, decided to face the issue. 'It is well known that, during the American civil war, John Mitchell was strongly for the South and for slavery, while the great majority of Irish men were as strongly for the union and abolition.'[26] Several prominent abolitionists supported Home Rule—James Redpath compared Irish tenants to slaves and the RIC to the Ku Klux Klan.

This was a serious issue. After all, it was conventional for Irish nationalists to point out, and condemn before American audiences, W. E. Gladstone's phrase that the North had fought for 'mere' power while the South fought for liberty. It was emblematic of the reactionary and corrupt nature of the British state that its Prime Minister could have said such a thing:[27] it was proof of the moral superiority of Irish nationalists that they would not say such a thing, but here was John Mitchel saying such a thing. But John Mitchel somehow avoided a similar condemnation. Dillon noted: 'But while we may find several acts in Mitchel's public life which have been regretted by men who were his sincere friends, we can find nothing which any countryman or admirer need feel ashamed of.' The book was seen, perhaps surprisingly, as part of a new emergent Anglo-Irish reconciliation, thanks to its prestigious

London publisher. The *St James's Gazette* commented. 'We believe we can say with truth that the hatred which Mitchel felt towards this country and nation have never been surpassed. Again and again he manifests his desire to witness a bloody extermination of the English people. Yet an eminent firm of English publishers brings out the life at this time and the English people are challenged to read it and admire.'[28] The unionist *Dublin Daily Express* cynically noted: 'It certainly seems curious that one who thought freedom for Irishmen was worth fighting for should have fought to maintain the slavery of negroes.'[29] The *Pall Mall Gazette*, bothered perhaps by this problem, hailed the objectivity of the biographer: William Dillon's conception of the duty of the biographer was just to tell the story of his subject's life, without stopping to excuse or to explain.[30] But the message of William Dillon's book was clear enough: John Dillon was right to promote the 'savage wrath' of Irishmen as they contemplated genocidal British policy during the Famine.

There is an irony here. In 1888, John Dillon was increasingly drawn to Elizabeth Mathew, the daughter of Sir James Mathew, a High Court judge and well-connected Liberal.[31] Sir James Mathew was also the nephew of the celebrated Franciscan apostle of temperance, Father Mathew. Father Mathew was a friend of Charles Trevelyan, the most important British official during the Famine: it was Father Mathew, and *not* Trevelyan—who disputed it—who supported the 'providentialist' thesis that God was punishing the Irish for sin during the Famine. He was also a militant opponent of all forms of Irish revolutionaries of the Mitchel type.[32] Perhaps caught up in the general bout of historical reflection,[33] Gladstone decided at this moment to work out his own ideas in Irish history. His analysis paid scant attention to the Mitchel story: but it did owe a lot to Daniel O'Connell. Gladstone's historical note at this point is of some interest. 'The growth of Irish nationalism has been singular or not quite easy to trace...the penal laws forced Irish nationalism to live feebly underground without air or light, in the Roman Catholic body before the Union.' O'Connell was the almost solitary prophet. The nationalism of the Protestants had both life and vigour. Gladstone correctly noted the success of the Union in destroying

Protestant nationalism but, notably, fails to discuss precisely why the Union won over those substantial sections of Ulster Presbyterian society which had supported the United Irishmen revolt of 1798. But then Gladstone produced a fascinating formulation:

> But the old spirit migrated into a larger and freer body namely that of what is after all the Irish nation. It became detached from all ideas of privilege and preference and held and holds the large and open platform on which it was placed by the genuine liberalism of O'Connell.
>
> The land question far from its basis is an incidental, unhappy and hampering accompaniment.[34]

This is a fascinating and revealing analysis. It reveals Gladstone's unwillingness to see agrarian agitation as anything other than incidental: the profound effect of these remarks is to downplay, display, and marginalize the land question—to treat it as not the 'basis' of the Irish question. Conceivably, land was not the 'basis' of the Irish question, but it was certainly not 'incidental' or 'hampering'. The really important aspect of the Irish question for Gladstone is the 'migration' of the 'old spirit' of nationalism under the guidance of the 'genuine Liberalism of O'Connell'. Gladstone had been troubled by nightmares occasioned by his role as a member of the Cabinet which jailed O'Connell in 1844; now he exorcised these nightmares in spectacular fashion. Irish nationalism was a pure form of patriotism. Old questions about the nature of Catholic public opinion in Ireland—including those raised sharply by his own anti-Vatican pamphlets of the mid 1870s—were suppressed in favour of a gamble on the 'migration' of the 'old spirit' and its effective permeation by the 'genuine liberalism' of O'Connell. This intellectual step established, the Irish question became a question of the destiny of Liberalism—all questions reduced to one: if Ireland could only be governed by authoritarian repressive means by Westminster surely the best outcome was self-government? Considerations as to the exact settlement of the land question which so bothered Parnell in 1890 and 1891, and, indeed, Parnellite considerations as to the opposing mentality of the north-east of the island, were essentially secondary. Even to his closest friends, Gladstone was perceived now to have become obsessive about the Act of Union—'worse than the French terrorists', he told Edward Hamilton. The idea here is that Jacobin Terror was morally superior to British terror in Ireland in 1798 and 1799. But the most remarkable aspect of Gladstone's thinking about Ireland is the way he reconceptualized the history of Ireland in which the real process of development is obscured in exchange for a concept of *migration* of a viable concept from eighteenth-century elite Irish Protestantism to nineteenth-century popular Irish Catholicism. In this re-imagination there is essentially no place for famine rage and no place for John Mitchel's anti-liberalism. Gladstone amidst all his vast reading on Ireland does not appear to have engaged seriously with William Dillon's 1888 biography.[35]

Not everyone in Ireland was impressed by Gladstonian 'history': in particular, not everyone could excuse Gladstone's own previous record as easily as he did. Edward Hamilton noted: 'Looking back on his own budgets, Mr. G. said he ranked his budget of 1853 highest. It cost him more trouble than any other; he regarded it as his greatest effort in every sense.' Gladstone extended income tax to Ireland as offset for forgiving Famine loans. 'He believed he was the first Chancellor of the Exchequer who took pains to master his subject.'[36] But in the late 1880s Irish nationalists still took a very different view. O'Neill Daunt commented: 'Mr. Gladstone has been justly and ably denouncing the Union in the *Westminster Review* and other periodicals. He has given many unanswerable arguments against it. He might add, however, if you want to appreciate the evils of the union, look at me, W.E.G. When Ireland lay crushed and prostrate beneath the misery of a seven years' famine, when multitudes had perished by starvation, and when all who could obtain the passage money were flying to America, I, W.E.G. seized the propitious moment to give a spur to the exodus by adding to the previous taxation of Ireland, and pleaded the terms of the Union as my justification for inflicting this scourge on the suffering people.'[37] But O'Neill Daunt kept his criticism private—after all, Gladstone was now an effective ally of the Irish party.

Gladstone's increasing acceptance of his version of the Irish nationalist world view (as redefined in the Gladstone way) was widely noticed.
The *Economist* concluded: 'Mr. Gladstone's letter upon the imprisonment of Mr John Dillon is calculated to justify and encourage, evasion
and defiance of law.'[38] In September 1888, the government, pushed by
*The Times*, put into play the judge-led Parnell Commission of inquiry
into the ramifications of the Parnell movement. It was widely seen as an
attempt to criminalize a popular political movement. What led to such
a drastic step? It is fair to note the dangers: the overt politicization of the
justice system, always political to some extent, and the many conse-
quent manipulative actions behind the scenes. There was stunning
overconfidence involved in placing strong reliance on Richard Pigott, a
shady Dublin character—hardly, after all, a close student of Parnell.
(Pigott's memoir places Parnell, for example, as an Oxford student.)[39]
But it is important to recall also the relatively rational reasons for this
confidence. The world of Gordon and Sheridan was well known to the
authorities, for example, and their connections to Parnell personally
were all publicly visible. Nationalists themselves were inclined to gossip
that Parnell in Kilmainham knew of plans for violent action. It was easy
to believe that something would break decisively in favour of *The Times*
and the government: not the least of the reasons for this miscalculation
was the ignominious collapse of Dillon's account of the party's relationship with Sheridan in the summer of 1887. The world was divided
between those who expected the Parnell Commission to destroy Parnell
and those who believed it would not. On his release from prison in
September, Dillon maintained a resolute stance. 'On the subject of
armed rebellion,' Dillon said, 'there was not a Tipperary man on the
earth who did not regret that he was not allowed to meet on equal terms
and with arms in the hand the malignant enemies of his race.'[40]

Of particular significance here was P. J. Sheridan. Sheridan was now
living in some style, possessing two ranches in Colorado and some
three thousand head of sheep. Everyone knew him to possess dangerous secrets. Would he decide to give evidence? Parnell was known to be
very concerned indeed on this point,[41] and he would not have been

pleased to read in November this story in the UK media from the hand of Alfred (later Sir Alfred) Robbins, with whom Parnell himself cultivated contacts:

> Upon authority to which considerable weight attaches, the London correspondent of the *Birmingham Post* learns that one of the next 'sensations' to be provided for the special commission by the *Times* is the evidence of P. J. Sheridan, the 'well known organiser of the West'. That individual is positively stated to be now on his way to England, and he may be expected to be placed in the witness box at no distant date to testify concerning the connections which the *Times* alleges to have between the Land League and the promoters of outrage.[42]

In early December, Dillon struck out on a new theme. He was now absolutely opposed to separation: William Dillon's introduction to the John Mitchel biography had left a touch of ambiguity on that point. At a major event in the Westminster Palace Hotel, Dillon was given an illuminated address hailing his triumphs, signed by 150 Liberal MPs, seventy of whom were in attendance.[43] The Mitchelite revolutionary was now truly *salonfähig*. In Oxford in late 1887, John Dillon had declared his desire to 'unite in patriotism' the people of the two countries.[44] In his emotional speech of thanks, Dillon went further as he rejected 'the idea that he had fostered hatred': 'What we have done is this. We have pointed the hatred of our people not against the people of this country but against the system of government from Dublin Castle, on the head of which, we have, I think, justly laid all the misfortunes of our countrymen.'[45] He added: 'If it is true that our ulterior object has been and is to maintain and to perpetuate the enmity between the Irish and the English people, how can any man deny that there does not exist at this moment a greater degree of friendliness between the peoples of England and Ireland than there ever existed before? (Applause).'[46] Happily, in view of such language, it became clear just before the end of the month that *The Times* had failed to secure P. J. Sheridan's appearance in London.[47]

Here is the paradox, as both Katharine O'Shea and F. H. O'Donnell pointed out. Parnell in 1882 promised Gladstone to bring about agrarian peace in Ireland: in the 1880s he did everything he could in this respect, probably weakening his own personal authority within nationalism— though this should not be overstated: loyal Parnellites after the split like Luke Hayden MP and Tim Harrington were strong supporters of the Plan of Campaign.[48] But in the changed circumstances of a Tory government, Gladstone was not keen to see the promise kept: he was more happy to see the Conservative government forced into repression in Ireland thus to argue that the Union was discredited. He was even happy to argue that coercion in Ireland provoked popular Irish struggle which benignly infused English working-class agitation.[49] 'When Parnell kept the word he had pledged in Kilmainham to slack down agitation, Mr. Gladstone threatened to pose in his place as the fiery champion of Irish wrongs, and even excused the Plan of Campaign which Parnell had wanted to suppress.'[50] John Dillon became a kind of hero to Liberal MPs—whilst Parnell in 1886 had feared he would become a pariah.

On 20–22 February 1889, the hapless scoundrel Richard Pigott was unmasked as the forger of the letters published in *The Times*. The Parnell Commission was rendered a non-event and a Liberal/Irish victory. A new commonplace was born. 'What was new in the evidence before the Parnell Commission was not true and what was true was not new.' The Liberal–Irish alliance was, it seemed, set fair.

In mid March 1889, the Liberal infatuation with Parnell reached the level of passion: he addressed a great Liberal gathering in St James's Hall. Gladstone was unfortunately ill but Parnell was introduced by John Morley, without, of course, any hint of the private tensions in their relationship. Morley's vision was clear: Ireland was to be an 'integral, reconciled and equal member of the Empire'. Parnell then 'confronted' his audience, pale, tall, with his left arm in a sling following a chemical experiment accident at Avondale. The *Pall Mall Gazette* reported in an explosion of the nonconformist conscience: 'In a moment everyone was up, for the next five minutes St James Hall was even as Exeter Hall when the Salvation Army had one of its greatest field days, when the General [William Booth] has brought the soldiers up to the highest pitch of ecstasy. Cheer followed cheer in endless succession.'[51] Parnell was unmoved. So they sang 'For he is a jolly good fellow'. Parnell's speech played into this emotionalism: the Irish tenant facing his land-lord was like a 'fly' trying to oppose an 'elephant'. More truthfully, he claimed that the Parnell Commission had not produced a single fact or substantiated accusation which was not known to Lord Salisbury and Lord Carnavon at the moment in 1885 when Lord Carnavon opened up discussions with him about the future government of Ireland.

Gladstone's historic achievement is clear. In 1876–80, he shifted popular Liberalism towards emotional crusades for humanitarian causes 'above' party politics: by the mid 1880s Ireland had become his leading non-negotiable crusade. In the discourse, the Irish cause came to be identified with democracy, constitutional freedom, and the laws of humanity.[52] All this had a high moral tone. But, for Gladstone, the conceptual problem was even more profound: English issues tended to reduce themselves to Irish issues. When the public appeared to support strikes in 1889 Gladstone clearly insinuated that the cause of the new sympathy which had given the working class their new force was opposition to coercion in Ireland.[53] It was a classic reductionism which contained a double danger: a failure to accept the complexity of English social issues and also, for those fearful of the rise of the labour move-ment, an enhanced feeling that Liberalism's Irish policy sent out a clear sign that it was an unreliable ally on domestic issues, especially those that touched on the role of law and defence of property rights. Sir Robert Ensor noted: 'What turned the Liberal business class of 1870 into the Conservative or Liberal-Unionist business class of 1895 really was the Irish agrarian movement—not fear of the [English] proletariat at all.'[54]

Of course, other factors were involved in Conservative electoral hegemony—for example, a new class sentiment fuelled by the growth of suburbs.[55] But it is important to realize that political language and vision also has an impact on voting behaviour.[56] It is important also to consider the tone or structure of feeling in British politics. This passage in G. M. Young's classic work *Victorian England: Portrait of an Age* conveys the impact of Gladstone—uplifting for some[57] and tiresome for many others.

By 1886 every argument on either side of the Irish case had been stated, confuted, reiterated, and shredded to the last syllable. But still Mr. Gladstone was there, always ready to fan the tiring ardour of his followers with a moral emotion which may seem to us to be strangely in excess of the occasion. Surely it is possible to be a religious man and an intelligent man, and yet not deem it necessary to enter into the chamber of the soul, the recesses of the heart, yea, the presence of Almighty God, when the question at issue is whether in the last Irish tussle, the policeman or the Ribbonman hit the other first; be it in politics or in poetry, few English optics are fine enough to determine whether a pale light in the western sky is the birth of a star or the dust above a Dublin street fight. Released from power, the old man employed the most wonderful resources of voice, presence, experience, fame, of scholarly and religious accomplishment, ever given to an English statesman, to keep Ireland before the eyes of a people already stirring away from Liberalism towards an Imperialism or a collectivism of which he understood nothing.[58]

In short, Gladstone's growing pro-Irish style of rhetorical radicalism was widely noted. Gladstone had always insisted that the boycott was coercive and illegal and not to be compared with the practice of exclusive dealing. As Dicey explained: 'It is Mr. Gladstone who, after telling his followers, that exclusive dealing is not boycotting but a "totally different thing" then now revealed to them that boycotting means exclusive dealing.'[59] Remarkably, of course, this placed Gladstone in exactly the same place as John Dillon in his speech in Parliament in August 1882. Gladstone attended the Special Commission in May 1889 in solidarity with William O'Brien, Dillon's ally in the Plan of Campaign.[60]

In the summer and autumn of 1889, Parnell avoided the Liberal leader. He was anxious to win a Catholic university from the Tory government and thought that he had a good chance. By October, this strategy had failed—to Gladstone's jubilation. Gladstone renewed his invitation for Parnell to visit him at Hawarden. Parnell finally accepted and just before arrival at Hawarden he spoke at Nottingham. As 1889 came to a close, Parnell's Nottingham speech was characterized by a statesmanlike, but still expectant tone. 'We recognise that for the first time we are within the constitution and that within the constitution we are sure of victory.'[61] One aspect, however, amused his unionist critics. In front of Alderman Gripper and other local Gladstonian municipal worthies in Nottingham, Parnell turned himself into a practical man in a practical role—gone was all the exciting nationalist rhetoric of his earlier years. Commentators suggested Parnell's long periods of silence aided and assisted reinvention of his political persona. At Nottingham, Parnell presented himself as 'and was seriously accepted as an agricultural and industrial economist—the Arthur Young *de nos jours*; the man who has pondered deeply on arterial drainage; who has given days of thought to the improvement of harbours, and wrestled for sleepless nights with the revival of "languishing fisheries"; who has mapped out a complete plan of the extension of Irish inland navigation'.[62] In fact, this was a genuine part of Parnell's political personality even if it is not surprising that not every English commentator had noted it before.

On 18/19 December, Parnell was Gladstone's guest at Hawarden. Sir Edward Russell reported: 'He was evidently much pleased with the occasion, threw aside all such reserve, not to say shyness, as marked his manner in the House of Commons, and conversed most freely about the present and future.'[63] Gladstone's daughter asked him: '"Who is the greatest actor you have seen Mr Parnell?" Your "father" undoubtedly, he promptly replied.'[64] Mary Gladstone was very impressed by Parnell—only to be shocked all the more by the divorce court revelations.

It is perfectly clear that Parnell publicly signalled that the relationship with Gladstone was satisfactory from the Irish point of view. But there were discordances of tone. In February 1890, Parnell referred back to the Forster era: 'But at the same time I felt and believed and I believe that many of my colleagues felt with me, that his criticism of some of our action—sins as I have said of omission rather than commission, was justifiable.'[65] To a quite remarkable degree, Parnell is conceding the central charge made by Forster in 1883: a charge he had contemptuously dismissed when it was first made. Even more remarkable is the willingness to pay a certain justice to the dead Forster, who had now been cast into outer darkness by Gladstone and the Gladstonians.

Parnell's moderation on the land question was also increasingly marked. He said in April 1890:

> I think and I always have thought we might reasonably ask in view of the history of the Irish land question, in view of the fact that the Imperial taxpayer is the descendant of the men who placed these landlords in Ireland for the purpose of perpetuating and serving English rule in that country... how far will the Imperial taxpayer go?[66]

But how far would the English taxpayer go to help resolve the land question? Parnell feared that the evidence of the 1886 Land bill suggested that Gladstone would not go very far in that direction. In the same speech (col. 988), he returned to an old theme. Parnell's problem was that the larger tenants were absorbing a very large share of the public money made available for land purchase—whilst the largest, often non-residential landlords were also gaining the biggest share of the land purchase fund. Parnell insisted that he had always wanted the Irish gentry, following 'a suitable solution of the land question', to take the part for 'which they are so well fitted in the future regeneration of their country, in the future direction of affairs, and in the future national life of the country'. He added, with sharp effect: 'The land question is not so large a question as many will suppose...It is the trouble which has arisen in Ireland between the average sized tenancies and the smaller class of tenants and their landlords. The trouble has not been created as a rule by the larger class of tenants...they stand on a much more equal footing with their landlords to make their contracts freely and fairly, and it is not, in my judgement, necessary for the sake of settling the Irish land question you must include the class of tenants above £50 valuation in any Purchase Bill.'[67] John Dillon was less than impressed. He felt it necessary to rebuke Parnell. 'The Irish members listened to these proposals with the deepest regret; without enthusiasm, because they regarded them as some more of the proposals of compromise which, during the course of the Irish land war, have been made over and over again, by the man who will yet be regarded by the landlords of Ireland with feelings of remorse and regret, because they did not close with his offer when it was still in his power to restrain those forces which may make them bitterly sorry for their actions.'[68]

Political observers asked themselves the question—was it possible that the Irish party would assist Balfour's Tory Land bill to pass or, at any rate, the congested districts section of it?[69] On 11 July 1890 in Parliament, Parnell appealed again to Balfour: he made it clear his hostility to 'the terrible evil of a general agrarian struggle'. Parnell also appealed to the government to offer some helpful compromise to defuse the Plan. Dillon was unsure, at first, how to interpret Parnell but by 16 July he was clear that 'Parnell's speech was…a bad speech'.[70] Parnell tried to win Morley over to his approach. 'I impressed upon him the policy of the oblique method of procedure in reference to land purchase.'[71] But he did not succeed.

Then the divorce crisis broke. Captain O'Shea finally brought his wife's liaison with Parnell into the public domain. The image of the responsible statesman was replaced by Tory music-hall jokes about the fire escape. Catholic Ireland and Gladstonian nonconformity was now confronted with Parnell's 'desecration' of an Irish Catholic marriage. On 19 November 1890, William O'Brien and John Dillon on a fundraising trip in the USA told the press at a meeting at the Hotel Iroquois in Buffalo that they were strongly in favour of the continuance of Parnell's leadership. T. D. Sullivan, who was present, remained ominously silent.[72]

On return to Ireland following the crystallization of the split, O'Brien and Dillon moved to Sullivan's position; Parnell had to go as leader. The majority of Irish MPs agreed, as did Gladstone. The result was inevitable: a split in Parnellism. Dillon and O'Brien tried unsuccessfully to reach a compromise with Parnell and contain the feral clericalist T. M. Healy, whose verbal savaging of Parnell was assisted by several priests prominent in the Plan of Campaign. In a discussion over party funds, there was a particularly awful personal break with Dillon: 'Don't you think Dillon it will answer all purposes if the funds are placed in your name and mine?' 'Yes, indeed,' was Dillon's reply. 'Yes, indeed, and the first time I am in a fix to leave me without a pound to pay the men.'

Parnell rose to his feet, white with passion. 'Dillon, that is not the kind of observation I had a right to expect from you after the way I have behaved to you.'[73] John Redmond wrote later to William O'Brien: 'I am afraid John's [Dillon's] interview with P at Calais had a *very bad effect* and accounts for much of recent events.'[74] It soon became clear in bitter electoral contests, however, that Parnell had lost the bulk of Irish public opinion outside Dublin and parts of the west, both at elite and mass level. Dillon continued to insist that Katharine was personally responsible for Parnell's refusal to accept his defeat at the polls.[75] But as his forces lost key by-elections in Ireland, Parnell maintained his pragmatic line on the land question. In Claremorris, a centre of the Land League movement, he described that movement as a 'spontaneous uprising' against oppression, therefore owing little to the leadership of Michael Davitt, who was now denouncing Parnell in terms reminiscent of Tim Healy. He insisted that 80 per cent of Irish farmers would benefit from the Balfour Land bill. He recalled his long-term opposition to those who wished to maintain the land issues as a grievance to benefit nationalism.[76] On 7 May 1891, Parnell was quite explicit: 'When we come to the large tenants in Connaught I think we ought to make a distinction where we find the large graziers having 2, 3 or 4 holdings, coming to values of several hundreds of pounds. I think that such holders ought not to take money which might be used to enable a much larger number of small tenants to become owners of their own holdings.'[77] The Mayo Land Leaguer and grazier James Daly noted angrily that Parnell was clearly showing his true landlordist colours.[78]

On 21 May, Parnell in Parliament extended his analysis of the place of the Irish land question in British politics. He judged that the 'temper' of the English and Scottish constituencies in the 1886 general election and since was clear. There was no willingness to fund a sufficiently generous land purchase for Ireland. His conclusion was decisive: 'It has been evident to me that if we are to do any good for the great mass of the Irish tenant farmers by land purchase some means must be found for curtailing the area to the amount of the sum to be expended on carrying it out.'[79] Parnell was well aware that he was annoying his old colleagues and even commented wryly when their criticism was moderate. Towards the end of that month, Tim Healy told his brother: 'I let him down so easy in the House on the grazing exclusion that he whispered to Sexton, what have you done to Tim tonight that he is so polite to me?'[80]

Ironically there was a grace in Parnell's last (indirect) exchange with Healy, a famous tormentor, but not Dillon. In Belfast a few days later, Parnell returned to the Land bill in Parliament; he placed his opponents in the party alongside Ulster reactionaries: 'The seceders [i.e. anti-Parnellites] and the Ulster landlords and the Belfast Conservative paper the *Newsletter* had opposed the proposition but it had been carried against them, though somewhat altered, the limit being raised to the £50 which he had suggested last session. On the whole he thought that the extension was a remarkable one, and the Government quite right in agreeing to it. It would bring about a very great reform and one which he would hardly have ventured to look forward to when he commenced the agitation. (Cheers.)'[81] Parnell added: 'He had a shrewd suspicion that "Lord Salisbury would give Ireland as good a Home Rule bill as Mr. Gladstone", and that Salisbury had the capacity to reassure our "Orange brethren." '[82]

Parnell's speech in Belfast is most celebrated because of his remarkable comments on the Protestant and unionist community of north-east Ulster which may be said to foreshadow the 'principle of consent' in mainstream Irish nationalist doctrine. 'Until the religious prejudices of the minority are conciliated Ireland can never enjoy proper freedom, Ireland can never be united…the work of building up an independent Ireland will have upon it a fatal clog and fatal drag.'[83] He claimed, not without a certain poetic political licence, that every Irish nationalist since Wolfe Tone had accepted this. But the speech has a wider significance. It explains his broader disenchantment with the Liberals—it is clear that the substantive difference on the land question pre-dated the divorce crisis—and harks back to his preference for the 'class conservative government' in Ireland he tried to negotiate in the late summer of 1885. This, he makes absolutely clear, was his preference. 'He [Parnell] danced most with the Liberals, but always preferred to go home with a

Tory.' [84] Parnell's speech declared: 'If he was asked to point out any portion of the world where the population was suitably distributed upon the land he should point to the province of Ulster. (Cheers.)... No part of Great Britain, no part of Ireland, presented similar appearances to those they saw in Ulster in every direction—little houses and small tenantry all over the country. They saw the land tilled by this industrious population to the highest possible degree.'[85] E. T. Robinson covered the Parnell event for the *Northern Whig*. He later recalled his 'haggard and worn but still defiant personality on the platform'. Unionists felt a sympathy for Parnell as one would for a fox surrounded after a 'plucky' effort. Robinson was aware that he was watching 'one of the best cantos' in a 'political swansong'. In particular, he noted Parnell's praise for Ulster agrarian productivity, commenting that this was the sort of language to be found more usually on the lips of Salisbury and Balfour than from Irish nationalist agitators. In May 1891 in his remarkable Belfast speech, Parnell indicated that he would rather have done the deal with Lord Salisbury than Gladstone. To those who pointed out that he had after the Hawarden meeting with Gladstone declared no reservations about the G.O.M. he had a simple reply. He had hoped to improve upon Gladstone's offer; with a united party behind him this was likely but *without* a united party it was impossible. It was only right to say that Lord Carnavon in 1885 had offered a better deal. Balfour's first biographer, Bernard Alderson, picked up on Parnell's praise and support for the Land Purchase bill and noted that it 'must have been gratifying to Mr. Balfour'.[86] Alderson noted approvingly, in Parnell's words: 'What will this measure do? It will do two things. It will enormously benefit the Irish tenant farmers.' He added also that it will enormously help the Irish labourer 'by expanding financial support for the building of cottages'.[87] An era was opening up in which Tory generosity on the question of Irish land purchase would be routinely compared unfavourably with Liberal parsimony.[88]

But Tory reformism on the land issue was confined by a determination to protect the law. *The Times* argued that the 'fallen soldiers' (the evicted tenants) of the land war should receive no help: 'It is, however, a matter of paramount importance to teach the Irish peasants in a manner that can neither be mistaken nor forgotten, that those who lean on the promise of the declared enemies of the law lean upon a broken reed.'[89] Parnell knew this and asked how a broken Irish party would protect the evicted tenants. His nationalist opponents suggested that Liberals when returned to power would deal with the matter and that by attacking the Liberals, Parnell endangered evictees. At Thurles on 2 August 1891, Parnell declared: 'Mr. Dillon says he will draw the sword again if the Liberal Party deceive him. But what if he has no sword to draw?' Later on the same day, at the National Club, he expanded the point: 'But how are they going to draw the sword if they have thrown it away, if they handed it over to the captain of the other ship?' At a minimum, a divided nationalism held little capacity to put pressure on the British Parliament. On 16 August 1891, Parnell insisted: 'It will be easier for a camel to go through the eye of a needle than for Mr. Gladstone or Mr. Morley to restore any single evicted tenant to his holding.' He added concisely: 'Mr. Dillon knows this well.'[90]

John Mitchel had famously declared that O'Connell's leadership depended on the perception that he was more intensely Irish than other Irishmen. But, as the St James's Gazette noted, Parnell was the 'master of Irish politics' but he was the most 'unIrish of Irishmen'.[91] Even before the divorce crisis, there were some hints of popular unease on this score. In September 1888, the Wexford People published a profile of four Irish leaders. There was the Bishop of Ferns, the Most Reverend James Brown DD, descendant of the Gaelic lord, John Brown, who died fighting for faith and fatherland against Cromwell. Then there was the Most Reverend Dr Walsh, archbishop of Dublin—the first to hold this post 'without the pale', a reference to the belief that Walsh's predecessors had been West Britons in outlook. There was John Dillon, son of a '48 man and product of the Catholic university, 'impassioned' and 'intransigent' in the land struggle. Then there was C. S. Parnell, a slightly weird figure. Even when he knocked a man to the floor, as in his Cambridge days, he did so in a 'fit of abstraction' not passion. His greatest political gift was for silence. Then, due to his Ulster Protestant descent on his mother's side he was not only a Protestant but a landlord and, therefore, merely half an Irishman.

Again and again in her memoir, Parnell's wife insisted that he was not Irish at all. *The Times* noted at the end: 'It is not the least remarkable thing about him but the Irish people do not seem to have missed the note of spontaneous and enthusiastic love of Ireland which might have been thought to be the key to their hearts.'[92] But, in truth, this claim could not be made of Irish nationalist attitudes in 1891. Irish commentators openly noted this absence in Parnell's emotional make-up. The *New Ross Standard* expressed the majority attitude quite well: Parnell had the appearance of an English gentleman, 'a purely English accent', and the rather 'costive habit of speech of the English'.[93] He had become for many an alien excrescence in Irish politics.

There is one important element in Parnell's final crisis. The 'uncrowned King' of Ireland never lost his pride, bearing, and sense of personal worth. A unionist like E. T. Robinson admired him that night in the Ulster Hall but so also did a nationalist like Alice Milligan. Parnell was fascinated by Macbeth, but he was never defeated in the way Macbeth was: 'Now does he [Macbeth] feel his title | Hang loose upon him, like a Giant's robe | Upon a dwarfish Thief' (*Macbeth* 5.2.20–2). Parnell never felt unworthy and never conveyed a sense of unworthiness—a defiant pride sustained him to the end and gave birth to the later cult of his personality in Irish politics.

The influence of R. Barry O'Brien's 1899 biography of Parnell—which survived the publication of F. S. L. Lyon's modern scholarly biography in 1977—has weakened in recent years. O'Brien saw Parnell essentially as a progressive liberal with early youthful Fenian leanings—rather like O'Brien himself. By 1978, things were changing. F. S. L. Lyons noted a greater complexity: '[Parnell's] favourite *nostrum* in these critical years was to bring the younger and more progressive landlords into the Home Rule movement so as to give a sufficient cachet to convince the British legislators in London.'[94] It had become commonplace to note Parnell's practical concern to ensure a soft landing for Irish landlords in the 1885/6 Home Rule crisis. His refusal to endorse anti-landlord militancy thereafter was clear, as was his willingness in May 1891 to address sympathetically the Unionist community in the north-east. Parnell became much less of a class renegade: but it remained the case that many scholars rightly noted that he had played a major role in the destruction of landlord hegemony in Ireland.

How then to explain this paradox? The answer lies in the reconstruction of Parnell's social and economic thinking and its connection with his political world view. Parnell felt sure that the status of Irish landlordism was unsustainable in a changed political and economic context. But he did hope for the younger landlords' survival as individual 'points of light' in the reconstruction of a new Home Rule Irish economy assisted by protection living alongside an efficient farming economy like that which Parnell felt was already prefigured in the north-east corner of the island. Francis Hackett saw Parnell as a true idealist: the ultimate refutation of the Marxist approach to history because he embraced the cause of the tenantry against his own class interest. Such a genial romantic view is understandable. Hackett's father, Dr Hackett, had sucked the lime from Parnell's eye following one of the most bitterly violent moments of the split. But we lose something when we fail to realize that Parnell saw himself as a scientist (like Lord Salisbury), an entrepreneur, a driving force in Irish development,[95] as well as a statesman.

In 1891, Parnell told Henry Lucy that, 'should his struggle to retain his political position fail, he would retire to his ancestral estate at Avondale and give up his time to the development of the mineral resources on his estate. These always had a fascination for him.'[96] Perhaps too much of a fascination. In the years from 1886 to 1891, he spent vast sums on this project, employing two hundred men in his mines and quarries. He was well aware that they did not earn their wages but justified the expenditure to himself by reference to his future hope. He was in thrall to the tradition that in the sixteenth century, magnetic ore was worked at Avondale: Parnell's hope was for a continuation of this lode. Henry Lucy concluded his account: 'Even whilst the fight was going on in Committee Room no.15 he received an intimation that his men were close upon the track. Had appearances been maintained Parnell would have found himself one of the wealthiest men in Ireland.'[97] Henry Lucy's final comment brings out the wider considerations which inspired Parnell: 'In private conversation he spoke hopefully of the prosperity his discovery would bring to a large district in Co. Wicklow. This dream, like Alnaschar's, was shattered in the sudden wreck of his fortunes.'[98]

In early 1891 also, Parnell spoke at Arklow. He was received surprisingly warmly by Canon Dunphy—in deference, in part, to Parnell's role as a local employer. In his speech, he declared that visiting Arklow 'always does my heart good'. He added: 'When I come here I see the evidence of prosperity, of work and industry.' He noted wryly that he wished there were 'many more such towns in Ireland'. Parnell concluded: 'I hope to spend the remaining years of my life in Wicklow.'[99]

# 8

# Dillon's World 1891–1918

## *Banquo's Ghost Again*

> Mr. Parnell seemed to have stalked like Banquo at Macbeth's feast
> through the House of Commons.
>
> *Spectator*, 'Banquo's Ghost', 15 April 1893.

For John Dillon, the personal costs of the 'split' were considerable.
Dillon (and his brother) had been close to the great Irish American
nationalist, John Devoy, since the late 1870s. Dillon had gone out of his
way to defend Devoy's name in the British Parliament. As late as
February 1890, an informer's report of the Dillon/Devoy dialogue was
sent to Arthur Balfour. In this document, Dillon apparently, in a letter
to Devoy, engaged in a pleasant fantasy of the possible role of force in
promoting Ireland's cause—'a hundred good men skilled in modern
warfare could make the demands of Ireland in a true and loud sounding
noise and in unequivocal terms'.[1] The British agent who reported this
story stressed the closeness of Devoy and Dillon. But the Parnell divorce
crisis drove the two friends apart. Devoy took Parnell's side, much to
Dillon's anger. But it is worth noting that even before Parnell's death,
Devoy accepted in effect that Parnell was beaten and that John Dillon
should be the next chairman of the Irish parliamentary party.[2] It has to
be said that this did not soften Dillon's anger with his old friend in
America. Why could John Devoy not see how absurd and hypocritical
Parnell's positions were—in particular Parnell's denunciation of a
Liberal alliance which he, Parnell, had promoted until the divorce

crisis? For Dillon, the Parnellite cries of English dictation were 'dishonest' and 'hollow': he believed with his whole soul that 'he was never more truly fighting in the cause of Irish nationality'.[3]

The split transformed Dillon's political identity. Up to that point he had a clearly defined stance on Parnell's agrarian left: this was entirely compatible with a deepening relationship with British Liberalism, also anti-landlord. After the split—at least partly determined by the need to maintain British Liberal support for Home Rule—the Liberal alliance became even more important in Dillon's political personality and the perception of that political personality. It was the logic of the choice he had made in 1891: his close friends like John Morley and Philip Stanhope (later Lord Weardale) had helped to intensify the Liberal rejection of Parnell. The agrarian militancy remained but it was now joined by a new (for Dillon) doctrine of party. When Parnell, in late 1882, with T. P. O'Connor's support, began to articulate a doctrine which placed the Irish parliamentary leadership in the decisive place in the leadership of Irish nationalism—as opposed, for example, to popular organizations or 'Leagues' of any sort—Dillon had been visibly unhappy. He did not like the 'top-down' rather than 'bottom-up' model. This unhappiness was widely perceived to be at the heart of his resignation from Irish political life and his two-year sabbatical in the United States. But in the 1890s John Dillon himself placed all value on a coherent party structure, ideology, and organization which could act in alliance with British Liberalism. Dillon feared a return to pre-Parnell localism, clientelism, and clericalism. He shared with the post-split Parnellites a suspicion that the clergy wanted weak lay leaders and structures they could control—hence, though Dillon was a committed Catholic and had many clerical allies, he acquired an aura of anti-clericalism. However, Tim Healy MP, who had supported Parnellism in the 1880s, now argued that the political context had changed: the dramatic phase of success and expansion of the Parnell era was over and the top-down model was no longer viable. Dillon sharply disagreed; for him the stability of the party was essential. In the 1892 general election, the Liberal landslide, much hoped for in Ireland, failed to materialize. The election resulted in a small majority of forty for the Liberals and Nationalists combined. This was enough to pass a Home Rule bill—with some difficulty—in the Commons in 1893. Remarkably, Gladstone appeared on 5 May to flirt with partition, to the dismay of the Dillonites and the amazement of the Redmondites. Nevertheless the Lords felt secure in dismissing the bill, which clearly lacked a wider UK resonance.

After Parnell's death, the principal responsibility of constructing Parnellism without Parnell fell to John Redmond, the leader of the Parnellite minority. He solved it by echoing if not actually integrating two aspects of Parnell's political personality—his respect for extreme men and his latent conservative interest in internal Irish reconciliation. This meant a certain coolness towards British Liberalism. For the one-third of Irish nationalists who remained loyal to the Parnellite credo it was axiomatic to dismiss the 'British democrat' as a self-interested, manipulative false friend. The *Parnellite* editorialized: 'It cannot be disputed by any other than an extremely ignorant person that the average British democrat is the fattest, best clothed and best paid Democrat in the wide world ... every additional benefit now conferred on the British democracy is another nail in the coffin of Home Rule.'[4] For the Parnellite it was absurd to think that the British democracy could be rallied against the Lords. For the Dillonite majority in the 1890s the opposite was the case. Home Rule passed in the Commons in 1893, therefore, only the reactionary House of Lords stood in the way. There was no need to change policy—rather it was essential to wait for the inevitable collapse of British oligarchy and work with the Liberals. Redmond, on the other hand, insisted that only an unlikely English revolution would destroy the House of Lords. It was better, therefore, to seek an internal Irish reconciliation of creeds and classes which might then soften the hostility of the Lords: a hostility underpinned by a sense that mainstream UK opinion feared Catholic bigotry in Ireland. Redmond also felt a conflicting responsibility to maintain Parnellism's appeal to its urban republican constituency in Ireland. On the fringe, Healy argued the Liberal alliance ended with W. E. Gladstone and the Liberal party should make what deals it could get with whoever could deliver.

The ghost of Parnell continued to haunt not just the streets of Dublin but the Palace of Westminster as well. As the Home Rule bill progressed through the House of Commons, the Liberal government and the Irish party decided on a strategy of not extending debate by responding to every anti Home Rule speech or claim. But this policy proved impossible for either Gladstone or Dillon to implement—so great was their emotional involvement in the proceedings, and, indeed, their sense of righteousness. As a result Joseph Chamberlain, for example, found it easy to goad both men into time-consuming displays of (ineffectual) self justification. Chamberlain's favourite trick was to cite Gladstonian texts which seemed to raise real doubt about the good faith of the Liberal party's nationalist allies. After all, said Chamberlain on 10 April 1893, he (Gladstone) 'hesitated to place this [Home Rule] government into the hands of men who...preached the gospel of plunder'.[5] The 'gospel of plunder' was a direct quotation from Gladstone: Gladstone fell for it; he insisted that he had used this sort of language against Parnell *alone*, not the Home Rule party as such, in the autumn of 1881. Gladstone never enjoyed these essays in historical recollection, and now that Chamberlain had raised his condemnation of Parnellite lawlessness in his Leeds speech on the eve of his arrest of Parnell, the Premier snapped. Partly out of irritation, partly out of a desire to provide a character reference for the Irish party members in the House, he insisted that the Leeds speech was a condemnation only of Parnell. Willie Redmond cried out with passion: 'They put all the blame on Parnell because he is dead.'[6] In point of fact, Gladstone had *some* truth on his side. He had exempted moderate home rulers, moderate land leaguers, and even John Dillon from his Leeds critique; but he did *not* blame Parnell alone. 'Mr. Parnell with his myrmidons around him in his Land League meetings in Ireland, has instructed the people of Ireland that they are not to go into the court which the Parliament of the country has established in order to do justice.' Gladstone had added: 'the men who preach what I am going to describe...[as] sheer lawlessness'. Chamberlain was, therefore, correct to insist Gladstone's remarks at Leeds were not confined simply to a condemnation of Parnell the individual.

It is hard not to sympathize a little with Gladstone here. His general recollection of the circumstances of October 1881 was reasonably good. His letter to John Bright on 29 September provides a kind of proof. 'My inclination is to denounce outright Parnell (not the Irish party, nor even the Land League) and his works and ways.'[7] But his intention was not executed with precision and, indeed, such a precision in the nature of things may not have been possible. Perhaps inevitably Gladstone's language drifted more widely and his purely personal focus on Parnell gave way to a larger, more generalized picture which embraced the wider Parnellite movement. There is also a slight issue of common sense here. Could Gladstone have considered it even a remote possibility that Parnell should be made to carry the *sole* burden for the lawlessness of the wider movement? It is hard not to resist the intuition that Gladstone's *genuine* recollection of his feeling towards Parnell in October 1881 became mixed up with an (ill-judged) desire to whitewash his Irish nationalist allies in the House in 1893. Gladstone was moved to apologize to Willie Redmond. The Prime Minister stated that he had believed in 1881 that Parnell was trying to frustrate the Land bill. 'I may have been right or wrong but it was under that impression that I made that very heavy charge.'[8] Willie Redmond replied gracefully but in a way which, of course, substantiated Chamberlain's argument: 'I confess that at the moment I thought an attempt was, unwittingly perhaps, being made to put blame upon Mr. Parnell from which I do not think any Members who served under him at the time would wish to dissociate themselves.' Willie Redmond returned again to the topic later in the debate because 'whatever blame might attach to the late Mr. Parnell must be shared to the fullest extent by everyone of the hon Members on the Irish benches'. In a final clinching observation, he completed Gladstone's discomfiture: 'There were few men in Ireland who did not feel proud to associate themselves with all the actions of Mr. Parnell to which the Prime Minister had taken exception.' A flustered Gladstone then stated that after 1882 he found Parnell a conservative and moderate figure. The *Spectator* noted an element of guilt in Gladstone's demeanour—as the man who had played a key part in destroying

Parnell: the periodical recalled again the image of Parnell as Banquo's ghost. Gladstone apologized to Willie Redmond but 'in reality' he was apologizing to the dead Parnell.[9] 'Thou canst not say I did it; never shake | Thy gory locks at me', the guilty Macbeth had said to Banquo; now it seemed Gladstone was saying the same to Parnell. He had not executed Parnell just as Macbeth had not personally executed Banquo: Gladstone, like Macbeth, had found another agent, in this case, the Irish party.

In early May 1893, Gladstone managed to embarrass the Irish party once again. In the midst of a decision about the importance of local conditions in determining mining legislation, he suddenly lurched back to Ireland. His remarks were taken as a kind of admission that some form of local opt-out from Home Rule for north-east Ulster was a reasonable suggestion.[10] It seemed like an admission of the case for partition; Redmond exploited it against the Irish party while Dillon winced.

Later in the year, as was becoming quite a tradition, Dillon's inaccurate and misleading words again caught up with him. Chamberlain on 20 June raised the Castlerea threat of 1886 that a Home Rule government would 'remember the police and other enemies'. Dillon said in Parliament that he was not in the least ashamed.[11] 'Pleading that he had spoken emotionally after the Mitchelstown massacre, Dillon misled the House.'[12] Prompted by T. W. Russell, the Irish Liberal Unionist MP, Chamberlain was able on 3 July to point out that the Castlerea speech was given nine months before the Mitchelstown affray. The next day Dillon apologized for his mistake, but it was not easy to eradicate the impact—the sense, especially following the Sheridan affair in 1887, that Dillon was rather inclined to make things up in Parliament, or, more accurately, that he was so fuelled by a sense of self-righteousness that he neglected inconvenient realities. Dillon admitted that he had been 'betrayed by his memory into a gross mistake'. He added: 'Every Hon. Member who reflects on the character of the mistake will be convinced that I spoke in good faith.' After all, said Dillon, if he had not believed what he said, why would he say something it was so easy to refute? It was not the most impressive of replies.[13] Parnell once said rather foolishly to the Special Commission that a remark of his may have been intended to mislead the House, but he was never actually caught out in the humiliating way Dillon was. Henry Lucy, the great parliamentary journalist, in his 'Behind the Speaker's Chair' column for the *Strand* magazine recalled sarcastically how Dillon had 'remembered Mitchelstown nine months and four days before that historic event ever happened'.[14]

The anti-Parnellite majority was bitterly split between the supporters of Dillon and Tim Healy. In November 1895, Healy and his allies were expelled from the committee of the Irish party; John Dillon, at last, married Elizabeth, who had been besotted with him for a decade, at the Brompton Oratory. In 1896, Dillon replaced Justin McCarthy as leader of the anti-Parnellites. At this moment of triumph, Dillon's want of self-discipline in 1893 was sharply recalled by the Healyite press. The *Dublin Weekly Nation* in 1896 noted

> an unhappy exhibition made by Mr. Dillon during the Home Rule debates. The policy of the Irish supporters of Mr. Gladstone's measure was to remain silent and not to assist in the obstruction by the Unionists... Mr. Dillon would not hold his tongue. His want of self-control led to a most hurtful scene, which greatly injured both the Government and the Irish Party, and gave Mr. Chamberlain, the arch-enemy of the Home Rule Bill, great personal triumph.[15]

An article in the *Contemporary Review* in 1897 argued that the 'want of self-control' was a defining feature of Irish political life. The *Spectator* was not sure about the generalization but felt that it was an accurate description of John Dillon.[16]

Dillon appeared—to other nationalists—to be obsessed with the maintenance of the Liberal alliance at all costs and in the face of all disappointments. In 1894, the Liberal government had failed to deliver to Dillon support for the 'wounded soldiers' (the evicted tenants) of the land war—just as the Parnellite press had predicted—but Dillon remained loyal to the Liberals. In 1894, he was prepared at Edinburgh and Coatbridge to defend the pro-Home Rule credentials of Lord Rosebery, rather than admit the erosion of the old Gladstonian spirit in the Liberal leadership.[17] Only this loyalty to the Liberal party can explain his parliamentary intervention against Redmond in 1899. Dillon seemed to place the Liberal alliance at the very top of his concerns. Redmond in February 1899 in Parliament was in full flow offering an expansive vision of the powers of a future Dublin Parliament: 'Mr. Parnell...repeatedly declared that there should be no veto except the veto of the Crown, which should be exercised there as in England, on constitutional principles, and in conformity with the wishes of the Irish ministers of the sovereign.' Suddenly Dillon intervened unhelpfully: 'Can you give me the date of that?'[18] Redmond was amazed: here was Dillon implying that Parnell had a restrictive vision of Home Rule's remit, a restrictive vision potentially more compatible with mainstream British Liberalism. The Parnellite press in the 1890s devoted much effort to claiming Dillon was as bad as Healy—Healy continued to ridicule Dillon and even ally with Redmond against him.

By the end of 1899, it was clear that William O'Brien's new agrarian movement, the United Irish League, had changed the mood in Ireland; by bringing in local Parnellite leaders—O'Brien had never been so hated amongst them as Dillon—O'Brien laid the basis for the reconstruction of the formal unity of the Irish parliamentary party in 1900 under Redmond's leadership. Dillon remained, however, the parliamentarian with most influence and the largest personal following amongst MPs. The defining feature of the UIL movement was its emphasis on land redistribution—as opposed to peasant proprietorship—as such, it threatened the interests of Irish strong farmers, in particular, graziers as well as landlords. Dillon's former secretary, Larry Ginnell, was to play a role as a Westmeath MP after 1900. Dillon proudly introduced Ginnell to his constituents: 'The question the electors of North Westmeath had to decide here was, were they to smash the United Irish League in the interests of the graziers or support the League in the interests of the people.'[19] In 1902, the UIL agitation seemed to have reached its natural limits: not least because of opposition from Irish strong farmers. But the Tory government and landlords were in the mood for real reform.

Captain Shawe-Taylor—despite of, or perhaps because of, the fact that he had been, in effect, a witness of Colonel Walter Bourke's murder—was a key figure on the landlord side in favour of the theme of conciliation. John Dillon was not an admirer of Shawe-Taylor. The brutality of his denunciation is striking: 'Mr Shawe-Taylor had in his veins some of the worst blood in Galway ... we do not believe that a man with the black blood of Clan Cromwell in his veins can ever be otherwise than an enemy of Ireland.'[20] Shawe-Taylor wrote to Dillon in mid August 1904 that he hoped to see absolute confidence between 'man and man' and 'so self-government would have been demanded by a united Ireland'. But he had little impact on Dillon's thought process.[21]

The Wyndham Act of 1903 was indisputably a major victory for the cause of the tenants in the establishment of a peasant proprietorship in Ireland. Both O'Brien and Redmond saw it as a triumph for the classic Parnellite approach, especially as it had been preceded by a conference embracing the leaders of the landlords and tenants. 'Conference' plus business was now, it was declared, the way forward in Ireland.[22] But John Dillon, in effect, placed his veto against such a move—there was to be no new era of 'good feelings'. Above all he explicitly felt that Irish nationalism could not afford to lose the momentum given to it by an unresolved land issue—in this view he was supported by important MPs such as Joe Devlin and John Roche.[23] He disliked also the arch conciliator on the landlord side, Sir Horace Plunkett, a cousin of Lord Cloncurry, his arch enemy at Murroe. As a complication, Dillon noted critically Plunkett's link to Father Thomas Finlay SJ who was in turn linked to Tim Healy. This was the message of Dillon's 'Swinford revolt' following a speech in his own East Mayo constituency. In his memoir, William O'Brien saw this moment as a profound comment on Dillon's political mentality—recalling the problems he made for Parnell at the time of the 1881 Land Act: 'Twenty years later when there was a question of making the best use of an Act which supplied the means of abolishing landlordism altogether, and realising Parnell's dream of the union of classes, there was still enough of the same perverse tendency to be uncompromising at the wrong moment.'[24] The ardent conciliator

Sir Horace Plunkett noted at this juncture that Dillon was 'so narrow he might be honest. I never knew a mind so dominated by inherited prejudices.'[25]

The Wyndham Act appeared to many nationalists—certainly John Redmond and William O'Brien—as the apotheosis of Parnell's strategy: a posthumous triumph of the highest order. It opened the way for an new consensual way of working *within* Irish politics—because the most divisive issue, land, had been removed. They saw Dillon's refusal to accept the possibilities of a new era as sterile dogmatism. For O'Brien it was proof that Dillon had never really been a Parnellite at any stage of his career. The failure to opt for a policy of conciliation within Ireland meant a continuation of some form of agrarian agitation. This tended to reduce the cohesion of nationalism. A significant number of Irish farmers were buying their land with British support and joining the rural bourgeoisie. John Dillon's former secretary, Larry Ginnell MP, promoted the campaigns of those left behind; William O'Brien saw them as essentially dysfunctional. It remains the case that there remained considerable conflict over the price landlords were prepared to accept and which tenants were prepared to pay.[26] This allowed a significant space for a continuing viable land agitation led by the Irish party—with John Dillon's sanction above all—but this agitation could never achieve the resonance of previous agitations. Even in its heyday (1879–82) the Land League's functioning was marred by class divisions, but by 1910 these class divisions in nationalism were even more marked.[27] Erstwhile close allies like his brother William, and even John Devoy, the great Irish American nationalist, did not back Dillon's stance on the Wyndham Act.[28] But he never seems to have had any doubts. He doubled down on his opposition to compromise when the Tory concept of devolution entered into serious political calculations in 1903. As Dr Philip Bull has expressed it: 'With the defeat of William O'Brien's conciliation, however, the nationalist party was now dominated by those who saw no need to build bridges to minorities.' For many scholars, the key development here is Dillon's close alignment with Joe Devlin, the Belfast MP. Devlin had placed his all-Catholic Ancient Order of Hibernians organization at the heart of the party, which, for example, used rough methods against O'Brienite conciliators. As Dr Bull has added: 'This set in train a sequence of events that climaxed in 1911, created political and social havoc in Ireland during subsequent years, ending with the partition of the country.'[29]

But how could the party have operated without Joe Devlin and did not the Unionists have their Orange Order? It is worth considering here the analysis of Stephen Gwynn, the Galway MP, a Protestant Home Ruler who opposed sectarianism strongly on the nationalist side. In Gwynn's view, the Irish party leadership in this period was a joint leadership of Dillon and Redmond, essentially a co-chairmanship. Such a leadership needed the prop provided by the deferential Joe Devlin—who did not understand the land question but who did draw northern nationalists, especially the Belfast Catholic working class, into the party. Devlin had the 'kind of loyalty which sweetens the air';[30] he never favoured Dillon over Redmond, or vice versa. Both Dillon and Redmond, neither of them 'men easily moved to affection'[31] in Gwynn's words, loved Devlin, and post-1916 Devlin sank with them rather than disown them.

The Liberal electoral landslide of 1906 appeared to transform Dillon's political prospects. It was clear that Liberals were no longer animated by a Gladstonian passion for Home Rule; but equally clear that they intended some substantive moves in that direction. Dillon was, however, hit by a double blow in early summer of 1907. Tragically, his wife Elizabeth died. More prosaically, Irish public opinion rejected the Irish Council bill. 'Latin for Home Rule', T. P. O'Connor called it, but Irish public opinion turned out to be indifferent, and even hostile in a way even Dillon failed to anticipate, to such oblique messaging. Nevertheless, Dillon was an intimate of Augustine Birrell, the Irish Chief Secretary, from 1907 to 1916 and, therefore, in a good position to exert influence on other issues: particularly that of higher education.

John Dillon had long been a harsh critic of Trinity College Dublin and its Protestant, unionist tradition. In 1901, he had declared: 'I do not believe these [patriotic] movements will ever succeed...until that fortress of English domination and anti-Irish bigotry, Trinity College, is forever swept away or there is placed opposite to it a truly National University where the most honoured classes will be the classes of Irish literature and history.'[32] But it should not be thought that Dillon had forgotten the liberalism of his 1874 intervention on Catholicism and modern science. At the beginning of 1905, he addressed the Catholic Graduates' and Undergraduates' Association at the Mansion House in Dublin. He warned against any tight clerical control of any new university. The *Morning Post* noted: 'He has travelled and he has seen that no Catholic nation of the world tolerates the educational strait-waistcoat which Maynooth demands as an indefeasible right of Catholicity for the unfortunate laity of Ireland.'[33] In the aftermath of the Liberal victory in 1906, Dillon had his chance to help create a 'truly national university'. He worked closely with intelligent and practical academics like Bertram Windle.[34] He developed a relationship with the Chief Secretary, Augustine Birrell.[35] Dillon's Liberal friend Richard Burdon Haldane played a key role.[36] Dillon's brother, a Franciscan monk, helped to weaken the influence of Bishop O'Dwyer, still a strong Dillon opponent, who tended to fear that the bill was a nonconformist conspiracy to obtain control of the education of the Catholic clergy.[37]

In his *Observer* review of the sympathetic biography of John Redmond by Warre B. Wells, Stephen Gwynn, a Redmond rather than Dillon *aficionado*, felt it proper to acknowledge that 'the establishment of the National University which Mr. Wells ranks highest among Redmond's political triumphs was, essentially Dillon's victory because the solution to the problem was on lines which he had laid down'.[38] At this moment, it is worth recalling, Edward Carson resisted Orange hostility to Irish university reform along Dillon's lines.[39] The Irish Universities bill was introduced on 31 March 1908 and was enacted on 1 August 1908: the same day as the Old Age Pensions Act, which Dillon regarded as a great material boon for Ireland. Dillon defined it as 'one of the greatest services to the Irish nation which it has ever been given to an English statesman to render'.[40] This legislation in essence constituted the foundation of Irish higher education for almost a century. Trinity

College remained unchanged, the Queen's College in Belfast became free-standing, the colleges at Galway and Cork, augmented by the Catholic University in Dublin, were clustered into the National University of Ireland. The National University was given substantial state funding. Dillon might have reflected wryly that in 1874, when he made his intervention following Tyndall's Belfast speech, the Catholic hierarchy had blocked Gladstone's Irish university reforms in part because of its unease about the spread of intellectual liberalism. In 1908, Dillon had survived long enough to be the patron of a new historic compromise on the issue. Dillon's friend, Haldane, recalling Gladstone's failure in 1874, made the point: 'In those days the religious question predominated over the educational question. Today, we have an indication that the educational question is predominating over the religious question.'[41]

Sir Edward Carson's speech was a classic of Irish liberalism calling for a 'spirit of generosity'. He acknowledged that the Irish Universities bill did not observe the principles of classical liberalism and non-sectarianism but he accepted that Catholic objections to the Protestant atmosphere of Trinity were not unreasonable—however much John Redmond, who also spoke in this debate, or John Dillon's father had been able to survive and even flourish within that context. Carson insisted it was essential to remedy the perceived grievance of Catholic Ireland—inadequate provision for higher education—and not remodel it or redefine or dismiss it. It was wrong to insist that people feel comfortable in a context where they clearly did not. This was, after all, the classic case for Ulster Unionism. He ended, however, with a plan for a future reconciliation: 'I look forward to the day when these great, successful liberal seats of learning, having made their way and formed their constituencies, showing themselves worthy in the great race of science and art, will come forward and say, as I hope Trinity College will: "Let us join together and make one great national university." I believe it is the duty of every Irishman, of whatever creed or politics, to wish Godspeed to these universities, and do his best in a spirit of noble generosity to make them a great success; and I hope that bringing of them into existence may be a step forward in the union of all classes and religions in Ireland for the progress of our country and its education.'[42] Birrell quickly expressed his strong admiration for Carson's speech. It is little wonder that a nationalist journal like *The People* of Wexford, then edited by Francis Cruise O'Brien, would take great pleasure in the unity of Dillon, Carson, Haldane, and Birrell in favour of benign educational reform and little wonder that it would note also with satisfaction the isolation of their Orange and Ulster Unionist critics.

The university reform was Dillon's great triumph but it prepared the way for his first great defeat as a populist leader of Irish nationalism. When the National University was established and founded, the Gaelic League demanded that a knowledge of Irish be necessary for matriculation. A resolution endorsing this demand was carried at a convention of the Irish party's own organization, the United Irish League; John Dillon argued it with all his power. Probably two thousand delegates were present and perhaps only one hundred of them had learned any Irish, but they had made up their minds that the next generation should not be ignorant. The Senate of the National University was much opposed to the demand, but was forced to accept it by the attitude of the Irish county councils, who declared that unless this were conceded they would not levy a rate to provide scholarships. Dillon's eloquent argument that it was unfair to the 'Protestant boy' fell on deaf ears.[43] (Protestant schools were less likely to teach Irish and their products would therefore be shut out from any chance of a scholarship.) John Pius Boland MP, a leader on the other side, noted: 'had Dillon used the big shots in his locker, appealed to his thirty years record, used all the arts of a demagogue to win his point at all costs, he might have carried the meeting with him'.[44]

It is hard to deny that Dillon's first defeat in this sort of contest was significant. He found himself on the wrong side of mainstream nationalism: a mainstream nationalism which was explicitly taking up in his view an intolerant position. His close allies in the struggle for educational reform—Matthew Minch or Sir Christopher Nixon[45]—were all Catholic liberals and moderate Home Rulers. They all shared a hostility to compulsion in these matters. But this was not a widespread view. There was no obvious change in Dillon's style and tone. It is remarkable how he managed to speak on the land question as if in a time capsule. Nothing had changed over three decades, it seemed. Dillon spoke at Thurles in 1909, rather in the manner of 1879: 'Until they smashed landlordism it was idle to hope that Ireland could be free. How was it possible to lead the people successfully through a struggle for their liberty of their country if every agent and landlord could walk over them and drive them out of their homes?'[46] But, in fact, the impression that nothing had changed was an illusion. This can be seen most clearly in Dillon's relationship with his loyal satrap Larry Ginnell. By 1909, Ginnell perceived that he was being left to maintain the Irish party's tradition of agrarian activism on his own. He was right—John Redmond felt strongly enough to write to Dillon that he was no longer obliged to defend Ginnell when he got into trouble with the authorities on agrarian matters.[47] In February 1909, at the Dublin convention of the UIL, Dillon sought to allow Ginnell a fair hearing, but Ginnell was now out of control: he insisted on a proper public accounting of the use of party funds and was forcibly ejected as he threw punches at other Irish party MPs.[48] Whatever his private feelings for Ginnell, Dillon backed Redmond at this moment: soon he was voting at Westminster for an increase in the Irish police budget partly necessitated by the need to police Ginnell's agrarian activism.[49] Ginnell was denied official party accreditation in 1910 but still retained his seat before transferring in 1917 to Sinn Fein. The point is that Dillon was no longer prepared to invest substantively in agrarian radicalism.

The year 1909 was a critical turning point in Dillon's career. It marked a change in his political tone. He achieved a great victory for the cause of Catholic education in Ireland—with the support of Edward Carson. He then found that compulsory Irish enthusiasts diluted the broad liberalism of approach he espoused. The Birrell Land Act also saw a new major land reform which was more favourable to tenants and less to landlords—rightly, in his view. The two general elections of 1910 revealed no loss in Irish party support—and a switch in the focus of politics to 'high politics' (the People's Budget or Lords reform) at Westminster and the looming issue of intense Ulster Unionist opposition to Home Rule. These weighty constitutional issues, in a sense, freed Dillon from his own self-imposed constraints. Worryingly, though few saw the significance at the time, the language issue saw Dillon outflanked by a more 'patriotic' position for the first time. Nonetheless, it was liberating that the land question—after taking up so much of his life for three decades—was now waning. Dillon gave a favour to the Birrell Land Act of 1909 he never gave to Wyndham in 1903, though both clearly were steps along the same road to a peasant proprietorship.

Dillon could afford now to employ to good effect his reading on the subject of British foreign affairs. His interventions were wide-ranging. The newly arrived Labour MPs looked up to him as a progressive statesman—who could advise them on the basis of his long experience on how best to exploit the rules of the House for their causes. What is remarkable is the way in which Dillon, released from his old constraints, now became a much more conventional, liberal, and consensual politician. The (always present) intellectual liberalism in his temperament seemed to take control.

Dillon embraced unreservedly the concept of a progressive alliance with the Liberals. There is an irony that he now appeared to stand for the policy of alliance with the English masses which Parnell had promoted in early 1881 but which he, Dillon, had then opposed. Dillon at Ballyhaunis in November 1912 declared: 'If the representatives of the working classes of England pass a satisfactory Home Rule Bill, the Nationalists will do their work for them; they will be by their side when they are endeavouring to overthrow the monopolists.'[50] As the popular English Liberal sentiment and electoral appeal of 1906 dropped, the Liberal party became more and more dependent on Irish support at Westminster. Dillon, Joe Devlin, the West Belfast MP, Redmond, and T. P. O'Connor constituted a kind of collective leadership of the Irish party. The failure of the two general elections of 1910 to transform Parliament left the Irish party with the effective balance of power and the ability, at least, to move the Liberals towards implementation of a Dublin Parliament. But this was not the core of the problem: the core of the problem was the refusal of Ulster Unionists, dominant in the north-east of Ireland, to accept the legitimacy of this Parliament. The Liberal cabinet did not have the resolve to defeat the Unionists by force. The implication therefore was that the nationalists should see the need to compromise. From 1912 to 1914, Ireland witnessed 'a strategy of tension' as the Liberal government hoped that the Irish party would eventually see the need to dilute their historic demand not to lose 'a single Irishman'.

When the Home Rule crisis opened up, Winston Churchill, a key member of the Liberal cabinet, made a speech in Belfast defending Home Rule partly on the basis that the Dublin Parliament would be dependent financially on Westminster. It would not, therefore, be dangerous or Anglophobic. Many nationalists were infuriated but not Dillon or Redmond. John Dillon belonged to that group of Home Rule leaders who had no problem with the acceptance of British money: he supported happily the National Insurance Act and the application of the Old Age Pension Act to Ireland: 'What I look forward to is this, and I look forward to it with confidence, that with the aid of the National Insurance Act and the money that is coming to us under it, and the Old Age Pensions Act, we should be able to completely sweep the whole poor law system of Ireland and reduce, and substantially reduce, the rates of the country. (cheers.).'[51] Dillon made it clear he did not accept the main Ulster Unionist argument—'we are told that all they want is to be left alone...they want no ascendancy'.[52] He had a point. He insisted that any serious analysis of Unionist rhetoric revealed supremacist themes. J. H. Campbell, a southern Unionist MP, replied to Dillon that the Unionists desired to live in 'perfect equality with their neighbours'[53] but Dillon could not accept that argument. But, on the other hand, Dillon did seem to accept that it was unwise to attempt to coerce the Ulster Unionists. On 2 March 1913, Redmond and Dillon, along with O'Connor and Devlin, reluctantly agreed to the proposal raised by Lloyd George that individual Ulster counties could opt out from Home Rule for a period of three years. Redmond was later prevailed upon to extend this period to six years. The Unionist leader, Edward Carson, rejected the idea as merely a stay of execution. Dillon's perceived flexibility on this issue may have reduced his popularity. Lovat Fraser described the Limerick city demonstration attended by 15,000–20,000. Joe Devlin attracted more interest than Redmond. But it should also be noted that Lovat Fraser wrote privately to Geoffrey Robinson of *The Times* on 12/13 October: 'Dillon is regarded with much affection but is no longer a great power, and did not sway the crowd much.'[54]

However, the Home Rule crisis soon settled into an anguished stalemate—in which neither Ulster unionist nor Irish nationalist could contemplate the future with any equanimity. Inevitably the arch conciliationist William O'Brien's All For Ireland League tried to help by coming up with imaginative solutions. As the crisis deepened, the AFIL made one last vain attempt to act as a force for compromise. D. D. Sheehan, the Cork MP, published an article in the *Daily Express* on 27 January 1914. The headline was 'Nationalist Help for Ulster?' Sheehan made it clear that 'we do not ignorantly declare with Redmond that there is no Ulster difficulty. We do not short-sightedly with the Irish leader seek to irritate the susceptibilities of our fellow countrymen in Ulster by telling them all their warlike preparation are nothing but bluff and blackmail.' Sheehan insisted that Catholic sectarianism—not just Protestant sectarianism—was a real issue. He called for a conference to discuss new O'Brienite proposals: the essence of O'Brien's strategy was to seek ways in which the political power of the Irish Protestant minority would be enhanced above the natural level due to 'roughly one fourth of the population'. Sheehan argued that the Ulster Unionist members in the Westminster Parliament should have a 'exercisable veto' over all Irish legislation until it was approved by a resolution of the House of Commons. Sheehan also argued that 'Ulster' should have sixty out of 164 representatives in the Irish Parliament and that this was a position of substantive power and influence. The interesting concept here is the way in which continuing Irish representation at Westminster, as encouraged in the third Home Rule Bill, is being utilized as a means of reassuring unionists—Redmond was later to adapt this same concept as a political means of reassuring nationalists in the partitioned area.[55] But by this stage, only the mainstream leaders on either side could strike a deal. Tim Healy recorded in February 1914: 'My impression is that the exclusion of Ulster will be proposed by the Government and accepted by Redmond. To-night Dillon cheered Lloyd George very pointedly at a passage which showed this would be the plan.'[56] Two days later he recorded: 'Dillon is going about talking to the Liberals in favour of the exclusion of Ulster. They all know that but for Devlin it would be arranged. Dillon has been saying the contrary up to this. He now says, "How can we coerce Ulster with our record against coercion?" and that we can not face civil war as a beginning to Home Rule.'[57]

Dillon was well aware of the weakness of the Ulster Unionist case: 'What has been the condition of Ulster for the last two years? They have done everything they like. They have marched and drilled, and armed, and have grossly outraged and insulted the Catholic population. The Catholics have been obliged to utterly obliterate themselves.'[58] He added: 'If you break out, you must do something and attack somebody. Who are they to attack? Are they to attack British soldiers or police or their Catholic neighbours?'[59] This was perfectly true but Carson had countered it: British forces could defeat unionists militarily, he said, but where would that leave everybody?[60] 'And what then?' Parnell had asked Davitt when Davitt outlined the revolutionary project of 1878. Carson now asked the same question of British Liberalism and Irish nationalism. Were they really prepared to govern the Ulster unionists as a 'conquered people'? Buckingham Palace talks in July 1914 broke down—Carson and Redmond were in tears. James Craig asked to shake Dillon's hand, saying he hoped to do half as much for Ulster as Dillon had done for Ireland. It should be recalled that the men had worked together on the issue of teachers' salaries and pensions.[61] These were exceptional scenes indeed. In the afternoon of 24 July, Asquith, Lloyd George, Birrell, Redmond, and Dillon met at No. 10. Asquith announced that he intended to go on with the Amending bill without a time limit. Dillon and Redmond, the Prime Minister noted, 'after a good deal of demur reluctantly agreed to try and persuade their party to assent'.[62] These negotiations eventually concluded in the enactment of 18 September 1914 of the Home Rule bill, accompanied by a suspensory Act that prevented its coming into operation until the end of the war.

When the First World War broke out, Dillon loyally supported Redmond's support for the British war effort; he criticized radical Irish nationalists who tended to support Germany:

> These gentlemen profess to be horribly shocked and outraged (laughter) because Mr. Redmond has declared himself to be on the side of England in the present war. Their principle is, I assume, whether England is right or wrong, Ireland must be against her—at least that is all one can gather from their writings and speeches. There was a time when that feeling was pretty general among Irish nationalists but that day is passed (applause)...[63]

In April 1915, Dillon spoke on a recruiting platform in Coatbridge. He opened his speech by recalling the Duke of Wellington's claim that Waterloo could not have been won without the valour of Irish Catholic soldiers; yet, he made it clear, he was not sentimental on such a point—the Irish, after all, had been driven by English misrule to serve in many Continental armies. Rather he had two very precise reasons for his support for the British war effort. The first was that Ireland simply could not afford to betray its traditional Home Rule pledge to stand beside Britain in such an international conflict: 'small nations like the Irish' cannot afford to set a 'matter of broken faith' in such a matter. The second reason was that Germany, for all its greatness in the art of civilization, lacked true respect for the spirit of liberty. In one respect, 'they were not great, they have not been great in the practice of liberty', 'If Germany prevails there cannot be the slightest doubt that a death blow would be struck at democracy for which so many generations have died fighting. For many generations to come, Europe would be completely controlled by a military bureaucracy.'[64] This is a remarkable speech, coming, as it did, from a man who had been locked up three times by the British government. He did, however, have less hope than Redmond that the war effort would have a reconciling effect on Irishmen: 'In my opinion the form and the fate of the Amending Bill will be determined mainly by two things. First by the unity and stead-fastness of the Irish people between now and the introduction of the bill, and, secondly, by the power and preparedness of the nationalists of Belfast to meet and defeat the military plot to destroy Home Rule by force.'[65] Dillon said, as Redmond would not here have done, that Ulster opposition might still be overcome by force applied by the 'forty thou-sand true Irish nationalists in the new army'.[66] In 1915, Vivian Herbert called in on Dillon in Dublin. He was very pessimistic about 'precipi-tate' young men who considered him a 'back number' and were in the process of undoing his life's work. Dillon made a point of reading the radical nationalist press—in a way that John Redmond did not—and this perhaps explains his pessimism about the party's fortunes which far exceeded that of Redmond at this point.[67] Herbert asked him why Dubliners still accepted a statue of William III in their city. Dillon enjoyed the joke: 'We are a very forgiving people.'[68] Is it possible he was wryly recalling to himself the *Spectator*'s disbelieving comment of 28 December 1881, on his statement that the Irish 'had a fatal facility to forgive and forget'? It stated: 'The one thing Irish never seem to do is forget and the rarest thing for them to do is forgive.'

As the war became more unpopular in Ireland, W. B. Wells noted the difference between Dillon and Redmond:

> The attitude of Mr. Redmond and Mr. Dillon towards the vigorous propa-ganda conducted by Sinn Fein during the latter part of 1915 and the early part of 1916 was the same; but their motives were entirely different. Both opposed the repressive measures fitfully and ineffectually undertaken by the Irish Executive. Mr. Dillon, however, opposed them because he felt that the revolutionary movement was so strong that repression could only precipitate an outbreak. Mr. Redmond, on the other hand, opposed them because he felt that the revolutionary movement was weak enough to be ignored with safety.'[69]

Dillon believed firmly that the executions after the Easter Rising of 1916 had been decisive. He believed that if the leaders had been kept in prison until after the war, a settlement would have been made and accepted. In the immediate aftermath of the Rising, Dillon, aided by his

ally and deferential friend Sir Matthew Nathan,[70] Birrell's undersecretary, went to see General Maxwell and warned against execution.
Dillon, at first, seems to have felt—according to the letter he immediately drafted for Redmond—that he had been heeded with respect and
his points understood. He wrote to Redmond on 2 May 1916: 'we parted
on friendly terms and I hope my visit may have some effect.'[71] But it was
not to be, and Dillon's later version of this conversation reflects his disappointment. He told Lady Gregory:

> Then we went to General Maxwell and I protested against the executions,
> and he said, 'Mr. Dillon, these men have shot English soldiers and I have
> come to Dublin first to put down the Rebellion.'
> 'But the Rebellion is over now.'
> 'Yes, and I am going to punish the offenders, four of them are to be shot
> tomorrow morning. I am going to ensure that there will be no treason
> whispered, even whispered, in Ireland for a hundred years.'
> 'You have been trying to do that for years.'
> 'Well, I am going to do it now. There will not be a whisper.'[72]

Dillon's speech in Parliament on the Easter Rising of 1916 in Dublin is a
classic. It was brave and honest: it accurately reflected how the tough
British response was helping the insurrectionaries, who had initially
little support. But there was the great and crippling omission: the failure to mention the fact that the insurrectionaries had hailed the
Germans as their gallant allies. It was a characteristic Irish form of self-
obsession. As English reviewers liked to point out, Tim Healy's memoir
included sixty-five pages on the First World War without mentioning
European realities like the German or French military leadership.[73] But
was this quite fair? Tim Healy had arranged through Winston Churchill
for his son, Joe, to take up a commission in the British army.[74] In Dillon's
case, the Coatbridge speech reveals precisely *why* he had to suppress the
German alliance of the 1916 insurrectionaries, if he wanted simply to
praise their bravery. He could not admit the full ambiguity of the
moment even though he was perfectly well aware of it. Dillon's dramatic
reaction perfectly captured the mainstream Irish reaction to the repression which followed the Easter Rising. The executions of the principal

leaders, for example, horrified a nationalist population used to a soft and sympathetic Liberal administration in Dublin Castle since 1906. Of course, Britain was engaged in a wider perilous struggle for national survival and the Irish insurrectionaries had chosen to side with Germany. The British might say with Orlando in *As You Like It*: 'The thorny point | Of bare distress hath taken from me the show | Of smooth civility.' But repeatedly in the struggle that followed, the level of repression was exactly the right amount to infuriate and not so extreme as to intimidate—a losing formula until finally the combination of back-channel negotiation and repression brought peace in 1921. Even Rosamond Stephen, intensely devoted as she was to the concept of reconciling Irish Protestant and Catholic—accepting also Dillon's historic view of Irish landlords—found the Dillon speech on the Rising exasperating. On 12 May, she asked her sister Dorothea: 'Did you see Dillon's speech? He said, *inter alia*, that the government might be damned glad if their troops fought as well in France as the Sinn Feiners did in Dublin. Was he sober?'[75]

But such a comment, understandable though it was, does not catch the full significance of the moment. Dillon was, in fact, attempting one last great effort to save the Irish party project. The alternative at this moment—and the most likely means of saving his influence—was to offer 'common cause' with Sinn Fein and help to restrain the 'more extreme elements'. For W. B. Wells, the failure to take this option was an 'extraordinary miscalculation of political forces'.[76] Instead, John Dillon bonded with Lloyd George on the subject of British military stupidity in Ireland. 'Maxwell is a brute,' Dillon said to Lloyd George. 'No, he is an ass,' Lloyd George replied.[77] The objective of Dillon's choice was somehow to get a Home Rule Parliament into play, which meant not antagonizing the British who could deliver it. The problem was that the Rising had already antagonized them. This obviously required some kind of partition. It was the only possible means of heading off the Sinn Fein drive. On 6 June 1916, Dillon spoke to Lloyd George. Lloyd George noted: 'Dillon has just called in after an interview with the Ulster bishops who are hostile and think the Ulster conference will reject the proposals. The bishop of Belfast did put forward a county option;

Redmond's reply that it would be useless... Thinks proposal would be carried but for the priests. Redmond and Dillon likely to attend. Devlin more hopeful than he was.'[78] On 23 June 1916, Devlin delivered for Redmond and Dillon—Ulster nationalist delegates at a convention in Belfast agreed to an acceptance of partition terms likely to be acceptable to Ulster Unionists and thus pave the way for Home Rule.[79] However, grass-roots Irish opinion was moving fast away from any compromise on partition. It was simply too late for this type of accommodation. There were Derry and Tyrone Sinn Fein people who never forgave Dillon for the support for Devlin's illusory triumph in 1916. Convinced correctly that Lloyd George did not have the will or capacity to settle the Irish question in the aftermath of the 1916 Rising, Dillon stepped down from high politics in Westminster to lead the Irish parliamentary party's ground campaign against the inexorable rise of Sinn Fein in Ireland and, more controversially, refused to participate in the Irish convention in July 1917. He strongly supported the anti-conscription campaign in Ireland. But he was now a secondary figure, forced to accept that funds intended for the anti-conscription movement went to the suspects in English jails.[80] At the Mansion House Conference in April 1918 he encountered old foes Tim Healy, William O'Brien, and the new leaders of Sinn Fenn.

Dillon's attempts to contest Sinn Fein's growing ideological hegemony were a complete failure. He claimed that he had never stood on a recruiting platform in Ireland. But what was he doing standing beside Asquith at Asquith's Dublin meeting? It seemed a typical example of Dillon's long-established capacity to re-invent his own past. Dillon rightly claimed to have defended the heroism of the 1916 insurrectionaries, but the *Catholic Bulletin* asked why he did not protest against the claims made by his colleague, Stephen Gwynn, at Galway concerning 'the men who shot down every man in khaki in the streets of Dublin... whether he was able to defend himself or whether he was hobbling down the street on a crutch'.[81] In fact, Gwynn himself retreated from the tone of this intervention; anyway John Dillon had made perfectly clear his own view of events in Dublin at this moment.

On 20 March 1917, Dillon made a classic speech in which he accused Sir Edward Carson of pouring 'hot shot and poisoned gas into the ranks of the government until he smashed it'. Carson had indeed played a role in replacing Asquith with Lloyd George. Dillon went on to speak of anti-Irish feeling in England, and blamed the British War Office for the lack of recruits enlisting in Ireland, and finally for the failure to involve the dominions and the USA. These points all have a certain validity. But Dillon's speech had its polarizing effect: a key figure in Ulster unionism—capable later of respect for John Redmond—Wilfrid Spender declared: 'I cannot imagine Ulster being such a fool as to put her head in the noose of such a hangman.'[82] Meanwhile Sinn Fein propaganda also compared Dillon to a hangman, blaming him for war deaths and executions. John Dillon, who had once wielded such influence both in Parliament and outside it, was now an isolated figure. (The senior British politician, Austen Chamberlain wrote on 29 July 1918 to his sister: 'I do not think Dillon evokes any support in the House or country.'[83]) As the Irish party became more hostile to the British government, Sinn Fein gloated: 'Perhaps they would have denied that their new departure was an acceptance of Sinn Fein, but to us it looked very like it.'[84] But even now, when it was too late, press reports circulated of a possible Dillon/Carson rapprochement. 'Do not be surprised if before Parliament compromise is arranged between the nationalists and the Government over Home Rule. The points of difference between Mr John Dillon and Edward Carson are being gradually whittled down, and the situation is more hopeful than it has been for years.'[85] But there is no sign either in Carson's or Dillon's papers of this wonderful development, though Dillon's enemies within nationalism believed that he would do a deal with Unionists to gain a Dublin seat on the next Parliament. There was no breakthrough in October 1918. On 5 November 1918, in what Carson's biographer described correctly as the dying speech of Irish nationalism in the British Parliament, Dillon proclaimed with great bitterness: 'the real moral of this debate is that Sir Edward Carson has been acclaimed King of Ireland; the government obey his orders.' 'May I say,' Carson replied, with some factual inaccuracy, 'this is the tenth year of my reign.' Dillon continued with a reference to Ulster Unionism's pre-war gun-running: 'He has reached the height of his power, it is the tenth year of his reign based upon German rifles and revolution. There would have been no rebellion in 1916 but for Sir Edward Carson and Mr Bonar Law.'[86] There is a bitter irony here. It had all started so well; ten years before, Dillon and Carson stood together in support for major Irish educational reform: Carson all the time resisting Orange opinion on that issue. On 21 November, Bonar Law and Lloyd George in a joint manifesto stated their policy. The objective of the British state was now stated to be Irish self-government. There were, however, 'two paths which are now said to be closed— the one leading to the complete severance of Ireland from the British Empire and the forcible submission of the six counties of North-East Ulster to a home rule parliament against their will'.

John Dillon, as it happened, fully accepted these positions. But he could neither work with the British government and/or the unionists nor repel Sinn Fein. He was weakened by his sense of the Irish party's historic achievement on the land question, now largely taken for granted: 'One of the new doctrines preached by Sinn Feiners is: "Don't recognise English law." (laughter.) I would like to ask you this—how do you hold your farms? Are they not held under the Land Acts? Where were the Land Acts passed? If the principle were logically and honestly enforced, not one of you today would have any rights to your farms because the only title you have is under English law.'[87] It requires a moment here to stop and recall Dillon's historic attitude towards these same Land Acts from 1881 to 1903, to recall also the Kilmainham party's hostility to any acceptance of English influence on Irish agrarian outcomes. But he was, of course, accurately noting the Irish party's great achievement in transferring the ownership of the land of Ireland from the landed class to their own support base of tenant farmers. Dillon was perceptive also as to the likely future: 'If they [Sinn Fein] can get an independent republic and separate this country completely from England, and by way of a *hors d'oeuvre* squelch Carson and the Ulstermen (laughter) they will be very remarkable men.'[88] Dillon was so sure of the

obvious absurdity of Sinn Fein's policy[89] that he may have had a linger-
ing hope, until the Treaty was signed, that the Irish public would accept
his critique. W. B. Wells believed as much:

> Right down to the opening of the Irish Conference in London, if you could
> penetrate the gloomy house in North Great George's Street and induce
> John Dillon to talk to you about politics, he would tell you that, though he
> loyally accepted the verdict of the country for the time being, the sweep-
> ing success of Sinn Fein was only a temporary aberration, and Nationalist
> Ireland would in time return to its allegiance to the Parliamentary Party
> and the policy for which it stood. It was a delusion pathetic in a man to
> whom politics were an all-sufficing interest and excitement, the very
> breath and meaning of his life, and who now in his old age, at the close of
> a career spent in the service of his country, found himself left on the shelf,
> a mere ghost lingering superfluous on the political scene.[90]

# Conclusion

Parnell, Dillon and Mazzini form, or would have formed, a very curious trio. Parnell is all coldness and caution; John Dillon is all fire and impetuosity; Mazzini was a zealot but in some ways a philosopher.

*Aberdeen Herald*, 26 November 1887.

Probably no parliamentarian has ever figured in more thrilling and historic scenes than John Dillon. As he leapt up from the benches below the gangway his tall spare frame, his severely earnest face, black hair and flowing beard, seemed too much like the ideal to be actually there in a prosaic Anglo-Saxon assembly.

Thomas Cox Meech, 'John Dillon',
*Birmingham Daily Gazette*, 5 August 1927.

During his early parliamentary career, John Dillon maintained a considerable personal charisma. He was certainly always capable of winning admiration *outside* the ranks of the Irish nationalist party; indeed, inside that movement there was a steady flow of criticism but that had been the case from the start of his career. On 25 February 1881, Florence Arnold-Forster recorded, her father, William Forster, the Chief Secretary, spoke of John Dillon 'with the respect that is generally felt for this honest and melancholy desperado'.[1] In the early 1880s, the Tory MP and former admiral Sir John Hay—a scourge of the great Chinese pirates of the era—liked to say that Dillon ought to be hanged but he would be damned sorry to do it.[2] In 1886, the *Spectator* opined: 'No one who knows Mr. Dillon attributes to him any selfish or corrupt motives.'[3] In 1887, the Liberal W. F. Conybeare called him the 'Bayard of the League'[4]—after the legendary French knight, the Chevalier de Bayard (1473–1524), who was *sans peur* and *san reproche*. Tim Healy was not as generous: 'Vanity lurks in every man's knapsack, but Dillon's self-esteem, I thought, outdistanced his power of vision.'[5] Even as the decades passed, with the inevitable wear and tear inflicted by critics like Tim Healy on a politician's reputation, Dillon retained not only a certain respect but also an image of glamour. The Spanish image of Dillon was still in play in the 1890s but gradually it came to be replaced with a more Italianate one. Dillon, it was increasingly said, was modelled upon—both physically and intellectually—the great Italian patriot Mazzini. Mazzini was a resonant figure for Irish nationalists. There was an irony and complexity here. Dillon's great enemy of the Land League era, W. E. Forster, was in the 1860s a great supporter of Mazzini. Forster indignantly refuted *The Times* when it accused Mazzini of willingness to contemplate assassination. Why, Irish nationalists cried, was Forster not willing to apply the same moral standard to Parnell? It was a typical case of British double standards—surely both men were the innocent victims of the crude propaganda of *The Times*?[6]

The *New Age* in October 1913 saw John Dillon as the 'disciple of Mazzini' on the verge of victory. Madame Venturi for one insisted on the strong likeness between Mazzini and Dillon.[7] Emilie Ashurst Venturi (1821–93) had known 'all the Italian patriots' and was Giuseppe Mazzini's English translator. According to Alfred Webb, she took Parnell's side during the split but forgave Dillon for his anti-Parnellite stance. Webb, the Quaker Irish nationalist MP, reported: 'She, however, bore with John Dillon. She had some idea that Mazzini's spirit had passed into him, and she bequeathed to him most of her library of Italian books.'[8] In fact, she also left Dillon her fashionable London house:[9] but he refused to accept it and passed it back to her family. Others disagreed sharply: St. Loe Strachey pointed out that Dillon's willingness to accept a long-term British subsidy for an independent Ireland was hardly reminiscent of Mazzini.[10] F. W. H. Myers, author of a celebrated essay on Mazzini,[11] felt that Dillon's character was markedly inferior to that of the noble-souled Italian patriot: 'Mazzini resembled Mr. Dillon as much, and almost as little, as he resembled

Nebuchadnezzar.'[12] In response, the *Pall Mall Gazette* pointed out that Myers might be an expert on the character of Mazzini, but was he an expert on the character of John Dillon?[13] The Ulster-born Liberal scholar and politician James Bryce, part of an Oxford coterie which knew and admired Mazzini, insisted that Mazzini and John Dillon were alike, praising both highly as men not like the rest of mankind.[14] This was an Oxford/Cambridge divide: Cambridge aficionados of Mazzini (like Myers) did not like the Dillon association.[15] But the interesting question is this: how did Dillon deal with Mazzini's rejection of Irish independence? Mazzini was moved by the historical sufferings of the Irish people: it follows, therefore that his rejection of independence was based on the idea that Irish independence had no likely positive agenda, no 'mission'. 'What did Mazzini say?', said Douglas Hyde in an important 1892 address which foreshadowed the Gaelic League a year later: 'That we ought to be content as an integral part of the United Kingdom because we have lost the notes of nationality, our language and customs.'[16] Independence might be a debt owed to history, a salving of centuries of suffering, but what was its future?[17] D. P. Moran devoted much thought to this subject. In his *The Philosophy of Irish Ireland*, first published as a series of articles between 1898 and 1900, he was deeply worried that Mazzini was right. He argued that since Grattan, the leading Irish political elites—he explicitly named both Parnell and Dillon—'threw over Irish civilisation whilst they professed in perfect good faith to fight for Irish Nationality'.[18]

Not every nationalist was as worried as Moran on this score. T. P. Sexton's words on that topic are axiomatic: 'Ireland has every mark and token of a nation, the token of a race, the token of creed, the token of special interest, the token of will, of mental distinction.'[19] Mazzini would have accepted much of this but asked, what would Ireland's special role be in the progress of humanity?[20] What was Ireland's 'distinctive principle of life'? What would Ireland contribute as a nation state that could not be contributed as part of the UK? For Dillon and even Gladstone such questions were in some sense irrelevant. They 'the Irish' wanted to be governed by their own laws and not our laws, good though they may be, Gladstone declared in the Home Rule debate of 1886. There can be little doubt that this criticism of Irish nationality by Mazzini has hardly stood the test of time. It is clear that a strong imagined community of Irishness trumps all. It is also clear that Ireland has moved in a distinctive journey away from emphasis on its 'spiritual empire'—as the largest English-speaking Catholic country—towards a more profound identification with the secular European ideal. But it does serve as a caution against narrow nationalism by inserting a concern with the broader progress of humanity[21] as against moments of communal self-satisfaction.

What after all was the deeper point, if any, of Irish independence? Was it simply to allow a greater efflorescence of Irishness in all its manifestations, perhaps most particularly in this period, Catholicism? In his speeches at Arklow, Nottingham, and Liverpool Parnell had stressed the lack of serious thought in Ireland on how to achieve practical improvements in economic and social life. Dillon, a small government liberal, on the other hand, had tended to emphasize Irish control of Irish affairs rather than any particular purpose for Irish control once in operation. Self-government was above all simply a democratic 'popular' necessity: perhaps even, as some alleged, a means to revenge. At Oldham in February 1888, he had declared: 'It was more important to the life of the nation to have the administration of the law under the control of the representatives of the nation than it was to give law.'[22] But when Irish independence was actually achieved, it became clear that this type of remark merely reflected Dillon's frustration caused by Balfour's ability to govern like an 'Egyptian pasha' in Ireland. Dillon really did care profoundly about the purposes and activities of a Dublin government beyond merely its possession of democratic legitimacy. Sir Robert Anderson recalled a conversation with John Morley in which Morley argued that Ireland 'must be granted self-government'. Anderson asked the question, 'And what kind of government will it be?' To which Morley promptly replied, 'The worst government in the world; that does not affect the principle.'[23] Anderson was an opponent of Home Rule, but William O'Brien also made it clear that this was indeed Morley's view. Dillon alongside O'Brien clearly rejected such a negative prognosis—he insisted that the long experience of fighting English MPs in Westminster was likely a good preparation for self-rule.[24] Dillon was not alone. Michael MacDonagh, in a book co-authored with Emily Lawless, sister of Dillon's bête noire Lord Cloncurry, asked: 'Indeed had not their preachers and writers often said that in freedom they would develop an Irish civilisation which would dazzle the world?'[25] Not everyone was convinced. Richard Arnold Bermann, in his *Ireland 1913*, accepted that the new Irish nation would be more Catholic but otherwise would be a 'lively, colourful variety of Irishness-Britishness with a touch of musical flair. If you say this to an Irishman right now, he will scream his head off at you, full of hatred but it's true.'[26]

However, in the actual case no Irish nationalist was more visibly and volubly depressed by the achievement of Irish independence than John Dillon. On 2 April 1922, he had a long lunch with Lady Gregory. She recalled the conversation in which Dillon referred back to 1918/19:

> He takes a gloomy view, hates Griffith—'a liar,' thinks better of Collins 'because he knows nothing about him;' has seen a good deal of De Valera after the Mansion House Conference, doesn't think him honest (the first I have heard him say this) but not so dishonest as Griffith. De Valera had asked him to join them when he proclaimed his Republic and set up Dail Eireann, 'but I said, you cannot fight in open war, you must end by organised murder and I will never countenance that.'[27]

Dillon felt sure that Sinn Fein policy aggravated sectarian tension in the north; he, on the other hand, appears less than realistic:

> Whenever the trouble in Belfast slackens Sinn Fein sends men to stir it up again to keep it going. The Belfast Catholics would be ready to go into the Northern Parliament but the priests won't allow it. Devlin would have gone in but the priests would have prevented his election. Craig told me he wished to come in with the South but he couldn't get support at present.[28]

On 27 December 1922, he sent a public letter to an old colleague, P. Jaguers of the Australian National League, insisting that the 'settlement of the national demand' which the party had negotiated 'was unquestionably in all aspects much better than that acquired under the Treaty signed on 6 December 1921'. He appeared to be indifferent to the achievement of Michael Collins—a 'republic in all but name', to quote a key UK Foreign Office official, with Ireland possessing its own army and navy. He cannot have enjoyed it when his house in Ballaghaderreen was taken over as a billet by Free State army troops in April 1923, who covered it in sandbags and barbed wire.[29] Even so he did not retreat into a political retirement; he was often seen at the edges of political meetings in Dublin.[30]

At the beginning of 1925, Dillon told a meeting of the National Club in Dublin: 'When we look back on the days when we were oppressed by England it would look like Paradise if we could get the same sort of oppression now.' His great biographer, F. S. L. Lyons, comments: 'This was an extraordinary conclusion to have reached at the end of a lifetime spent in opposing British rule in Ireland, and there can be little doubt that the speech embarrassed some of his friends.'[31] William O'Malley, the former Connemara MP, disagreed with Dillon but acknowledged: 'I think his feeling was that no good could come out of Sinn Fein—as it was said of old that no good could come out of Nazareth.'[32] The *Spectator* had called Sinn Feiners the 'nightmare children of an illicit union between ultramontanism and Jacobinism'.[33] Dillon spoke as if he agreed. He received interesting support from Horace Plunkett, an old enemy.[34] Plunkett had been in effective alliance with Redmond and William O'Brien in pursuit of the conciliation strategy vetoed by Dillon's Swinford revolt in 1903. A unionist, he had later advocated a dominion settlement. But he assumed that Dillon shared his concerns about the College of Science and vocational education under the new order. 'Yesterday I heard of a county council which had voted £1,400 for the teaching of Irish and £200 for technical education. I gave it up.'[35] It was a comment designed to evoke a sympathetic response from the John Dillon who in 1874 had challenged Catholic Ireland to treat modern science with respect.

But it is clear that for the man who defended modern science against Catholic obscurantism in the 1870s this was a painful moment. It was perhaps an even more painful moment for the mature politician who steadfastly opposed the use of compulsory Irish against the Protestant community and whose son, Professor Myles Dillon, was to become Ireland's greatest Celtic scholar and most eloquent opponent of the misuse of the language as a means of cultural discipline. John Dillon was not short of contemporaries who felt that he had brought his defeat upon himself. Florence Arnold-Forster had called him a 'melancholy desperado' in 1881, but long before the end of his career his 'gloomy and rather self-righteous temperament led to the hostile nickname 'the melancholy humbug'.[36] In fact, Tim Healy's 'melancholy humbug' jibe, sometimes wrongly attributed to Parnell, really stuck, appearing in the press in 1894[37] and in all parts of the country and abroad[38] until after his death. The *Globe* correspondent said that not even a new Boswell who knew Dillon could pen a better description.[39] The *Larne Times*, though, liked to call him a 'preposterous humbug'.[40] The *Belfast Newsletter* insisted four years after his death that even Dillon's friends admitted the truth of Healy's jibe.[41] At every point his record was subject to corrosive criticism during his lifetime. The London *Times* obituary noted that he was the only Irish MP with an interest in foreign policy and he certainly had maintained radical independent views on the Boer War and Egypt and Persia. Dillon brilliantly exposed British moral standards during the Boer War—'capturing women and children by the thousand'.[42] Warre B. Wells sneered that 'he was a friend to democracy in every country except his own'.[43] But was this fair? William O'Malley insisted English Labour MPs regarded John Dillon as their guide, philosopher, and friend;[44] they were hugely impressed by his knowledge both of foreign affairs and procedure. In fact, Dillon had learnt the hard way, failing on a technicality, for example, to force the government to debate the humanitarian crisis in Martinique as late as 1902. This gave him the fund of knowledge which he passed on to Labour MPs. On the other hand, Dillon's pleasure in fighting his Ballaghaderreen employees in a bitter strike in 1925 rather supports the Wells verdict.

At the end of July 1927, in his last significant political engagement, Dillon attended a private tea party at the National Liberal club given in his honour by F. W. Hirst, the former *Economist* editor. He asked that the meeting be kept out of the newspapers. The *Westminster Gazette* later reported: 'He was one of few Radicals in the Parnell band. Thus his influence among Liberal members and journalists was among his best gifts to the Irish cause. That he should have died in London after a gathering with some of these old political comrades was not unfitting.'[45] At one level, the connection with F. W. Hirst, a former distinguished editor of the *Economist*, is surprising. The *Economist* in the 1880s had loathed the young Dillon and welcomed his early retirement from politics. But Hirst was a true old-school free market liberal of the Gladstone type. He was fired as *Economist* editor in part because he supported Dillon's analysis of British military repression in Dublin in 1916.[46] Hirst was, in fact, a borderline liberal, 'on the verge of alienating itself from the progressive variety and allying itself with middle-class economic conservatism', embracing a 'mid Victorian interpretation of the right of private property'.[47] The meeting of minds with Dillon is obvious, as *Irish Society* observed in 1913: 'Mr Dillon is a Liberal of the Gladstone kind.'[48]

One of the most devastating criticisms of Dillon was made by Michael MacDonagh, an ally of William O'Brien:

> Dillon regarded himself as a stern, unbending Nationalist. What he was really, was a formalist—one who had a closed mind in regard to new ideas who adhered strictly to traditional methods and condemned any break-away from the long pursued and beaten groove, even though, so far it had led nowhere near the end that was looked for.[49]

It should be recalled that MacDonagh was an experienced journalistic observer of the Irish party in the House of Commons. One hundred years after Dillon's political eclipse the utility of his effective embrace of the Ancient Order of Hibernians—a mass Catholic organization at the heart of the Irish nationalist political machine—has attracted increasing criticism from young Irish scholars. After all, had not Dillon insisted at the time of the Papal rescript against the Plan of Campaign that it was essential for Irish nationalists to resist clerical dictation? Dr James Doherty has recently observed: 'If Dillon's support for the A.O.H. was indeed intended to thwart O'Brienite conciliation, the creation of a militantly Roman Catholic mass movement achieved its longer term goal. The longer term consequence of the tactic's success, however, was to widen the cultural and sectarian gulf in Irish society particularly between the Protestants of north-east Ulster and the rest of the country, with damaging implications for the attainment of unitary self-rule.'[50] Perhaps too Dillon accepted the logic of this analysis—and this helps to explain his early acceptance of the principle of consent.

But these criticisms do not fully catch the complexity of John Dillon. The man who launched the Swinford revolt against conciliation was the same man who argued against the political weaponization of the Irish language. The man who attacked Sir Edward Carson and Ulster unionism—sometimes, though not always, in exaggerated terms— was the same man who conceded the principle of consent in 1914. The man who was widely seen as the most emotionally conservative nationalist of his generation was the man who did not take satisfaction from the emotional and ethnic satisfaction of the achievement of self-government and instead asked Mazzini's question of all narrow nationalists: how does this make for the broader progress of humanity? What is Ireland contributing to that end, which it could not contribute under the union?

In the last eighteen months of his political career, Parnell with part of his mind made an attempt to re-imagine the future of Irish nationalism. It would have a new focus on material improvement. It would be a nationalism which was not to be dictated to by the Catholic Church. It would be conciliatory towards the unionists of the north-east corner. It would consider unhooking from land agitation and the alliance with radical liberals in favour of a state-subsidized compromise on the land question and an understanding with the British Conservatives. John Dillon, in effect, opposed all these positions in 1891. Parnell's views were widely disliked within Irish nationalism in 1891. Dillon can hardly have felt that they had any resonance. He endorsed a rejection of the politics of internal Irish conciliation and placed intense reliance on the Liberals. In the end they failed him, as he honestly admitted. Parnell would not have been surprised.

John Dillon's political career ended in failure but it cannot be said to be a failure. He helped drive the cause of Irish nationalism out of stagnant waters. Ireland won self-government by violent methods which he had flirted with but could not in the end morally sanction. The actual achievement of self-government was for him to be a profound disappointment, bringing none of the wider benefits he had assumed. But he was one of the victors of the land war which he first supported in 1879; by the time of his death, it was clear that the Land League slogan of peasant proprietorship had won out in Ireland. The National University of 1908 was a substantial achievement and it owed more to John Dillon than any other politician.

The Northern Irish troubles have tended to generate a more sceptical attitude towards his record. John Dillon blocked the moment of possible reconciliation of 'creed' and 'class' generated by the 1903 Wyndham Act. It seemed to both John Redmond and William O'Brien that he had missed the chance to implement Parnell's vision in favour of the maintenance of a grievance culture; worse still, that grievance culture no longer united but divided nationalist Ireland. William O'Brien felt that this was anticipated by Dillon's persistent failure to comprehend Parnell's motives in the 1880s. Dillon was too close, it seems, to agrarian agitators like Larry Ginnell MP, but he was also embroiled more profoundly in the toils of the alliance with British liberalism.

After 1886, the British Liberal party and the Irish parliamentary party engaged in a dance of death which effectively destroyed both parties as serious forces by 1921. For much of the time it was a joyous dance, infused with much mutual admiration and even love, but that was precisely the problem. The Irish party reinforced the worst side of the Liberals and the Liberals reinforced the worst side of the Irish party. The Liberals encouraged the Irish party not to take seriously the Ulster unionist community. The Irish, in effect, imposed Home Rule on the Liberals to the extent that it reduced their capacity to respond to the rise of Labour, whilst simultaneously pushing a substantial section of the erstwhile Liberal bourgeoisie towards the Conservatives.

Neither connection helped Dillon to gain the direct focus on the primary problem of Home Rule—the division within the Irish people. But, it has to be admitted, neither John Redmond in the 1890s nor William

O'Brien (from 1905 to 1914), who at different times had such a direct focus, came close to resolving the problem. It also has to be admitted that Dillon's campaign for the 'rights of the Protestant boy' in the face of massive pressure from Irish language enthusiasts is impressive, as is his explicit commitment from 1914 onwards to the acceptance of the principle of consent with respect to the Ulster unionist community. Dillon did a great deal to define Irish nationalism over some four decades. On all sides his honesty was accepted—this despite the fact he was sometimes capable, through an excess of self-righteous passion, of misleading Parliament. No one who knows John Dillon, the *Spectator* famously said, can doubt his integrity, and it is for that reason that his career reveals so much about the nature of Irish nationalism: its dignity, rationale, and its limitations. Parnell, it is said, became, by a complex route, the hero of the Irish bourgeoisie; John Dillon in his prime was its incarnation.

The clue to understanding Dillon's political career is his hostility to the Irish Protestant landed aristocracy and its professional allies, the only class in Ireland who appeared to assume a superiority over the upper reaches of the Catholic bourgeoisie. It was not a simple anti-Protestant bigotry which motivated him. Far from it—as early as 1879, he attempted to moderate the Land League programme to take account of the Presbyterian tenant farmers in the north. In 1909, he refused to allow the Irish language to be used as a weapon against the 'Protestant boy'. In 1914, he accepted quicker than most Irish MPs the need to avoid any hint of a desire to coerce the north-east. But the Protestant landed aristocracy attracted his ire, as did its Trinity College—in Dillon's eyes and TCD's own—cultural citadel. The bitter language Dillon employed throughout the Land League, the Plan of Campaign, and Wyndham Act controversies was entirely compatible with the 'hearts and minds' alliance within the Liberal party. But this political agreement based on a unity of values against landed aristocratic arrogance was inadequate in the face of that deeper search for cultural meaning for Irish nationalism which inspired those who destroyed the Irish party in 1918.

# NOTES

## Foreword

1. Paul Bew, 'John Hume modified Parnell's vision to bring about peace', *Irish Independent*, 8 August 2020.

## Chapter 1

1. *Northern Daily Mail*, 20 February 1896.
2. Ged Martin, 'Parnell and Cambridge: The Education of an Irish Nationalist', *Irish Historical Studies*, vol. 19 (March 1974), 72–82.
3. Conor Cruise O'Brien, *Parnell and his Party* (Oxford, 1957), 30.
4. *Freeman's Journal*, 3 February 1874.
5. William O'Brien, *The Parnell of Real Life* (London, 1926).
6. Thomas Barnes, *Parliamentary Portraits* (London, 1815), 199.
7. Roy Foster, *Charles Stewart Parnell: The Man and his Family* (Hassocks, 1977), 6–9, is still the classic source.
8. F. H. O'Donnell, *A History of the Irish Parliamentary Party* (London, 1910), i. 420.
9. Ibid. 421.
10. W. J. O'Neill Daunt, *A Life Spent for Ireland* (London, 1896), 395.
11. Arthur Baumann, *The Last Victorians* (London, 1927), 271.
12. *Charles Stewart Parnell: A Memoir* (New York, 1914), 38.
13. Brendan Ó Cathaoir, *John Blake Dillon, Young Irelander* (Dublin, 1990), 5.
14. 'Ireland', *The Spectator*, 7 June 1856.
15. J. G. Swift MacNeill, *What I Have Seen and Heard* (Boston, 1925), 32.
16. Andrew Kettle, *Material for Victory* (Dublin, 1958), 35.
17. *Irish Independent*, 13 February 1986.
18. *Weekly Irish Times*, 15 March 1902.
19. *People's Advocate*, 31 July 1897.
20. *Irish Independent*, 19 November 1917.
21. *Vide*, Maurice Manning, *James Dillon: A Biography* (Dublin, 1999).
22. Liz Pahl (ed.), *Signe Toksvig's Irish Diaries 1926–37* (Dublin, 1994), 270–1.
23. Katharine O'Shea, *Charles Stewart Parnell* (London, 1914), ii. 50.
24. *Gloucester Mercury*, 24 June 1882.
25. Historians, 'The Best Hundred Irish Books' (Dublin, 1886), 37.

26. *Northern Whig*, 6 October 1891.
27. 'Versatile Public Men', *Paisley and Renfrewshire Gazette*, 23 May 1896.
28. William O'Brien, *Evening Memories* (Dublin and London, 1920), 63.
29. Thomas Cox Meech, John Dillon, *Birmingham Daily Gazette*, 5 August 1927; T. P. O'Connor, *Memoirs of an Old Parliamentarian* (London, 1929), i. 140.
30. The Supplement to the *New Ross Standard*, 23 August 1890, *Free Studies from Life: Parnell*.
31. F. S. L. Lyons, *Charles Stewart Parnell* (London, 1977), 19.
32. *Illustrated London News*, 22 February 1896.
33. London, 1874, p. 63.
34. See Cardinal Newman's *My Campaign in Ireland* (Aberdeen, 1896). John Dillon was one of a group of Dublin students who wrote to Newman congratulating him when he became a Cardinal.
35. Greta Jones, 'Catholicism, Nationalism and Science', *Irish Review*, no. 20 (Winter/Spring 1997), 51.
36. O'Brien, *The Parnell of Real Life*, 46.
37. O'Brien, *Evening Memories*, 190.
38. O'Brien, *The Parnell of Real Life*, 46.
39. Katharine O'Shea, *Charles Stewart Parnell* (London, 1914), i. 192. For the politics of this group, see Greta Jones, 'Scientists and Home Rule', ch. 10 in Boyce and O'Day (eds.), *Defenders of the Union* (London, 2001).
40. Brendan Ó Cathaoir (ed.), *The Diary of Elizabeth Dillon* (Dublin, 2019), 521–2.
41. *Gloucester Mercury*, 24 June 1882. The story first appeared in *Truth* and then was widely reprinted; Parnell at this time was spending a lot of time in the company of Labouchere.
42. *Weekly Freeman's Journal*, 25 June 1881.
43. Roy Foster, *Charles Stewart Parnell: The Man and his Family* (Hassocks, 1977), 38.
44. Professor Ged Martin, in his important *Martinalia* essays, available on his website (https://www.gedmartin.net/), has thrown much light on this topic.
45. Margaret Frances Sullivan, *Ireland of Today: The Causes and Aims of the Agitation* (Philadelphia, 1881), 356.
46. Kettle, *Material for Victory*, 63–4.
47. *Gloucester Mercury*, 24 June 1882.
48. Foster, *Charles Stewart Parnell*, 156–9 is superb on this point.
49. Again, I owe the analysis to Professor Ged Martin, in his fascinating *Martinalia* essays, available on his website (https://www.gedmartin.net/).
50. *Londonderry Sentinel*, 26 May 1891.
51. Kettle, *Material for Victory*, 134.
52. John Dillon, *Dictionary of Irish Biography* entry.
53. Roy Foster, 'Parnell and "his people": The Ascendancy and Home Rule', in *Paddy and Mr Punch: Connections in Irish and English History* (London, 1993).
54. Baumann, *The Last Victorians*, 272.

55. *Daily News*, 19 November 1881.
56. *Dublin Gazette*, 2 May 1883.
57. A Woman of No Importance, *Memories Discreet and Indiscreet* (London, 1917), 273.
58. Baumann, *The Last Victorians*, 270.
59. Thomas Cox Meech, *Birmingham Daily Gazette*, 5 August 1927.
60. *The Perthshire Constitutional & Journal*, 6 June 1887.
61. *Sunderland Daily Echo*, 16 May 1902.
62. *Reynold's Newspaper*, 7 August 1927; *Aberdeen Press Journal*, 5 August 1927.
63. A Woman of No Importance, *Memories Discreet and Indiscreet*, 273.
64. Baumann, *The Last Victorians*, 269–70.
65. *Hull Daily Mail*, 6 February 1924.
66. O'Brien, *The Parnell of Real Life*, 63.
67. See the present author's essay, 'The Paradoxes of Parnell', in Joep Leersen (ed.), *Parnell and his Times* (Cambridge, 2020).
68. John Howard Parnell, *Charles Stewart Parnell, A Memoir* (New York, 1914), 104.
69. 'John Dillon', *Roscommon Messenger*, 13 August 1927.
70. Sergeant A. M. Sullivan, *Old Ireland: Reminiscences of an Irish KC* (London, 1928), 135.
71. *The Diary of Elizabeth Dillon*, 24 June 1888, p. 323.
72. *Drogheda Argus*, 5 August 1927.
73. *Derry Journal*, 5 August 1927.
74. F. S. L. Lyons, *John Dillon* (London, 1968), 35.
75. *The Times*, 3 July 1886; J. A. Froude here states this thesis.
76. John Savage, *'98 and '48: The Modern Revolutionary History and Literature of Ireland* (New York, 1856), 344.
77. Margaret Frances Sullivan, *Ireland of Today: The Causes and Aims of Irish Agitation* (Philadelphia, 1881).
78. William O'Brien, *Recollections* (London, 1905), 110.
79. T. P. O'Connor, *Memoirs of an Old Parliamentarian* (London, 1929), 139 (1881, *aet.* 30).
80. *Common Sense in Ireland*, 16 October 1897, p. 4.
81. Lennox Robinson (ed.), *Lady Gregory's Journals* (Dublin, 1946), 169 (2 April 1922).
82. For example, Liam O'Flaherty, *Life of Tim Healy* (London, 1927); Michael MacDonagh, *The Life of William O'Brien: The Irish Nationalist* (London, 1928); F. Sheehy Skeffington, *Michael Davitt* (London, 1908); Denis Gwynn, *The Life of John Redmond* (London, 1932).
83. J. V. O'Brien, *William O'Brien and the Course of Irish Politics 1881–1918* (Berkeley, 1976); Sally Warwick Haller, *William O'Brien and the Irish Land War* (Dublin, 1990).
84. Laurence Marley, *Michael Davitt: Freelance Radical and Frondeur* (Dublin, 2007); T. W. Moody, *Davitt and Irish Revolution 1846–82* (Oxford, 1987); Carla King, *Michael Davitt* (Dublin, 2009), and the same author's *Michael Davitt: After the Land League 1882–1906* (Dublin, 2016); Fintan Lane and Andrew G. Newby (eds.), *Michael Davitt: New Perspectives* (Dublin, 2009).

85. J. P. Finnane, *John Redmond and Irish Unity* (Syracuse, 2004); Dermot Meleady, *Redmond: The Parnellite* (Cork, 2018); Dermot Meleady, *John Redmond: The National Leader* (Dublin, 2014); Chris Dooley, *Redmond: A Life Undone* (Dublin, 2015).
86. Frank Callanan, *T. M. Healy* (Cork, 1996).
87. Manchester, 2016, p. 261.
88. James Doherty, *Irish Liberty and British Democracy: The Third Home Rule Crisis 1909–14* (Cork, 2019), 227.
89. Philip Bull, 'Writing about Irish Land against the Background of Northern Ireland', ch. 4 in Fergus Campbell and Tony Varley (eds.), *Land Questions in Modern Ireland* (Manchester, 2013).
90. Trevor Wilson (ed.), *Political Diaries of C. P. Scott* (London, 1970), 202.
91. Francis Hackett, *Ireland: A Study in Nationalism* (New York, 1918), 330.
92. E. Biagini, *British Democracy and Irish Nationalism* (Cambridge, 2007), 202, 229.
93. Ó Cathaoir, *Elizabeth Dillon*, refers to Ginnell as Dillon's 'poor little secretary' (p. 624) but Lyons does not mention him at all despite Ginnell's later role as a radical agrarian MP and, indeed, the only Irish party MP to make a successful transition to Sinn Fein.

## Chapter 2

1. 'The Romantic Element—1830 to 1850', in J. H. Plumb (ed.), *Studies in Social History: A Tribute to G. M. Trevelyan* (London, 1955), 235.
2. Liam Kennedy, 'Irish Folklore', *Spectator*, 23 January 2021.
3. *United Irishman*, 4 April 1848; Justin McCarthy, *Reminiscences* (1910), i. 71.
4. Bryan P. McGovern, *John Mitchel: Irish Nationalist, Southern Secessionist* (Knoxville, 2009), 216–17.
5. *Freeman's Journal*, 17 October 1873.
6. *Cork Constitution*, 9 February 1874.
7. Ibid.
8. *Nation*, 2 January 1875.
9. *Nation*, 6 February 1875. John Martin to Charles Kickham, 30 January 1875.
10. *Irishman*, 13 February 1875.
11. *Nation*, 27 February 1875.
12. *The Times*, 8 February 1875.
13. Ibid.
14. J. R. Vincent (ed.), *The Diaries of Edward Henry Stanley, 15th Earl of Derby between September 1869 and March 1878* (London, 1994), 196.
15. *Irishman*, 20 February 1875; James Quinn, *John Mitchel* (Dublin, 2008), 85.
16. R. V. Comerford, *Charles J. Kickham* (Dublin, 1979), 14.
17. *Hansard*, 18 February 1875, vol. 222, col. 529.
18. Alan O'Day, *Irish Home Rule* (Manchester, 1998), 43.
19. *Tralee Chronicle*, 9 February 1875.

20. *Irishman*, 20 February 1875.
21. William O'Brien, *Recollections* (London, 1905).
22. *The Times*, 18 February 1875.
23. Ibid.
24. *The Times*, 27 February 1875.
25. Stefan Collini, *Public Moralists, Political Thought and Intellectual Life in Britain 1850–1930* (Oxford, 1991), 216.
26. P. A. Sillard, *The Life of John Mitchel* (Dublin, 1901), 278.
27. *Nation*, 13 March 1875.
28. *Irishman*, 13 March 1875.
29. *The Political History of John Dillon*; *Dublin Weekly Nation*, 22 August 1895; *Pall Mall Gazette*, 2 September 1896.
30. William Dillon assumed that he could ensure—if Gavan Duffy wanted it—that Parnell would be prepared to bow out. Charles Gavan Duffy, *My Life in Two Hemispheres* (London, 1898), ii. 348–50.
31. Myles Dungan, *The Captain and the King: William O'Shea, Parnell and Late Victorian Ireland* (Dublin, 2009), 21.
32. Margaret Frances Sullivan, *Ireland of Today: The Causes and Aims of Irish Agitation* (Philadelphia, 1881), 431.
33. Patrick Maume (ed.), John Mitchel, *The Last Conquest of Ireland (Perhaps)* (Dublin, 2005), pp. xvi–xxi.
34. Ciaran Brady, *James Anthony Froude: An Intellectual Biography of a Victorian Prophet* (Oxford, 2013), 265.
35. *Irishman*, 14 December 1881.
36. *United Irishman*, 6 May 1848.
37. R. V. Comerford, *The Fenians in Context* (Dublin, 1986), 141–2.
38. Stephen Koss, *The Rise and Fall of the Political Press in Britain* (London, 1981), 233.
39. *St James's Gazette*, 14 June 1888.
40. Ibid.
41. *Irishman*, 13 March 1875.
42. *Irishman*, 14 June 1888.
43. Ibid.
44. Paul Bew, *Ireland: The Politics of Enmity 1789–2006* (Oxford, 2009), 213.
45. This statement was greeted with pleasure by the pro-Gladstone press, *Northern Echo*, 8 July 1889.
46. Duffy, *My Life in Two Hemispheres*, ii. 348.
47. Tim Healy, *Letters and Leaders of My Day* (London, 1928), 28 March 1877, p. 53.
48. *Spectator*, 6 March 1895; *The Times*, 27 February 1895.
49. *Drogheda Argus*, 24 April 1875.
50. P. J. P. Tynan, *The Irish National Invincibles and Their Times* (London, 1894), 51.
51. F. S. L. Lyons, *John Dillon* (London, 1968), 23.
52. In Edward Russell, *That Reminds Me* (London, 1899), 323. I owe this reference to Patrick Maume.

53. *The People (Wexford)*, 13 October 1877.

54. *Irishman*, 29 December 1877; quoted in Clare Murphy, 'Varieties of Crowd Activity', in Peter Jupp and Eoin Magennis (eds.), *Crowds in Ireland c.1720–1920* (London, 2000), 182–3. Italics added.

55. *Irishman*, 29 December 1887.

56. *Sheffield Independent*, 14 September 1877.

57. *Dublin Daily Express*, 10 December 1877.

58. T. W. Moody, *Davitt and Irish Revolution* (Oxford, 1981), 188 (Moody notes only two); Sullivan, *Ireland of Today*, 334–5.

59. Terence de Vere White, *The Road of Excess* (Dublin, 1946), 366, 374–5.

60. *Freeman's Journal*, 16 January 1878.

61. Lyons, *John Dillon*, 25.

62. *Hansard*, 16 May 1878, vol. 240, col. 76.

63. *Spectator*, 18 May 1878.

64. *Irishman*, 31 May 1875.

65. F. H. O'Donnell, *A History of the Irish Parliamentary Party* (London, 1910), i. 376.

66. *Nation*, 23 November 1878.

67. *Freeman's Journal*, 4 February 1879.

68. *Irish Times*, 18 March 1879.

69. Justin McCarthy, *The Story of an Irishman* (London, 1904), 200.

70. Conor Cruise O'Brien, *Parnell and his Party* (Oxford, 1957), 30.

71. Patrick Maume, 'Parnell and the IRB Oath', *Irish Historical Studies*, xxix, no.115 (May 1995).

72. T. W. Moody, *Michael Davitt and Irish Revolution 1846–1922* (Oxford, 1981), 292–5; F. Sheehy Skeffington, *Michael Davitt* (London, 1908), 80; Liam Swords, *A Dominant Church: The Diocese of Achonry 1818–1960* (Dublin, 2004), 222.

73. Sheridan was to be the uncle of a distinguished Irish American athlete; a recent study by Margaret Molloy provides new information on the Sheridan family, who eventually married into the family of Michael Collins.

74. Frank Mayes, *Rural Tensions in 19th Century Knock, County Mayo* (Dublin, 2021), 44; for Sheridan, see also Leon Ó Broin, *The Prime Informer: A Suppressed Scandal* (Dublin, 1971), 87.

75. *Irishman*, 18 July 1879.

76. Donald Jordan, *Land and Popular Politics in Ireland: County Mayo from the Plantation to the Land War* (Cambridge, 1994), 239/241; *Irishman*, 16 July 1879; Terry Golway, *Irish Rebel: John Devoy and America's Fight for Freedom* (New York, 1999), 122.

77. Paul Bew, '"A vision to the dispossessed": Popular Piety and Revolutionary Politics in the Irish Land War 1879–82', in Judith Devlin and Ronan Fanning (eds.), *Religion and Rebellion* (Dublin, 1997), 136–51; Anne Kane, 'The Transcendent Role of Catholic Discourse in the Irish Land War', in Fergus Campbell and Tony Varley (eds.), *Land Questions in Modern Ireland* (Manchester, 2013), 209.

78. Andrew Dunlop, *Fifty Years of Irish Journalism* (London, 1911), 241.
79. *Economist*, 16 August 1879.
80. D. G. Boyce and Alan O'Day (eds.), *Parnell in Perspective* (London, 1991).

## Chapter 3

1. Alvin Jackson, *The Two Unions: Ireland, Scotland and the Survival of the United Kingdom 1707–2007* (Oxford, 2012).
2. Mitchell Henry MP, 'The National Convention', *Nation*, 20 September 1879.
3. *Aberdeen Press*, 11 November 1879.
4. *The Times*, 23 December 1907.
5. Paul Bew, *Land and the National Question in Ireland, 1858–82* (Dublin, 1978), 206–7.
6. *Nation*, 22 November 1879.
7. *Freeman's Journal*, 19 November 1879; *Nation*, 22 November 1879.
8. Andrew Kettle, *Material for Victory* (Dublin, 1958), 20.
9. *Freeman's Journal*, 19 November 1879.
10. *Belfast Morning News*, 24 November 1879.
11. See the important work of Paul Townend, *The Road to Home Rule: Anti-Imperialism and the Irish National Movement* (Madison, 2016).
12. The scholarship of Paul Townend has provoked an important debate on this point.
13. *Daily News*, 24 November 1879.
14. *Nation*, 22 November 1879.
15. William O'Brien and Desmond Ryan (eds.), *Devoy's Post Bag 1871–1828* (Dublin, 1948), 22 October 1879, p. 457.
16. *Dublin Evening Express*, 8 November 1877.
17. *Irish World*, 28 August 1880.
18. F. H. O'Donnell, *A History of the Irish Parliamentary Party* (London, 1910), 384–5.
19. *New York Herald*, 3 January 1880.
20. *New York World*—quoted in *The Times*, 20 June 1880.
21. See Ely M. Janis, *A Greater Ireland: The Land League and Transatlantic Nationalism in Gilded Age America* (Madison, 2015) for the broad context.
22. *Spectator*, 4 September 1886.
23. *The Times*, 20 January 1880.
24. John Howard Parnell, *Charles Stewart Parnell: A Memoir* (New York, 1914), 164.
25. E. Delany and D. MacRaild (eds.), *Irish Migration: Ethnic Identities since 1750* (London, 2005), 267.
26. *Irishman*, 20 April 1880.
27. Don Jordan, *Land and Popular Politics in Ireland: Co. Mayo from the Plantation to the Land War* (Cambridge, 1994), 261.
28. *Midland Counties Advertiser*, 13 December 1882.

29. 'Political Strife, Past and Present', *New Ross Standard*, 21 June 1935.
30. Daire Hogan and Patrick Maume (eds.), *The Reminiscences of Ignatius O'Brien, Lord Chancellor of Ireland 1913–18* (Dublin, 2021), 139.
31. 'John Dillon and the O'Conor Don', *Irish Times*, 27 November 1886.
32. *Nation*, 22 November 1879.
33. *Dublin Weekly Nation*, 20 March 1880.
34. *Freeman's Journal*, 22 April 1880.
35. F. H. O'Donnell, *A History of the Irish Parliamentary Party* (London, 1910), i. 386.
36. T. D. Sullivan, *Recollections of Troubled Times in Irish Politics* (Dublin, 1905), 17.
37. *Dublin Evening Telegraph*, 21 July 1908.
38. Bew, *Land and the National Question in Ireland, 1858–82*, 109.
39. F. H. O'Donnell, *A History of the Irish Parliamentary Party* (London, 1910), ii. 466.
40. *Nation*, 12 June 1880.
41. T. P. O'Connor, *Memoirs of an Old Parliamentarian* (London, 1929), 140.
42. *Wexford People*, 24 July 1880.
43. H. O. Arnold-Forster, *The Truth about the Land League* (1883), 21; Rainsborough, 1 July 1880.
44. *Parnellism and Crime*, revised edn. (London, 1887), 10.
45. Dana Hearne and Margaret Ward (eds.), introduction to Anna Parnell, *The Tale of a Great Sham* (Dublin, 2020), p. xxxvi.
46. Henry James, *The Work of the Irish Leagues* (London, 1890), 263–4.
47. John Dillon, Kildare, 18 August 1880, ibid. 264.
48. F. S. L. Lyons, *John Dillon* (London, 1968), 38–9.
49. *Irish Times*, 25 August 1880.
50. *Irishman*, 28 August 1880.
51. Ibid.
52. *The Times*, 10 August 1880.
53. 'Character and Destiny', *Westminster Gazette*, 13 July 1925.
54. *Daily Record*, 18 May 1914.
55. Tim Healy, *Letters and Leaders of My Day* (London, 1928), i. 98.
56. *Hansard*, 26 August 1880, vol. 256, col. 124.
57. T. W. Moody and R. A. J. Hawkins (eds.), *Florence Arnold-Forster's Irish Journal* (Oxford, 1988), 12–13 (10 September 1880).
58. *Liverpool Echo*, 30 August 1880.
59. *Northern Whig*, 25 March 1875.
60. *Irish Times*, 29 December 1973.
61. H. O. Arnold-Forster, *The Truth about the Land League* (1883), 23; 31 October 1880, Tipperary.
62. *Freeman's Journal*, 28 December 1880.
63. *Newry Reporter*, 21 September 1880.
64. *Dublin Daily Express*, 18 October 1880.

65. *Roscommon Messenger*, 13 April 1929.

66. See Patrick Maume's essay on Tom Steele, 'The Head Pacificator and Captain Rock: Sedition, Suicide and Honest Tom Steele', in K. Hughes and D. MacRaild (eds.), *Crime, Violence and the Irish in the Nineteenth Century* (Liverpool, 2017), 239–59.

67. *The Graphic*, 'Parnell at Limerick', 6 November, 13 November 1880.

68. *Clonmel Chronicle*, 7 December 1880.

69. 'Parnell, Wicklow and Nationalism', in Donal McCartney (ed.), *Parnell: The Politics of Power* (Dublin, 1990), 30.

70. *Waterford Standard*, 8 December 1880.

71. John Augustus O'Shea, *Roundabout Recollections* (London, 1892), ii. 69–73.

72. *Aberdeen Free Press*, 26 March 1883.

73. L. P. Curtis, 'Stopping the Hunt 1881–2: An Aspect of the Irish Land War', in C. H. E. Philpin (ed.), *Nationalism and Popular Protest in Ireland* (Cambridge, 1987), 367–70.

74. *British High Politics and a Nationalist Ireland: Criminality, Land and the Law under Forster and Balfour* (Cork, 1994), 146.

75. *Jersey Independent and Daily Telegraph*, 11 December 1880.

76. Then picked up in *Aberdeen Press and Journal*, 14 December 1880; *Daily Chronicle*, 13 December 1880.

77. *Irishman*, 8 January 1881.

78. *Parnellism and Crime*, 10.

79. *Hansard*, 17 January 1881, vol. 257, col. 913; see also the report in the *Irishman*, 22 January 1881.

80. *Spectator*, 22 January 1881.

81. Dana Hearne (ed.), *Anna Parnell, The Tale of a Great Sham* (Dublin, 2020), 76. See also ch. 5, 'Rent at the point of a bayonet'.

82. J. L. Hammond, *Gladstone and the Irish Nation* (London, 1938), 215; R. Barry O'Brien, *The Life of Charles Stewart Parnell, 1846–1891* (London, 1898), ii. 358–9.

83. *Hansard*, 9 February 1881, vol. 258, col. 452.

84. Sir Herbert Maxwell, *The Life and Times of the Rt Hon William Henry Smith* (London, 1893), ii. 50.

85. Lord George Hamilton, *Parliamentary Reminiscences and Reflections 1868–1885* (London, 1916), 192.

86. *Fife Herald*, 17 February 1881.

87. Moody and Hawkins (eds.), *Florence Arnold-Forster's Irish Journal*, 68 (6 February 1881).

88. See Parnell's letter from Paris dated 13 February to the Land League in Dublin, *Dundee Courier*, 16 February 1881.

89. Kettle, *Material for Victory*, 45.

90. *Spectator*, 19 February 1881.

91. *Dundee Courier*, 16 February 1881.

## Chapter 4

1. William O'Brien, *The Parnell of Real Life* (London, 1926), 318.
2. F. S. L. Lyons, *John Dillon* (London, 1968), 48.
3. *North Devon Journal*, Editorial, 10 March 1881.
4. 'Parliamentary Notes', *Belfast Newsletter*, 5 March 1881.
5. *Hansard*, 4 March 1881, vol. 259, cols. 335–6.
6. *Liverpool Daily Post*, 5 March 1881.
7. Moody and Hawkins (eds.), *Florence Arnold-Forster's Irish Journal*, 88 (6 March 1881).
8. *Glasgow Evening Citizen*, 18 March 1881.
9. Paul Bew, *Land and the National Question in Ireland, 1858–82* (Dublin, 1978), 156, 173.
10. *The Times*, 18 April 1881.
11. *United Irishman*, 11 April 1848.
12. Conor Cruise O'Brien, *Parnell and his Party* (Oxford, 1957), 66.
13. *Hansard*, 2 May 1881, vol. 260, col. 153.
14. *Derry Journal*, 4 May 1881.
15. *Weekly Freeman's Journal*, 7 May 1881.
16. *Northern Whig*, 15 February 1881.
17. Moody and Hawkins (eds.), *Florence Arnold-Forster's Irish Journal*, 127.
18. This *Express* report is reprinted in the *Irishman*, 7 May 1881.
19. Moody and Hawkins (eds.), *Florence Arnold-Forster's Irish Journal*, 132.
20. *Hansard*, 10 May 1881, vol. 261, col. 163.
21. Michael Davitt, *Full of Feudalism* (New York, 1904), 318.
22. *Derry Journal*, 4 May 1881.
23. See the vivid recall of Anna Parnell which rather stressed the way in which the male leaders of the League pressed her into the role. *Freeman's Journal*, 16 October 1906.
24. *Leeds Mercury*, 11 March 1881.
25. *Irishman*, 2 April 1881.
26. *Belfast Morning News*, 16 May 1891.
27. *Dublin Daily Express*, 20 June 1881.
28. *Nation*, 23 June 1881.
29. *Nation*, 28 May 1881; Donald Jordan, *Land and Popular Politics in Ireland: County Mayo from the Plantation to the Land War* (Cambridge, 1994), 302–3.
30. *Wexford People*, 25 June 1881.
31. *Dublin Daily Express*, 20 June 1881.
32. Jane McL. Côté, *Fanny and Anna Parnell: Ireland's Patriot Sister* (Dublin, 1991), 181.
33. See Paul Bew, *Land and the National Question in Ireland, 1858–82* (Dublin, 1978).
34. William O'Brien, *Recollections* (London, 1905), 304–5.
35. William O'Brien, *The Parnell of Real Life* (London, 1926), 71–2.
36. O'Brien, *Recollections*, 305.

37. Moody and Hawkins (eds.), *Florence Arnold-Forster's Irish Journal*, 202 (8 August 1881).
38. Lyons, *John Dillon*, 55.
39. O'Brien, *Parnell and his Party*, 5.
40. Moody and Hawkins (eds.), *Florence Arnold-Forster's Irish Journal*, 231.
41. *Freeman's Journal*, 20 August 1881.
42. *The Times*, 4 August 1881.
43. 'Mr John Dillon on the Land Act', *Derry Journal*, 31 August 1881.
44. *Shields Daily News*, 1 September 1881.
45. O'Brien, *The Parnell of Real Life*, 15.
46. O'Brien, *Recollections*, 330–1.
47. *Munster Express*, 8 October 1881.
48. *The Flag of Ireland*, 16 August 1881.
49. Moody and Hawkins (eds.), *Florence Arnold-Forster's Irish Journal*, 215 (19 September 1881).
50. *Freeman's Journal*, 4 October 1881.
51. *Freeman's Journal*, 5 October 1881.
52. William O'Connor Morris, *Present Irish Questions* (London, 1901), 351.
53. *Freeman's Journal*, 6 October 1881.
54. Morris, *Present Irish Questions*, 174.
55. Harold Spender, *Home Rule* (London, 1912), 30.
56. Irish Loyal and Patriotic Union, *The Work of the Irish Land Commission*, Third Series Leaflet
57. *The Times*, 14 October 1881.
58. Moody and Hawkins (eds.), *Florence Arnold-Forster's Irish Journal*, 273 (14 October 1881).
59. Katherine O'Shea, *Charles Stewart Parnell* (London, 1914), i. 207.
60. Ibid. 236.
61. James Bryce, *Studies in Contemporary Biography* (London, 1903), 239.
62. Michael Davitt, *Fall of Feudalism* (London, 1904), 481.
63. Paul Bew, *Ireland: The Politics of Enmity 1789–2006* (Oxford, 2009), 356.
64. *Hansard*, 18 April 1887, vol. 313, col. 1228.
65. Lyons, *John Dillon*, 60.
66. O'Brien, *The Parnell of Real Life*, 34.
67. *Freeman's Journal*, 18 October 1881.
68. O'Brien, *The Parnell of Real Life*, 35.
69. Dana Hearne (ed.), *Anna Parnell, The Tale of a Great Sham* (Dublin, 2020), 104.
70. *Sheffield Daily Telegraph*, 31 October 1881.
71. *Tablet*, 10 December 1881.
72. *The Times*, 10 January 1881.
73. 'Peasant Proprietorship in Ireland', *The Times*, 6 February 1882.
74. Burns Library, Boston College, Patrick Collins, Land League collection, Box 1/23.

75. *Flag of Ireland*, 11 February 1882.
76. Moody and Hawkins (eds.), *Florence Arnold-Forster's Irish Journal*, 370 (9 February).
77. J. L. Hammond, *Gladstone and the Irish Nation* (London, 1938), 254–5.
78. Moody and Hawkins (eds.), *Florence Arnold-Forster's Irish Journal*, 378.
79. This information is derived from the report of the later legal case taken by some of the tenants against the Land League solicitor.
80. *Freeman's Journal*, 1 February 1884, for a review of the Murroe conflict.
81. Hearne (ed.), *Anna Parnell*, 144.
82. H. C. G. Matthew (ed.), *The Gladstone Diaries*, vol. x (Oxford, 1990), 226.
83. A. B. Cooke and J. R. Vincent (eds.), 'Herbert Gladstone, Forster and Ireland 1881/2', *Irish Historical Studies*, xvii, no. 68–69 (March 1972), 230.
84. *Gladstone Diaries*.
85. O'Shea, *Charles Stewart Parnell*, i. 243.
86. *Freeman's Journal*, 25 March 1882.
87. O'Brien, *Parnell and his Party*, 77.
88. *Irish Times*, 22 April 1881.
89. *Herts. and Cambs. Reporter*, 2 November 1888.
90. Myles Dungan, *The Captain and the King: William O'Shea, Parnell and Late Victorian Ireland* (Dublin, 2009), 113.
91. Moody and Hawkins (eds.), *Florence Arnold-Forster's Irish Journal*, 447–8.
92. Carla King, *Michael Davitt after the Land League 1882–1906* (Dublin, 2000), 42.
93. *Reminiscences of John Adye Curran K.C.* (London, 1915), 131.
94. D. B. King, *The Irish Question* (Philadelphia, 1882).
95. *Irishman*, 28 May 1882.
96. This was widely reprinted in the English press: see, for example, *Banbury Advertiser*, 11 May 1882.
97. Shane Kenna, *War in the Shadows: The Irish American Fenians who Bombed Victorian Britain* (Dublin, 2014), 343. In his important recent essay in *Martinalia*, Professor Martin has stressed correctly that the time available for Parnell to have met Sheridan seems very constrained; but this problem would be solved if Sheridan was the 'special correspondent' acting for the *Irish World* to which he was at this point so close.
98. *St James's Gazette*, 24 March 1883.
99. *Economist*, 20 May 1882.
100. Curran, *Reminiscences of John Adye Curran K.C.*, 140.
101. F. H. O'Donnell, *A History of the Irish Parliamentary Party* (London, 1910), i. 488–9.
102. Quoted in Patrick Maume, 'Gerald Penrose Fitzgerald', *Proceedings of the Royal Irish Academy*, vol. 118c (2018), 312.
103. *Hansard*, 24 May 1882, vol. 269, col. 1545.
104. *Hansard*, 24 May 1882, vol. 269, col. 1537.
105. *Hansard*, 7 April 1881, vol. 260, col. 915.

106. An Irish Liberal, *The Speaker's Handbook on the Irish Question* (London, 1893), 161.
107. *Hansard*, 25 May 1882, vol. 269, col. 1623.
108. H. C. G. Matthew (ed.), *The Gladstone Diaries*, vol. x (Oxford, 1990).
109. Ibid.
110. *Hansard*, 25 May 1882, vol. 269, col. 1617.
111. Moody and Hawkins (eds.), *Florence Arnold-Forster's Irish Journal*, 506.
112. J. R. Vincent (ed.), *The Diaries of Edward Henry Stanley 1826–1893: Between 1878 and 1893* (Oxford, 2003), 427 (24 May 1882).
113. *Derby*, 26 May 1882, p. 428.
114. *Manchester Evening News*, 27 May 1882.
115. *Irishman*, 28 May 1882.
116. These two *New York Herald* reports were reprinted in the *Irishman*, 27 May 1882.
117. *Hansard*, 26 May 1882, vol. 269, cols. 1732–53.
118. *Nation*, 17 September 1881.
119. A. L. Thorold, *The Life of Henry Labouchere* (London, 1913), 166.
120. O'Shea, *Charles Stewart Parnell*, ii. 3–5.
121. *Midland Counties Advertiser*, 21 December 1882 for a good resumé of these events in a court hearing.
122. Fergus Campbell, *Land and Revolution: Nationalist Politics in the West of Ireland, 1891–1912* (Oxford, 2005), 77–8.
123. O'Shea, *Charles Stewart Parnell*, ii. 7.
124. D. B. King, *The Irish Question* (London, 1882), 224.

## Chapter 5

1. 'Mr Dillon's Retirement', *Economist*, 30 September 1882.
2. For this speech, see the excellent and original discussion by Alan O'Day, *Charles Stewart Parnell* (Dublin, 2012), 70–1.
3. *Spectator*, 23 December 1882.
4. *Irish Times*, 18 December 1882.
5. Julie Kavanagh, *The Irish Assassins: Conspiracy, Revenge and the Murders that Stunned an Empire* (London, 2021), 229.
6. *Hansard*, 20 February 1883, vol. 276, cols. 419–20.
7. T. P. O'Connor, *Memoirs of an Old Parliamentarian* (London, 1929), 276.
8. *Hansard*, 22 February 1883, vol. 276, col. 622; Shane Kenna, *The Invincibles: The Phoenix Park Assassinations and the Conspiracy that Shook an Empire* (Dublin, 2019), 148–9.
9. Tom Corfe, *The Phoenix Park Murders: Conflict, Compromise and Tragedy in Ireland 1879–1882* (London, 1968), 252.
10. *Freeman's Journal*, 6 March 1883.
11. *Mr Parnell's Position*, 15 December 1883.
12. Mark Tierney, *Croke of Cashel: The Life of Archbishop Thomas William Croke, 1832–1902* (Dublin, 1976), 144–9; *Dublin Weekly Nation*, 26 May 1883.

13. *Freeman's Journal*, 9 April 1883; Donal P. McCracken, *Inspector Mallon: Buying Irish Patriotism for a Five-Pound Note* (Dublin, 2009), 114.

14. *Dundee Courier*, 15 May 1883.

15. James H. Murphy, *Ireland's Czar: Gladstonian Government and the Lord Lieutenant of the Red Earl Spencer, 1868–86* (Dublin, 2014), 231–7.

16. Paul Bew, *Churchill and Ireland* (Oxford, 2016), 23–4.

17. The State Journal of Lincoln Nebraska, *Dublin Daily Express*, 6 July 1885.

18. William O'Brien, *Evening Memories* (Dublin and London, 1920), 406–7.

19. H. C. G. Matthew (ed.), *The Gladstone Diaries*, vol. x (Oxford, 1990), 302; *Irishman*, 27 February 1885.

20. O'Brien, *Evening Memories*, 97.

21. The *Times* review, 22 December 1886. T. P. O'Connor's treatment emphasized family background, physical beauty, and activism: 'The speeches of Mr Dillon are violent in their conclusions only. The propositions which startled or shocked unsympathetic hearers are reached by him through calculations of apparently mathematical frigidity, and are delivered in an unimpassioned monotone' (T. P. O'Connor, *The Parnell Movement* (London, 1886), 193).

22. Tim Healy, *Letters and Leaders of My Day* (London, 1928), i. 230.

23. Stephen Ball (ed.), *Dublin Castle and the First Home Rule Crisis: The Political Journal of Sir George Fottrell* (Cambridge, 2008), 113.

24. *Spectator*, 'The Crisis and Ireland', 20 June 1885.

25. *Spectator*, 25 July 1885.

26. *Spectator*, 1 August 1885.

27. L. P. Curtis, *Coercion and Conciliation in Ireland 1880–1892* (Princeton, 1963), 50; Peter Gordon (ed.), *The Political Diaries of the Fourth Earl of Carnarvon 1857–90*, 1 August 1885, p. 397.

28. See also *Special Commission Act, 1888: Report of the shorthand notes of the speeches, proceedings and evidence taken before the Commissioner appointed*, 12 February 1880, 5.155. Paul Bew, 'The Paradoxes of Parnell', in Joep Leersen (ed.), *Parnell and his Times* (Cambridge, 2020), 43. I am now less sure, as a result of Professor Ged Martin's work, that Parnell's protectionism owed quite as much to traditional Irish social republican thought, but it definitely owed something.

29. *Spectator*, 29 August 1885.

30. Ibid.

31. John Howard Parnell, *Charles Stewart Parnell, A Memoir* (New York, 1914), 282–3.

32. *Irish Weekly Independent*, 4 October 1941, p. 4.

33. Andrew Kettle, *Material for Victory* (Dublin, 1958), 63–4. Michael Davitt, however, felt that Parnell's project was 'absurd'; see the excellent discussion in Carla King, *Michael Davitt after the Land League 1882–1896* (Dublin, 2016), 144.

34. *Aberdeen Free Press*, 'Parnell at Dublin dinner', 25 August 1885. There is no serious evidence to support Parnell's suggestion, *vide* Niall Whelehan,

*The Dynamiters: Irish Nationalism and Political Violence in the Modern World* (Cambridge, 2020).

35. *Economist*, 29 August 1885.
36. *The Times*, 6 December 1885.
37. *St James's Gazette*, 6 October 1885.
38. F. S. L. Lyons, *John Dillon* (London, 1968), 47.
39. *Freeman's Journal*, 12 October 1885.
40. *The Times*, 22 December 1885.
41. 'John Dillon at Roscrea', *Freeman's Journal*, 12 October 1885.
42. Alan O'Day, *Parnell and the First Home Rule Episode* (Dublin, 1986), 109.
43. *Spectator*, 'Mr Parnell's Sermon', 17 October 1885.
44. Ibid.
45. Ibid.
46. J. L. Hammond, *Gladstone and the Irish Nation* (London, 1964 edn.), 28 September letter, pp. 408–9.
47. *St James's Gazette*, 'Childers at Pontefract', 13 October 1885.
48. Stephen Ball (ed.), *Dublin Castle and the First Home Rule Crisis: The Political Journal of Sir George Fottrell 1884–87* (Cambridge, 2008), Diary entry for 19 October 1885, p. 139.
49. *Spectator*, 14 November 1885.
50. A. B. Cooke and J. R. Vincent, *The Governing Passion: Cabinet Government and Party Politics in Britain, 1885–86* (Brighton, 1974), 20.
51. Margaret O'Callaghan, *British High Politics and a Nationalist Ireland: Criminality, Land and the Law Under Forster and Balfour* (Cork, 1994), 95, 102.
52. D. W. R. Bahlman, *The Diary of Sir Edward Walter Hamilton 1886–1906* (Hull, 1993), 31 July 1902, p. 421.
53. *The Times*, 2 January 1886.
54. Document dated 30 October 1885, Alan O'Day, *Irish Home Rule 1867–192* (Manchester, 1998), 317.
55. Parnell to K. O'Shea, 6 January 1886, *BL Gladstone Papers* Add MS 44,629; Parnell to E. D. Gray, 3 January 1886, *NLI* MS 5735.
56. *A Life Spent for Ireland: From the Memoirs of O'Neill Daunt*, edited by his Daughter (London 1896), 395; for O'Neill Daunt's unease about the New Departure, see his correspondence with Mitchell Henry, especially Henry to Daunt, *NLI* MS 11446.
57. *The Times*, 8 April 1886.
58. SPO/CB, Police Reports 1886–1915, no. 4, dated February 1887.
59. Professor Lecky on the 'Two Irelands', *St James's Gazette*, 26 April 1890.
60. *The Times*, 11 December 1885.
61. Tim Healy, *Letters and Leaders of My Day* (London, 1928), i. 234. For Sir Richard Temple's dislike of Blaine, see his *Letters and Characters Sketches from the House of Commons* (London, 1912), 251.

62. Alvin Jackson, 'The Rivals of C. S. Parnell', in Donal McCartney (ed.), *Parnell: The Politics of Power* (Dublin, 1991), 72–90. See also, more broadly, Alvin Jackson, *The Ulster Party: Irish Unionists in the House of Commons 1884–1911* (Oxford, 1989).

63. Mark Bonham Carter, *The Biography of Margot Asquith* (London, 1995), 103.

64. *Sale and Purchase of Land (Ireland) Bill*, p. 3.

65. Ibid. 4.

66. Ibid. 17.

67. Mark Bonham Carter (ed.), *The Autobiography of Margot Asquith* (London, 1991), 101.

68. On this whole topic, see Paul Bew, *Ideology and the Irish Question* (Oxford, 1994), but also, most recently, the excellent treatment in Dermot Meleady, *Redmond: The Parnellite* (Cork, 2008), 228.

69. Wallace's essay is included in a volume of Gladstone essays, Andrew Reid (ed.), *Ireland: A Book of Light on the Irish Problem* (London, 1886).

70. R. Barry O'Brien, *The Life of Charles Stewart Parnell, 1846–1891* (London, 1898), iii. 158.

71. *Wigton Advertiser*, 14 June 1886.

72. *The Times*, 3 July 1886.

73. Herbert Vivian, Recollections of John Dillon, *Truth*, 17 August 1927; Ged Martin, *The Cambridge Union and Ireland 1815–1914* (Edinburgh, 2000), 193–7.

74. *Hansard*, 24 August 1886, vol. 308, cols. 387–404.

75. *Spectator*, 28 August 1886.

## Chapter 6

1. *Hansard*, 20 September 1886, vol. 309, col. 999.

2. *Freeman's Journal*, 1 November 1886.

3. *Weekly Irish Times*, 17 November 1886.

4. Stephen Ball (ed.), *Dublin Castle and the First Home Rule Crisis: The Political Journal of Sir George Fottrell 1884–87* (Cambridge, 2008), 187–92.

5. William O'Brien, *Evening Memories* (Dublin and London, 1920), 164.

6. William O'Brien, *An Olive Branch in Ireland, and Its History* (Dublin, 1910), 300.

7. F. S. L. Lyons, *John Dillon* (London, 1968), 86–7. *Westminster Gazette*, 10 December 1913.

8. *Hansard*, 20 June 1893, vol. 13, col. 1510.

9. The Government of Ireland Bill Part 1, Section 21. Appendix 1 in Alan O'Day, *Parnell and the First Home Rule Episode* (Dublin, 1986), 244.

10. *Ulster As It Is* (London, 1893), ii. 181. But it is worth pointing out that Spencer in December 1886, as recorded by Labouchere, was visibly relaxed about Dillon's activism. H. W. Lucy, *Sixty Years in the Wilderness* (1912), 83.

11. O'Brien, *Evening Memories*, 178.

12. 'The Political Effects of Mr Dillon', *Irish Weekly Nation*, 18 December 1896.

13. *Freeman's Journal*, 21 February and 6 March 1882; Paul Bew, *Land and the National Question in Ireland, 1858–82* (Dublin, 1978), 199. This gives a complex picture of a failure which cannot be placed solely at Dillon's door.
14. O'Brien, *Evening Memories*, 182.
15. Andrew Kettle, *Material for Victory* (Dublin, 1958), 68.
16. O'Brien, *Evening Memories*, 181.
17. H. C. G. Matthew (ed.), *The Gladstone Diaries*, vol. xi (Oxford, 1990), 456.
18. Ibid. 452.
19. Brendan Ó Cathaoir (ed.), *The Diary of Elizabeth Dillon* (Dublin, 2019), 300 (23 December 1887).
20. Matthew (ed.), *The Gladstone Diaries*, xi. 638.
21. F. S. L. Lyons, *John Dillon* (London 1968), 189–90.
22. Brian Casey, *Class and Community in Provincial Ireland 1851–1914* (London, 2018), 200.
23. L. P. Curtis, *The Depiction of Eviction in Ireland 1845–1910* (Dublin, 2011), 137; A. Kerrin and B. Roche, *No Ornamental Member: A Life in Politics, John Roche M.P. 1848–1914* (London, 2017).
24. O'Brien, *An Olive Branch in Ireland*, 345.
25. *Dictionary of Irish Biography* entry by C. J. Woods.
26. L. M. Geary, *The Plan of Campaign* (Cork, 1986), 141.
27. Terence Dooley, *The Decline of the Big House in Ireland: A Study of Irish Landed Families 1860–1960* (Dublin, 2001), 94.
28. 'The Political Effect of John Dillon', *Economist*, 18 December 1886.
29. ILPV, The Recess Series 1887/8, '*Coercion' plus Lying: or, the Plan, the Parnellites and the Policy of Pecksniff*, 162 (January 1888).
30. *Freeman's Journal*, 14 December 1886.
31. *Evening Standard*, 16 December 1886.
32. *Pall Mall Gazette*, 2 November 1886.
33. Dillon, *Freeman's Journal*, 24 January 1887; Daire Hogan and Patrick Maume (eds.), *The Reminiscences of Ignatius O'Brien, Lord Chancellor of Ireland 1913–18* (Dublin, 2021), 167–8.
34. Marie-Louise Legg (ed.), *Alfred Webb: Autobiography of a Quaker Nationalist* (Cork, 1999), 50.
35. Ibid. 2.
36. Conor Cruise O'Brien, *Parnell and his Party* (Oxford, 1957), 251.
37. Richard Temple, *Letters and Character Sketches from the House of Commons* (London, 1912), 227.
38. *Nation*, 23 April 1887.
39. Sir Edward Russell, *That Reminds Me* (London, 1899).
40. *Hansard*, 18 April 1887, vol. 313, col. 1227.
41. *Hansard*, 18 April 1887, vol. 313, col. 1193.
42. *The Times*, 3 May 1887, Report dated 2 May, Dublin.
43. *A History of the Irish Parliamentary Party* (London, 1910), ii. 283.

44. *Hansard*, 8 April 1886, vol. 304, col. 1115.

45. *Hansard*, 22 April 1887, vol. 313, cols. 1634, 1641.

46. *The Times*, 21 May 1887.

47. *The Times*, 21 May 1887; *Irish World*, 3 March 1883, 13 October 1883.

48. Richard Temple, *Letters and Character Sketches from the House of Commons* (London, 1912), 315.

49. Margaret O'Callaghan, *British High Politics and a Nationalist Ireland: Criminality, Land and the Law under Forster and Balfour* (Cork, 1994), 119.

50. For an excellent assessment of the context, see Carla King, *Michael Davitt: After the Land League* (Dublin, 2016), 204–7.

51. T. W. Moody, *Davitt and Irish Revolution* (Oxford, 1981), 547; L. M. Geary, *The Plan of Campaign* (Cork, 1986), 73–5. Neither Moody nor Geary in their excellent accounts mention this phrase which appeared in *The Times*.

52. *The Scotsman*, 6 June 1887.

53. Sir Edward Russell, *That Reminds Me* (London, 1899), 323.

54. *Hansard*, 14 July 1887, vol. 317, col. 875.

# Chapter 7

1. *Spectator*, 10 September 1887.

2. *Bristol Mercury*, 15 September 1887; *Yorkshire Post*, 8 September 1887.

3. *Leinster Leader*, 17 September 1887.

4. F. S. L. Lyons, *John Dillon* (London, 1968), 89.

5. *Diaries*, 16 September 1887, p. 285.

6. *Hansard*, 13 September 1887, vol. 321, col. 530; *Spectator*, 17 September 1887.

7. *Dublin Daily Express*, 29 October 1887.

8. 'Boycotting at Mitchelstown', *The Times*, 1 October 1887.

9. Brendan Ó Cathaoir (ed.), *The Diary of Elizabeth Dillon* (Dublin, 2019), 321 (7 January 1888).

10. Quoted in *Freeman's Journal*, 18 January 1889.

11. Ibid.

12. *Ulster Examiner*, 2 February 1876.

13. *Hansard*, 15 February 1888, vol. 322, col. 351.

14. John Howard Parnell, *Charles Stewart Parnell, A Memoir* (New York, 1914), 219.

15. Ó Cathaoir (ed.), *The Diary of Elizabeth Dillon*, 317 (11 May 1888).

16. William O'Brien, *An Olive Branch in Ireland, and Its History* (Dublin, 1910), 356.

17. Andrew Kettle, *Material for Victory* (Dublin, 1958), 75.

18. Katharine O'Shea, *Charles Stewart Parnell* (London, 1914), ii. 43.

19. *Wexford People*, 29 December 1888.

20. *Cardiff Times*, 30 June 1888.

21. *Pall Mall Gazette*, 31 July 1888.

22. *Cardiff Times*, 4 August 1888.

23. *South Wales Daily News*, 28 July 1888.

24. *Weekly Freeman's Journal*, 28 July 1888.
25. William Dillon, *Life of John Mitchel* (London, 1888), pp. xiii, xiv; *St James's Gazette*, 14 June 1888; *Pall Mall Gazette*, 31 August 1888.
26. Preface, p. ix.
27. Margaret Frances Sullivan, *Ireland of Today: The Causes and Aims of Irish Agitation* (Philadelphia, 1881), 431.
28. *St James's Gazette*, 14 June 1888.
29. *Dublin Daily Express*, 16 June 1888.
30. *Pall Mall Gazette*, 31 August 1888.
31. Lyons, *John Dillon*, 92.
32. R. Haines, *Charles Trevelyan and the Great Irish Famine* (Dublin, 2004), 213, 438.
33. There was also, of course, a Unionist variant. *Vide* Isabella M. Tod, 'Some Historical Fallacies', *The Liberal Unionist*, August 1888.
34. H. C. G. Matthew (ed.), *The Gladstone Diaries*, vol. xii (Oxford, 1994), 4 July 1888, p. 130. For an early and impressive analysis of this facet of Gladstone's thinking, see James Loughlin, *Gladstone: Home Rule and the Ulster Question 1882–1893* (Dublin, 1986), 177.
35. Significantly, J. L. Hammond's massive tome, *Gladstone and the Irish Nation* (London, 1938), does not mention Mitchel.
36. D. W. R. Bahlman (ed.), *Diary of Sir E. W. Hamilton, 1885–1906* (Hull, 1993), 7 October 1894, p. 275.
37. W. J. O'Neill Daunt, *A Life Spent for Ireland* (London, 1896), 4 January 1888 diary entry, pp. 107–8.
38. *Economist*, 18 August 1888.
39. *Personal Recollections of an Irish National Journalist* (Dublin, 1883), 349.
40. *St James's Gazette*, 26 October 1888.
41. Myles Dungan, *The Captain and the King: William O'Shea, Parnell and Late Victorian Ireland* (Dublin, 2009), 320–1.
42. *Birmingham Evening News*, 26 November 1888.
43. *St James's Gazette*, 7 December 1888.
44. *Oxford Journal*, 3 December 1887.
45. 'The Liberal Party and Mr Dillon', *Freeman's Journal*, 7 December 1888.
46. Ibid.
47. 'The *Times* and P. J. Sheridan', *The Times*, 29 December 1888.
48. *Freeman's Journal*, 14 January 1887.
49. Spectator, *Mr Gladstone's Latest Speech*, 26 September 1889.
50. F. H. O'Donnell, *A History of the Irish Parliamentary Party* (London, 1910), ii. 469.
51. *Pall Mall Gazette*, 14 March 1889.
52. Eugenio F. Biagini, *British Democracy and Irish Nationalism 1876–1906* (Cambridge, 2007), 377.
53. *Spectator*, 26 September 1889.
54. R. C. K. Ensor, 'Some Political and Economic Interactions in Late Victorian England', *Transactions of the Royal Historical Society*, xxxvi (1949).

55. The *locus classicus* for the argument which sees the Irish question primarily as an issue for the elite is James Cornford, 'The Transformation of Conservatism in the Late Nineteenth Century', *Victorian Studies* (1963), 35–66.

56. John D. Fair, 'From Liberal to Conservative: The Flight of the Liberal Unionists after 1886', *Victorian Studies*, vol. 29, no. 2 (Winter 1986), 291–314; and brilliantly, Jonathan Parry, *The Rise and Fall of Liberal Government in Victorian Britain* (New Haven, 1993), 305.

57. As Professor Biagini has brilliantly demonstrated.

58. G. M. Young, *Victorian England: Portrait of an Age* (Oxford, 1936), 137.

59. *The Times*, 23 December 1890, Gladstonianism and Parnell.

60. *Willesden Chronicle*, 24 May 1889.

61. *St James's Gazette*, 19 December 1889.

62. Ibid.

63. Sir Edward Russell, *That Reminds Me* (London, 1899), 115.

64. O'Shea, *Charles Stewart Parnell*, ii. 43.

65. *Hansard*, 14 February 1890, vol. 341, col. 324.

66. *Hansard*, 21 April 1890, vol. 343, col. 983.

67. *Hansard*, 21 April 1890, vol. 343, col. 985.

68. Dillon, *Hansard*, 24 April 1890, vol. 343, col. 1365.

69. *St James's Gazette*, 19 March 1890.

70. F. S. L. Lyons, 'John Dillon and the Plan of Campaign 1886–1890', *Irish Historical Studies*, vol. xiv, no. 56 (September 1965), 342.

71. O'Shea, *Charles Stewart Parnell*, ii. 171.

72. T. D. Sullivan, *Recollections of Troubled Times in Irish Politics* (Dublin, 1905), 281.

73. Michael MacDonagh, *The Life of William O'Brien, the Irish Nationalist* (London 1928), 138–9. Frank Callanan has provided the best account of this moment, *The Parnell Split 1890–1* (Cork, 1992), ch. 6.

74. Dermot Meleady (ed.), *John Redmond: Selected Letters and Memoranda 1880–1918* (Dublin, 2018), February 1891, p. 28.

75. Jane Jordan, *Kitty O'Shea: An Irish Affair* (London, 2005), 191.

76. *Cork Daily Herald*, 20 April 1891.

77. *Hansard*, 7 May 1891, vol. 353, cols. 330–2.

78. Donald Jordan, *Land and Popular Politics in Ireland: County Mayo from the Plantation to the Land War* (Cambridge, 1994), 268; *Connaught Telegraph*, 9 May 1891.

79. *Hansard*, 21 May 1891, vol. 353, col. 828.

80. Tim Healy, *Letters and Leaders of My Day* (London, 1928), ii, 1 June 1891, p. 361.

81. *Londonderry Sentinel*, 26 May 1891.

82. *Sunderland Daily Echo*, 23 May 1891.

83. *Northern Whig*, 24 May 1891.

84. Michael Foley, 'Riddle Unwrapped', *Sunday Times*, 13 November 2011.

85. *Northern Whig*, 21 January 1925.

86. Bernard Alderson, *Arthur James Balfour: The Man and his Work* (London, 1903), 85.
87. Ibid. 84–5.
88. Tony Varley, 'Gaining Ground, Losing Ground: The Politics of Land Reform in Twentieth-Century Ireland', in Fergus Campbell and Tony Varley (eds.), *Land Questions in Modern Ireland* (Manchester, 2013), 30; K. Theodore Hoppen, *Governing Hibernia: British Politicians and Ireland 1800–1921* (Oxford, 2016), 'Doing it on the cheap: Liberals', ch. 8; 'Throwing money about: Conservatives', ch. 9.
89. *Londonderry Sentinel*, 26 May 1891.
90. Jenny Wyse Power (ed.), *Words of the Dead Chief* (Dublin, 2009), 163–4. Edited by Donal McCartney and Pauric Travers.
91. *St James's Gazette*, 13 August 1883.
92. *The Times*, 18 October 1891.
93. *New Ross Standard*, 20 December 1890.
94. 'The Land War', *Irish Times*, 12 May 1979.
95. As noted above, Professor Martin has forcefully made this point in recent years.
96. Henry William Lucy, *Sixty Years in the Wilderness, More Passages by the Way* (London, 1912), 316.
97. Ibid. 316–17.
98. Ibid. 317.
99. 'Parnell at Arklow', *Freeman's Journal*, 28 January 1891; Roy Foster has rightly noted: 'His industries, for instance, took up more of his time (and his money) than has been recognised, especially in the later years of his life' (*Charles Stewart Parnell: The Man and his Family* (Hassocks, 1977), 308).

## Chapter 8

1. National Archives, 30/60/13/2/70987. This document was sent by the spymaster Nicholas Gosselin to Arthur Balfour, 5 February 1890.
2. John Devoy to John Dillon, 30 August 1891, *Devoy's Post Bag*, vol. 2, p. 325.
3. Ibid. 328.
4. *The Parnellite*, 18 February 1895.
5. *Hansard*, 10 April 1893, vol. 10, col. 1853.
6. *Hansard*, 10 April 1893, vol. 10, col. 1855.
7. H. C. G. Matthew (ed.), *The Gladstone Diaries*, vol. x (Oxford, 1990), 134.
8. *Hansard*, 10 April 1893, vol. 10, col. 1857.
9. J. L. Garvin, *The Life of Joseph Chamberlain* (London, 1933), ii. 561.
10. Dermot Meleady, *John Redmond: The Parnellite* (Cork, 2008), 224.
11. *Hansard*, 20 June 1893, vol. 13, cols. 1511–12.
12. Garvin, *The Life of Joseph Chamberlain*, ii. 568 (3 July 1893).

13. *Hansard*, 4 July 1893, vol. 14, col. 514.
14. *Aberdeen Press and Journal*, 21 September 1893.
15. *Dublin Weekly Nation*, 22 August 1896; *Pall Mall Gazette*, 2 September 1896.
16. 'Common Sense in Ireland', *Spectator*, 16 October 1897.
17. *Freeman's Journal*, 19 March 1894; see Dillon's speeches in Edinburgh and Coatbridge.
18. *Hansard*, 16 February 1899, vol. 60, cols. 178–239.
19. *Irish News*, 4 October 1900.
20. Colin Reid, *The Lost Ireland of Stephen Gwynn: Irish Constitutional Nationalism and Cultural Politics, 1864–1950* (Manchester, 2011), 74–5.
21. Fergus Campbell, *Land and Revolution: Nationalist Politics in the West of Ireland 1891–1921* (Oxford, 2005), 76.
22. Paul Bew, *Conflict and Conciliation in Ireland: Parnellites and Radical Agrarians, 1890–1910* (Oxford, 1987), ch. 4.
23. Trinity College Dublin, Dillon papers, 6729/96, Devlin to Dillon, 7 September 1903; John Roche to Dillon, 19 October 1903.
24. William O'Brien, *Recollections* (London, 1905), 334.
25. L. P. Curtis, *The Depiction of Eviction in Ireland 1845–1910* (Dublin, 2011), 89.
26. This is the (correct) thesis of Fergus Campbell, *Land and Revolution: Nationalist Politics in the West of Ireland* (Oxford, 2005), 89–90.
27. Bew, *Conflict and Conciliation in Ireland*, ch. 5.
28. William Dillon to John Devoy, 28 September 1927, *Devoy's Post Bag*, vol. 2, p. 549.
29. Philip Bull, 'Writing about Irish Land against the Background of Northern Ireland', in Fergus Campbell and Tony Varley (eds.), *Land Questions in Modern Ireland* (Manchester, 2013), 85.
30. *Derry Journal*, 22 January 1934.
31. Ibid.
32. William O'Connor Morris, *Present Irish Questions* (London, 1901). 368; *Freeman's Journal*, 13 April 1901.
33. *Morning Post*, 'Education in Ireland', 14 January 1905.
34. Monica Taylor, *Sir Bertram Windle: A Memoir* (London, 1932), 194.
35. The increasingly relaxed nature of the Birrell/Dillon correspondence is worthy of a note: see TCD Dillon Papers, 679/168/171.
36. John Campbell, *Haldane: The Forgotten Statesman who Shaped Britain and Canada* (London, 2020), 213.
37. Augustine Birrell, *Things Past Redress* (London, 1937), 202.
38. *Observer*, 8 July 1919.
39. Paul Bew, *Ideology and the Irish Question: Ulster Unionism and Irish Nationalism, 1912–1916* (Oxford, 1994), 42.
40. Alan O'Day, *Irish Home Rule* (Manchester, 1998), 227.
41. *Hansard*, 11 May 1908, vol. 188, col. 745.
42. *Hansard*, 11 May 1908, vol. 188, col. 847.

43. S. Gwynn, *Ireland* (London, 1924), 144; Bew, *Ideology and the Irish Question*, 85–90.
44. J. P. Boland, *An Irishman's Day* (London, 1940), 133–4.
45. *Irish Times*, 14 December 1903.
46. *Spectator*, 24 April 1909.
47. Trinity College Dublin, Dillon MS 6748/24, Redmond to Dillon, 4 March 1908.
48. *Irish Independent*, 12 February 1909.
49. *Strabane Weekly News*, 29 September 1910.
50. *Spectator*, 26 November 1912.
51. *Weekly Freeman's Journal*, 18 May 1912.
52. *Hansard*, 9 June 1913, vol. 53, col. 1365.
53. *Hansard*, 7 July 1913, vol. 55, cols. 155–6.
54. Jane Marsland (introd.), *Lovat Fraser's Tour of Ireland* (Belfast, 1992).
55. I have used this particular example of O'Brienite conciliation—there could have been others—because it is the example drawn to my attention by Captain Sheehan's family in the early 1980s.
56. Tim Healy, *Letters and Leaders of My Day* (London, 1928), 538 (11 February 1914, Tim to Maurice Healy).
57. Ibid. 538 (13 February 1914).
58. *Hansard*, 19 March 1914, col. 864.
59. *Hansard*, 19 March 1914, col. 865.
60. Paul Bew, 'Edward Carson and the Principle of Consent', Leinster House lecture, 29 May 2019, as part of the Dail 100 series.
61. BNL, 12 June 1911.
62. B. B. Gilbert, *David Lloyd George: A Political Life—Organiser of Victory* (London, 1992), 105–6.
63. *Freeman's* Journal, 26 October 1914; Pat Walsh, *The Rise and Fall of Imperial Ireland* (Belfast, 2003), 447.
64. *Coatbridge Leader*, 24 April 1915. It should be noted Dillon was the great critic of British behaviour in the Boer war. *Vide Hansard*, 25 February 1901, cols. 1154–9.
65. Pat Walsh, *The Rise and Fall of Imperial Ireland* (Belfast, 2003); *Freeman's Journal*, 20 October 1914.
66. Belfast speech, 25 October 1914.
67. James McConnell, *The Irish Parliamentary Party and the Third Home Rule Crisis* (Dublin, 2013), 115.
68. 'Recollections of John Dillon', *Truth*, 17 August 1927.
69. W. B. Wells, *John Redmond: A Biography* (London, 1919), 173.
70. Keith Jeffrey (ed.), *Irish Experiences in War* (Dublin, 1999), 111.
71. Dermot Meleady, *Selected Letters and Memoranda, 1880–1918* (Dublin, 2018), 232.
72. Lennox Robinson (ed.), *Lady Gregory's Journals 1916–30* (London, 1946), 171.

73. *The Sphere*, 8 December 1928, pointed out that Healy failed to mention Joffre, Haig, or Hindenberg.

74. Frank Callanan, *T. M. Healy* (Cork, 1997), 515.

75. Oonagh Walsh (ed.), *An Englishwoman in Belfast: Rosamund Stephen's Record of the Great War* (Cork, 2000), 49.

76. W. B. Wells, *Irish Indiscretions* (London, 1922), 40.

77. Lennox Robinson (ed.), *Lady Gregory's Journals 1916–30* (London, 1946), 171.

78. House of Lords Archives, LG D/14/3/2, Note of message from Dillon to Lloyd George, 6 June 1916.

79. Charles Townshend, *The Partition: Ireland Divided 1885–1925* (London, 2021), 102–3. See also Conor Mulvagh, 'Ulster Exclusion and Irish Nationalism: Consenting to the Principle of Partition', *Revue Française de Civilisation Britannique*, vol. xxiv: 2/2019.

80. *Galway Express*, 31 October 1918.

81. *Irish Independent*, 10 February 1917.

82. Margaret Baguley (ed.), *World War I and the Question of Ulster* (Dublin, 2009), Wilfred to Lilian Spender, 24 March 1917, p. 208.

83. Robert C. Self (ed.), *The Austen Chamberlain Diary Letters* (Cambridge, 1995), 92.

84. J. Anthony Gaughan, *Memories of Senator Joseph Connolly* (Dublin, 1996), 146.

85. *Daily Mirror*, 25 September 1918.

86. Ian Colvin, *The Life of Lord Carson* (London, 1936), iii. 365–6.

87. *Weekly Freeman*, 3 November 1918.

88. John Dillon, *Weekly Freeman*, 14 December 1918.

89. Elaine Callinan, *Electioneering and Propaganda in Ireland 1917–1921* (Dublin, 2020), 190.

90. Wells, *Irish Indiscretions*, 38.

## Conclusion

1. Moody and Hawkins (eds.), *Florence Arnold-Forster's Irish Journal*, 80.

2. William O'Brien, *Recollections* (London, 1905), 248,

3. *Spectator*, 'The Dillon case', 18 September 1886.

4. *Hansard*, 5 May 1887, vol. 314, col. 1034.

5. Tim Healy, *Letters and Leaders of My Day* (London, 1928), i. 230.

6. Justin McCarthy, *Hansard*, 23 February 1883, vol. 276, col. 778.

7. *The Speaker*, 25 March 1893.

8. Marie-Louise Legg (ed.), *Alfred Webb: The Autobiography of a Quaker Nationalist* (Cork, 1999), 57.

9. *Leeds Mercury*, 30 March 1893.

10. *Spectator*, 20 May 1916.

11. F. W. H. Myers, *Essays: Modern* (London, 1883). For Myers, Mazzini was a scourge of assassins (p. 41) and decidedly not a violent revolutionary.

12. *The Times*, 16 December 1886, 'Mazzini and Mr. Dillon'.

13. *Pall Mall Budget 1886*, vol. 34, p. 3.
14. Brendan Ó Cathaoir (ed.), *The Diary of Elizabeth Dillon* (Dublin, 2018), 254 (4 March 1889).
15. Dennis Mack Smith, *Mazzini* (New Haven and London, 1994), 190.
16. Douglas Hyde, *The Revival of Irish Literature and other Addresses* (London, 1894), 80.
17. Nicholas Mansergh, *The Irish Question* (London, 1965), 55–60.
18. Patrick Maume (ed.), *The Philosophy of Irish Ireland* (Dublin, 2006), 96.
19. *Hansard*, 20 April 1893, vol. 11, col. 804.
20. Paolo Gerbaudo, *The Great Recoil: Politics after Populism and Pandemic* (London, 2021), 233.
21. This is the essential point of Mansergh's *The Irish Question*, 55–9.
22. *The Times*, 27 February 1888.
23. Robert Anderson, *Sidelights on the Home Rule Movement* (London, 1906), 199.
24. *Sligo Champion*, 29 June 1912.
25. Emily Lawless, *Ireland*, 3rd edn. (New York, 1923), 472.
26. R. A. Bermann, *Ireland 1913* (Cork 2021), 169.
27. Lennox Robinson (ed.), *Lady Gregory's Journal* (Dublin, 1946), 169–70 (2 April 1922).
28. Ibid. 170. Except for the point on Craig, this analysis is confirmed in Brian Feeney's book, *Antrim: The Irish Revolution 1912–23* (Dublin, 2021), 124–9.
29. *Sligo Independent*, 17 March 1923.
30. *Derry Journal*, 5 August 1927.
31. F. S. L. Lyons, *John Dillon* (London 1968), 477–8; Martin O'Donoghue, *The Legacy of the Irish Parliamentary Party in Independent Ireland 1922–49* (Liverpool, 2019), 65. See also Dillon's similar comments in letters to his brilliant academic son: J. Fischer and J. Dillon (eds.), *The Correspondence of Myles Dillon 1922–5* (Dublin, 1999), 157, 220.
32. *Roscommon Messenger*, 13 August 1927.
33. *Spectator*, 24 November 1917.
34. Trevor West, *Horace Plunkett, Cooperation and Politics* (Dublin, 1986), 78–85.
35. Dillon MS, TCD Library, 6798/49, Plunkett to Dillon, 21 January 1925.
36. Patrick Maume, *The Long Gestation: Irish Nationalist Life 1891–1918* (Dublin, 1999), 226.
37. *Dublin Daily Express*, 18 July 1894.
38. See, for example, *Buckingham Express*, 18 July 1894; *Yorkshire Evening Post*, 23 September 1898; *St James's Gazette*, 23 October 1901; *Shields Daily News*, 28 February 1903; *Belfast Weekly News*, 9 January 1913; *Ottawa Free Press*, 21 December 1912.
39. Quoted in *Dublin Daily Express*, 18 July 1894.
40. *Larne Times*, 13 March 1915.
41. *Belfast Newsletter*, 28 March 1931.
42. Simon Heffner, *The Age of Decadence: Britain 1880–1914* (London, 2017), 263.

43. W. B. Wells, *Irish Indiscretions* (London, 1918), 177–8.
44. William O'Malley, 'John Dillon', *Roscommon Messenger*, 13 August 1927.
45. *Westminster Gazette*, 5 August 1927.
46. Alexander Zevin, *Liberation at Large: The World According to the Economist* (London, 2019), 163.
47. Michael Freeden, *Liberalism Divided: A Study in British Political Thought 1914–39* (Oxford, 1986), 259.
48. *Irish Society*, 22 April 1923.
49. Michael MacDonagh, *The Life of William O'Brien, The Irish Nationalist: A Biographical Study of Irish Nationalism—Constitutional and Revolutionary* (London, 1928), 165.
50. James Doherty, *Irish Liberty, British Democracy: The Third Home Rule Crisis* (Cork, 2019), 44. See also Martin O'Donoghue, 'Faith and Fatherland? The Ancient Order of Hibernians, Northern Nationalism and the Partition of Ireland', *Irish Historical Studies*, xlvi, no. 169 (2022), 76–100.

# BIBLIOGRAPHY

Anderson, Robert, *Sidelights on the Home Rule Movement* (London, 1906).

Bahlman, D. W. R. (ed.), *Diary of Sir E. W. Hamilton, 1880–5* (2 vols., Oxford, 1992).

Bahlman, D. W. R. (ed.), *Diary of Sir E. W. Hamilton, 1885–1906* (Hull, 1993).

Ball, Stephen (ed.), *Dublin Castle and the First Home Rule Crisis: The Political Journal of Sir George Fottrell, 1884–1887* (Cambridge, 2008).

Bermann, R. H., *Ireland 1913* (Cork, 2021).

Bew, Paul, *Land and the National Question in Ireland, 1858–82* (Dublin, 1978).

Bew, Paul, *Conflict and Conciliation in Ireland: Parnellites and Radical Agrarians, 1890–1910* (Oxford, 1987).

Bew, Paul, *Ideology and the Irish Question* (Oxford, 1994).

Bew, Paul, '"A Vision to the Dispossessed"? Popular Piety and Revolutionary Politics in the Irish Land War, 1879–82', in Judith Devlin and Ronan Fanning (eds.), *Religion and Rebellion* (Dublin, 1997).

Bew, Paul, *Ireland: The Politics of Enmity, 1789–2006* (Oxford, 2007).

Bew, Paul, *Enigma: A New Life of Charles Stewart Parnell* (Dublin, 2012).

Bew, Paul, 'The Paradoxes of Parnell', in Joep Leersen (ed.), *Parnell and his Times* (Cambridge, 2020).

Bew, Paul and Maume, Patrick, 'Michael Davitt and the Personality of the Irish Agrarian Revolution', in Fintan Lane and Andrew Newby (eds.), *Michael Davitt: New Perspectives* (Dublin, 2009).

Biagini, Eugenio, *British Democracy and Irish Nationalism, 1876–1906* (Cambridge, 2007).

Blunt, Wilfrid Scawen, *The Land War in Ireland* (London, 1912).

Bogdanor, Vernon, *The Strange Survival of Liberal Britain: Politics and Power before the First World War* (London, 2022).

Bonham Carter, Mark (ed.), *The Autobiography of Margot Asquith* (London, 1995).

Bourke, Richard and Gallagher, Niamh, *The Political Thought of the Irish Revolution* (Cambridge, 2022).

Boyce, D. G. and O'Day, Alan (eds.), *Parnell in Perspective* (London, 1991).

Boyce, D. G. and O'Day, Alan (eds.), *Gladstone and Ireland: Politics, Religion and Nationality in the Victorian Age* (London, 2010).

Brady, Ciaran, *James Anthony Froude: An Intellectual Biography of a Victorian Prophet* (Oxford, 2013).

Bryce, J. V., *Studies in Contemporary Biography* (London, 1903).

Bull, Philip, 'Writing about Irish Land against the Background of Northern Ireland', in Fergus Campbell and Tony Varley (eds.), *Land Questions in Modern Ireland* (Manchester, 2013).

Burke, John, *Athlone in the Victorian Era* (Athlone, 2007).

Burrow, J. A., *A Liberal Descent: Victorian Historians and the English Past* (Cambridge, 1981).

Callanan, Frank, *The Parnell Split, 1890–1891* (Cork, 1992).

Callanan, Frank, *Tim Healy* (Cork, 1996).

Callanan, Frank (ed.), 'Charles Stewart Parnell', in *Dictionary of Irish Biography* (9 vols., Cambridge, 2009).

Callanan, Frank (ed.), 'John Dillon' in *Dictionary of Irish Biography* (9 vols., Cambridge, 2009).

Campbell, Christy, *Fenian Fire* (London, 2003).

Campbell, Fergus, *Land and Revolution: Nationalist Politics in the West of Ireland* (Oxford, 2005).

Campbell, Fergus, *The Irish Establishment, 1879–1914* (Oxford, 2009).

Campbell, Fergus and Varley, Tony (eds.), *Land Questions in Modern Ireland* (Manchester, 2013).

Campbell, John, *Haldane* (London, 2021).

Clare, James Tormey, *Priest and Patriot: A Short Sketch of the Life of Michael Tormey, C.C.* (Trafford, 2004).

Cole, J. A., *Prince of Spies: Henri Le Caron* (London, 1984).

Collini, Stefan, *Public Moralists, Political Thought and Intellectual Life in Britain 1850–1930* (Oxford, 1991).

Colombier-Lakeman, Pauline, 'Ireland and the Empire: The Ambivalence of Irish Constitutional Nationalism', *Radical History Review*, no. 104 (Spring 2009: special issue entitled *The Irish Question*).

Comerford, R. V., *Charles J. Kickham* (Dublin, 1979).

Comerford, R. V., *The Fenians in Context* (Dublin, 1985).

Cooke, A. B. and Vincent, J. R. (eds.), 'Herbert Gladstone, Forster and Ireland 1881–2', *Irish Historical Studies*, xviii, no. 69 (Mar. 1972).

Cooke, A. B. and Vincent, J. R., *The Governing Passion: Cabinet Government and Party Politics in Britain 1885–86* (Hassocks, 1974).

Corfe, Tom, *The Phoenix Park Murders: Conflict and Compromise in Ireland, 1879–82* (London, 1968).

Cornford, James, 'The Transformation of Conservatism in the Late Nineteenth Century', *Victorian Studies*, 7, no. 1 (1963).

Côté, Jane McL., *Fanny and Anne Parnell: Ireland's Patriot Sisters* (Dublin, 1991).

Curran, John Adye, *Reminiscences of John Adye Curran K.C.* (London, 1915).

Curtis, L. P., *Coercion and Conciliation in Ireland, 1880–1892* (Princeton, 1963).

Curtis, L. P., 'Incumbered Wealth: Landlord Indebtedness in Post-Famine Ireland', *American Historical Review*, lxxxv, no. 2 (1980).

Curtis, L. P., 'Stopping the Hunt 1881–2: An Aspect of the Irish Land War', in C. H. E. Philpin (ed.), *Nationalism and Popular Protest in Ireland* (Cambridge, 1987).

Curtis, L. P., 'Landlord Responses to the Irish Land War, 1879–87', *Éire–Ireland*, xxxviii–xxxix (2003).

Curtis, L. P., *The Depiction of Eviction in Ireland, 1845–1910* (Dublin, 2012).

Daunt, W. J. O'Neill, *A Life Spent for Ireland: From the Memoirs of O'Neill Daunt*, edited by his Daughter (London, 1896).

Davitt, Michael, *The Fall of Feudalism in Ireland, or The Story of the Land League Revolution* (London and New York, 1904).

Delany, E. and MacRaild, D. (eds.), *Irish Migration: Ethnic Identities since 1750* (London, 2005).

Dillon, William, *Life of John Mitchel* (2 vols., London, 1888).

Doherty, James, *Irish Liberty and British Democracy: The Third Home Rule Crisis 1909–1914* (Cork, 2019).

Dooley, Chris, *Redmond: A Life Undone* (Dublin, 2015).

Dooley, Terence, *The Decline of the Big House in Ireland: A Study of Irish Landed Families 1860–1960* (Dublin, 2001).

Duffy, Charles Gavan, *My Life in Two Hemispheres* (2 vols., London, 1898).

Dungan, Myles, *The Captain and the King: William O'Shea, Parnell and Late Victorian Ireland* (Dublin, 2009).

Dunlop, Andrew, *Fifty Years of Irish Journalism* (Dublin, 1911).

Dunne, T. J., 'The Political Ideology of Home Rule' (MA thesis, University College Dublin, 1972).

Ensor, R. C. K., 'Some Political and Economic Interactions in Late Victorian England', *Transactions of the Royal Historical Society*, xxxvi (1949).

Ervine, St John, *Parnell* (London, 1925).

Fair, John D., 'From Liberal to Conservative: The Flight of the Liberal Unionists after 1886', *Victorian Studies*, vol. 29, no. 2 (Winter 1986), 291–314.

Fischer, J. and Dillon, J. (eds.), *The Correspondence of Myles Dillon 1922–5* (Dublin, 1999).

Fitzpatrick, W. J., *The Life of the Very Rev. Thomas N. Burke OP* (2 vols., London, 1885).

Fleming, N. C. and O'Day, Alan (eds.), *Charles Stewart Parnell and his Times: A Biography* (Oxford, 2011).

Foner, Eric, 'Class, Ethnicity and Radicalism in the Golden Age: The Land League and Irish America', *Marxist Perspectives*, 1, no. 2 (Summer 1978).

Foster, R. F., *Charles Stewart Parnell: The Man and his Family* (Hassocks, 1977).

Foster, R. F., *Paddy and Mr Punch: Connections in Irish and English History* (London, 1993).

Foster, R. F., *The Irish Story: Telling Tales and Making It Up in Ireland* (London, 2001).

Freeden, Michael, *Liberalism Divided: A Study in British Political Thought 1914–39* (Oxford, 1986).

Garvin, J. L., *The Life of Joseph Chamberlain* (2 vols., London, 1932–3).

Gaughan, J. Anthony, *Memories of Senator Joseph Connolly* (Dublin, 1996).

Geary, Laurence M., *The Plan of Campaign* (Cork, 1986).

Gerbaudo, Paolo, *The Great Recoil: Politics after Populism and Pandemic* (London, 2021).

Golway, Terry, *Irish Rebel: John Devoy and America's Fight for Freedom* (New York, 1999).

Gordon, Peter (ed.), *Earl of Carnarvon: Political Diaries, 1857–1890* (Cambridge, 2009).

Hackett, Francis, *Ireland: A Study in Nationalism* (New York, 1918).

Haines, Robin *Charles Trevelyan and the Great Irish Famine* (Dublin, 2004).

Haldane, Richard Burdon, *An Autobiography* (London, 1929).

Hamer, F. E. (ed.), *The Personal Papers of Lord Rendel* (London, 1931).

Hamilton, Lord George, *Parliamentary Reminiscences and Reflections, 1868–1885* (London, 1916).

Hammond, J. L., *Gladstone and the Irish Nation* (London, 1938; 2nd edn., 1964).

Harrison, Henry, *Parnell Vindicated: The Lifting of the Veil* (London, 1931).

Healy, T. M., *Letters and Leaders of My Day* (2 vols., London, 1928).

Hearne, Dana and Ward, Margaret (eds.), *Anna Parnell: The Tale of a Great Sham* (Dublin, 2019).

Hogan, Daire and Maume, Patrick (eds.), *The Reminiscences of Ignatius O'Brien, Lord Chancellor of Ireland 1913–18* (Dublin, 2021).

Holland, Bernard H., *The Life of Spencer Compton, Eighth Duke of Devonshire* (2 vols., London, 1911).

Horgan, John J., *Parnell to Pearse*, ed. John Horgan (Dublin, 2009; first published 1948).

Hurlbert, W. H., *Ireland under Coercion* (Edinburgh, 1889).

Hynes, Eugene, *Knock: The Virgin's Apparition in Nineteenth-Century Ireland* (Cork, 2008).

Jackson, Alvin, *The Ulster Party: Irish Unionists in the House of Commons 1884–1911* (Oxford, 1989).

Jackson, Alvin, 'The Rivals of C. S. Parnell', in Donal McCartney (ed.), *Parnell: The Politics of Power* (Dublin, 1991).

Jackson, Alvin, *Home Rule: An Irish History, 1800–2000* (London, 2003).

Jackson, Alvin, *The Two Unions: Ireland, Scotland and the Survival of the United Kingdom 1707–2007* (Oxford, 2012).

Janis, Ely M., *A Greater Ireland: The Land League and Transatlantic Nationalism in Gilded Age America* (Wisconsin, 2015).

Jeffrey, Keith (ed.), *Irish Experiences in War* (Dublin, 1999).

Jones, D. S., *Graziers, Land Reform and Political Conflict in Ireland* (Washington, DC, 1995).

Jones, Greta, 'Catholicism, Nationalism and Science', *Irish Review*, 20 (Winter/Spring 1997).

Jones, Greta, 'Scientists and Home Rule', in D. G. Boyce and Alan O'Day (eds.), *Defenders of the Union* (London, 2001).

Jordan, Donald, 'John O'Connor Power, Charles Stewart Parnell and the Centralisation of Popular Politics in Ireland', *Irish Historical Studies*, xxv, no. 97 (May 1986).

Jordan, Donald, *Land and Popular Politics in Ireland: County Mayo from the Plantation to the Land War* (Cambridge, 1994).

Jordan, Donald, 'The Irish National League and the "Unwritten Law": Rural Protest and Nation-Building in Ireland, 1882–1890', *Past & Present*, 158 (1998).

Jordan, Jane, *Kitty O'Shea: An Irish Affair* (London, 2005).

Kane, Anne, 'The Transcendent Role of Catholic Discourse in the Irish Land War', in Fergus Campbell and Tony Varley (eds.), *Land Questions in Modern Ireland* (Manchester, 2013).

Kavanagh, Julie, *The Irish Assassins: Conspiracy, Revenge and the Murders that Stunned an Empire* (London, 2021).

Kee, Robert, *The Laurel and the Ivy* (London, 1993).

Kehoe, Elizabeth, *Fortune's Daughters* (London, 2004).

Kenna, Shane, *War in the Shadows: The Irish-American Fenians who Bombed Victorian Britain* (Dublin, 2014).

Kenna, Shane, *The Invincibles: The Phoenix Park Assassinations and the Conspiracy that Shook an Empire* (Dublin, 2019).

Kettle, A. J., *The Material for Victory: Being the Memoirs of Andrew J. Kettle*, ed. L. J. Kettle (Dublin, 1958) (from a manuscript prepared by A. J. Kettle a few years before his death in 1916).

King, Carla (ed.), *Parnell and his Island: George Moore* (Dublin, 2004).

King, Carla, *Michael Davitt: After the Land League 1882–1906* (Dublin, 2016).

King, Carla and McCormack, W. J. (eds.), *John Devoy: Michael Davitt: From the 'Gaelic American'* (Dublin, 2008).

King, D. B., *The Irish Question* (New York, 1882).

Koss, Stephen, *The Rise and Fall of the Political Press in Britain* (London, 1981).

Lane, Fintan (ed.), *Politics, Society and the Middle Class in Ireland* (Basingstoke, 2010).

Lane, Fintan and Newby, Andrew (eds.), *Michael Davitt: New Perspectives* (Dublin, 2000).

Larkin, Emmet, *The Roman Catholic Church and the Fall of Parnell* (Liverpool, 1979).

Lawless, Emily, *Ireland* (3rd edn., New York, 1923).

Lawlor, David, *Divine Right? The Parnell Split in Meath* (Cork, 2007).

Leerssen, Joep, *Parnell and his Times* (Cambridge, 2021).

Legg, Marie-Louise, *Newspapers and Nationalism: The Irish Provincial Press, 1850–82* (Dublin, 1994).

Legg, Marie-Louise (ed.), *Alfred Webb: The Autobiography of a Quaker Nationalist* (Cork, 1999).

Loughlin, J. P., Gladstone, *Home Rule and the Ulster Question, 1882–1893* (Dublin, 1986).

Lubenow, W. C., *Parliamentary Politics and the Home Rule Crisis* (Oxford, 1988).

Lucy, Henry, *A Diary of the Salisbury Parliament, 1886–1892* (London, 1892).

Lucy, Henry William, *Sixty Years in the Wilderness, More Passages by the Way* (London, 1912).

Lucy, Henry, *The Diary of a Journalist* (3 vols., London, 1920–3).

Lyons, F. S. L., 'John Dillon and the Plan of Campaign', *Irish Historical Studies*, xiv, no. 56 (September 1965).

Lyons, F. S. L., *John Dillon* (London, 1968).

Lyons, F. S. L., *Charles Stewart Parnell* (London, 1977).

Lyons, F. S. L., 'The Land War', *Irish Times*, 12 May 1979.

McCarthy, Justin, *The Story of an Irishman* (London, 1904).

McCartney, Donal (ed.), *Parnell: The Politics of Power* (Dublin, 1990).

McCartney, Donal and Travers, Pauric (eds.), *The Ivy Leaf: The Parnells Remembered* (Dublin, 2006).

McConnel, James, '"Fenians at Westminster": The Edwardian Irish Parliamentary Party and the Legacy of the New Departure', *Irish Historical Studies*, xxxiv, no. 133 (May 2004).

McConnel, James, *The Irish Parliamentary Party and the Third Home Rule Crisis* (Dublin, 2013).

McCracken, Donal P., *Inspector Mallon: Buying Irish Patriotism for a Five-Pound Note* (Dublin, 2009).

MacDonagh, Michael, *The Life of William O'Brien, the Irish Nationalist* (London, 1928).

McDonough, Terence (ed.), *Was Ireland a Colony? Economics, Politics and Culture in Nineteenth-Century Ireland* (Dublin, 2005).

McFarland, F. W., *John Ferguson (1836–1906): Irish Issues in Scottish Politics* (East Linton, 2003).

McGovern, Bryan P., *John Mitchel: Irish Nationalist, Southern Secessionist* (Knoxville, 2009).

MacKnight, Thomas, *Ulster As It Is* (2 vols., London, 1896).

Manning, Maurice, *James Dillon: A Biography* (Dublin, 1999).

Mansergh, P. N. S., *The Irish Question: 1840–1921* (London, 1965).

Marley, Lawrence, *Michael Davitt: Freelance Radical and Frondeur* (Dublin, 2007).

Martin, Ged, 'Parnell and Cambridge: The Education of an Irish Nationalist', *Irish Historical Studies*, xix (Mar. 1974).

Matthew, H. C. G., *The Gladstone Diaries*, ix (Jan. 1875–Dec. 1880) (Oxford, 1986); x (Jan. 1881–June 1883) (Oxford, 1990); xi (July 1883–Dec. 1886 (Oxford, 1990); xii (1887–91) (Oxford, 1994).

Maume, Patrick, 'Parnell and the IRB Oath', *Irish Historical Studies*, xxix, no. 115 (May 1995).

Maume, Patrick, 'An Irishwoman of Letters between Newman and Wagner, Geraldine Penrose Fitzgerald', *Proceedings of the Royal Irish Academy*, 118(c) (2019).

Maume, Patrick, 'Rebel on the Run: T. J. Quinn and the IRB/Land League Diaspora in America', ed. Jim Doan, 00–1, *Working Papers in Irish Studies* (Nova Southeastern University, Fort Lauderdale, Florida, 2000).

Maume, Patrick (ed.), *James Mullin: The Story of a Toiler's Life* (Dublin, 2000).

Maume, Patrick, 'The *Dublin Evening Mail* on Gladstone, 1868–98', in Mary Daly and K. Theodore Hoppen (eds.), *Gladstone: Ireland and Beyond* (Dublin, 2011).

Maume, Patrick, 'The *Dublin Evening Mail* and Pro-Landlord Conservatism in the Age of Gladstone and Parnell', *Irish Historical Studies*, xxvii, no. 148 (Nov. 2011).

Maume, Patrick, 'The Head Pacificator and Captain Rock: Sedition, Suicide and Honest Tom Steele', in K. Hughes and D. MacRaild (eds.), *Crime, Violence and the Irish in the Nineteenth Century* (Liverpool, 2017).

Maxwell, Sir Herbert, *Life and Times of Rt Hon. W. H. Smith MP* (2 vols., Edinburgh and London, 1897).

Mayes, Frank, *Rural Tensions in 19th Century Knock, County Mayo* (Dublin, 2021).

Meleady, Dermot, *Redmond: The Parnellite* (Cork, 2008).

Meleady, Dermot, *The National Leader* (Cork, 2013).

Meleady, Dermot (ed.), *John Redmond: Selected Letters and Memoranda 1880–1918* (Dublin, 2018).

[Menzies, Mrs Stuart], *Memories Discreet and Indiscreet by a Woman of No Importance* (London, 1917).

[Menzies, Mrs Stuart], *Further Indiscretions by a Woman of No Importance* (London, 1918).

Molloy, Margaret and Martin Sheridan, *Mayo's Favourite Son 1881–1918: A Forensic Account of an Irish NYPD Officer's Sporting Success* (Goring by Sea, 2018).

Montague, Robert, *Recent Events and the Clue to Their Solution* (London, 1886).

Moody, T. W., 'The New Departure in Irish Politics, 1878–79', in H. A. Cronne, T. W. Moody, and D. B. Quinn (eds.), *Essays in British and Irish History in Honour of James Eadie Todd* (London, 1949).

Moody, T. W., *Davitt and Irish Revolution* (Oxford, 1981).

Moody, T. W. and Hawkins, R. A. J. (eds.), *Florence Arnold-Forster's Irish Journal* (Oxford, 1988).

Morley, John, *Recollections* (2 vols., London, 1905).

Morley, John, *Miscellanies* (London, 1908).

Morris, William O'Connor, *Ireland 1798–1898* (London, 1898).

Mulvagh, Conor, *The Irish Parliamentary Party at Westminster 1900–18* (Manchester, 2016).

Murphy, Clare, 'Varieties of Crowd Activity', in Peter Jupp and Eoin Magennis (eds.), *Crowds in Ireland c.1720–1920* (London, 2000).

Murphy, James H., *Ireland's Czar: Gladstonian Government and the Lord Lieutenant of the Red Earl Spencer, 1868–86* (Dublin, 2014).

Murphy, Maura, 'Fenianism, Parnellism and the Cork Trades, 1860–1900', *Saothar*, v (May 1979).

Myers, F. H. W., *Essays: Modern* (London, 1883).

Newman, Henry, *My Campaign in Ireland* (Aberdeen, 1896).

Nic Dháibhéid, Caoimhe and Reid, Colin (eds.), *From Parnell to Paisley: Constitutional and Revolutionary Politics in Modern Ireland* (Dublin, 2010).

O'Brien, Conor Cruise, *Parnell and his Party, 1880–1890* (Oxford, 1957).

O'Brien, R. Barry, *The Life of Charles Stewart Parnell, 1846–1891* (2 vols., London, 1899).

O'Brien, William, *Recollections* (London, 1905).

O'Brien, William, *An Olive Branch in Ireland, and Its History* (Dublin, 1910).

O'Brien, William, *Evening Memories* (Dublin and London, 1920).

O'Brien, William, *The Irish Revolution* (Dublin, 1923).

O'Brien, William, *The Parnell of Real Life* (London, 1926).

O'Brien, William and Ryan, Desmond (eds.), *Devoy's Post-Bag, 1871–1928* (2 vols., Dublin, 1948–53).

Ó Broin, Leon, *The Prime Informer: A Suppressed Scandal* (Dublin, 1971).

O'Callaghan, Margaret, *British High Politics and a Nationalist Ireland: Criminality, Land and the Law under Forster and Balfour* (Cork, 1994).

Ó Cathaoir, Brendan, *John Blake Dillon, Young Irelander* (Dublin, 1990).

Ó Cathaoir, Brendan (ed.), *The Diary of Elizabeth Dillon* (Dublin, 2019).

O'Connor, T. P., *The Parnell Movement* (London, 1887).

O'Connor, T. P., *Charles Stewart Parnell: A Memory* (London, 1891).

O'Connor, T. P., 'Charles Stewart Parnell', *Kilkenny Moderator*, 1 Feb. 1899.

O'Connor, T. P., *Memoirs of an Old Parliamentarian* (2 vols., London, 1929).

O'Connor, T. P., *Reactions to Irish Nationalism, 1865–1914* (Dublin, 1987).

O'Connor, T. P., *Charles Stewart Parnell* (Dublin, 1998).

O'Day, Alan, *Parnell and the First Home Rule Episode* (Dublin, 1986).

O'Day, Alan, *Irish Home Rule* (Manchester, 1998).

O'Day, Alan, *Charles Stewart Parnell* (Dublin, 2012).

O'Donnell, F. H., *A History of the Irish Parliamentary Party* (2 vols., London, 1910).

O'Donoghue, Martin, *The Legacy of the Irish Parliamentary Party* (Liverpool, 2019).

O'Donoghue, Martin, 'Faith and Fatherland? The Ancient Order of Hibernians, Northern Nationalism and the Partition of Ireland', *Irish Historical Studies*, xlvi, no. 169 (2022).

O'Grady, Standish James, *The Crisis in Ireland* (Dublin and London, 1882).

O'Hara, Bernard, *Davitt* (Westport, 2006).

O'Leary, Patricia, *The Gentleman Saint: A Pilgrimage to Oxford, Dublin & Rome in the Footprints of St John Henry Newman* (Leominster, 2020).

O'Malley, William, Parnell obituary, *Tuam Herald*, 17 Oct. 1891.

O'Neill Daunt, W. J., *A Life Spent for Ireland* (London, 1896).

O'Shea, John Augustus, *Roundabout Recollections* (London, 1892).

O'Shea, Katharine (Mrs C. S. Parnell), *Charles Stewart Parnell: His Love Story and Political Life* (2 vols., London, 1914).

O'Sullivan, Niamh, *Aloysius O'Kelly: Art, Nation, Empire* (Dublin, 2010).

Pahl, Liz (ed.), *Signe Toksvig's Irish Diaries 1926–37* (Dublin, 1994).

Parnell, J. H., *Charles Stewart Parnell: A Memoir* (New York, 1914).

Parnell, J. H., *Charles Stewart Parnell: A Memoir* (London, 1916).

Parry, Jonathan, *The Rise and Fall of Liberal Government in Victorian Britain* (New Haven, 1993).

Paseta, Senia (ed.), *Uncertain Futures: Essays in Honour of Roy Foster* (Oxford, 2016).

Philpin, C. H. E. (ed.), *Nationalism and Popular Protest in Ireland* (Cambridge, 1987).

Pigott, Richard, *Recollections of an Irish National Journalist* (Dublin, 1883).

Plumb, J. H. (ed.) *Studies in Social History: A Tribute to G. M. Trevelyan* (London, 1955).

Powell, Enoch, 'Kilmainham—the Treaty that Never Was', *Historical Journal*, xxi, no. 4 (1978).

Power, John O'Connor, *The Anglo-Irish Quarrel: A Plea for Peace* (London, 1886).

Quinn, James, *John Mitchel* (Dublin, 2008).

Regan-Lefebvre, Jennifer (ed.), *For the Liberty of Ireland at Home and Abroad: The Autobiography of J. F. X. O'Brien* (Dublin, 2010).

Reid, Colin, *The Lost Ireland of Stephen Gwynn: Irish Constitutional Nationalism and Cultural Politics, 1864–1950* (Manchester, 2011).

Robbins, Sir Alfred, *Parnell: The Last Five Years* (London, 1926).

Roberts, Andrew, *Salisbury: Victorian Titan* (London, 1999).

Robinson, Sir John, *Fifty Years of Fleet Street* (London, 1904).

Robinson, Lennox (ed.), *Lady Gregory's Journals* (Dublin, 1946).

Roche, Brian and Aengus, Karen, *No Ornamental Member: A Life in Politics: John Roche MP, 1848–1914* (London, 2017).

Russell, Sir Charles, *Speech before the Parnell Commission* (London, 1889).

Russell, Edward, *That Reminds Me* (London, 1899).

Shaw, J. J., *Mr Gladstone's Two Irish Policies: 1868 and 1886* (Belfast, 1888).

Sheehy Skeffington, F., *Michael Davitt* (London, 1908).

Short, K. R. M., *The Dynamite War: Irish American Bombers in Victorian Britain* (Dublin, 1979).

Sillard, P. A., *The Life of John Mitchel* (Dublin, 1901).

Sullivan, A. M., *Old Ireland: Reminiscences of an Irish KC* (London, 1927).

Sullivan, M. F., *Ireland of Today: The Causes and Aims of Irish Agitation* (Philadelphia, 1881).

Sullivan, T. D., *Recollections of Troubled Times in Irish Politics* (Dublin, 1905).

Swift MacNeill, J. G. *What I Have Seen and Heard* (Boston, 1925).

Swords, Liam, *A Dominant Church: The Diocese of Achonry 1818–1960* (Dublin, 2004).

Thorold, Algar Labouchere, *The Life of Henry Labouchere* (London, 1913).

Tierney, Mark, *Croke of Cashel: The Life of Archbishop Thomas William Croke, 1832–1902* (Dublin, 1976).

*The Times, Reprint of Proceedings under the Special Commission Act* (London, 1890).

*The Times, The Parnellite Split: or, The Disruption of the Irish Parliamentary Party* (London, 1891).

Townend, Paul, *The Road to Home Rule: Anti-Imperialism and the Irish National Movement* (Madison, 2016).

Townshend, Charles, *The Partition: Ireland Divided* (London, 2021).

Tully, Jasper, 'How Parnell was Entangled with Mrs O'Shea', *Roscommon Herald*, 6 Jan. 1940.

Tynan, P., *The Irish National Invincibles and Their Times* (London, 1894).

Varley, Tony, 'Gaining Ground, Losing Ground: The Politics of Land Reform in Twentieth-Century Ireland', in Fergus Campbell and Tony Varley (eds.), *Land Questions in Modern Ireland* (Manchester, 2013).

Vaughan, W. E., *Landlords and Tenants in Mid-Victorian Ireland* (Oxford, 1994).

Vincent, J. R., *Gladstone and Ireland* (London, 1979).

Vincent, J. R. (ed.), *A Selection from the Diaries of Edward Henry Stanley, 15th Earl of Derby, between September 1869 and March 1878* (London, 1994).

Vincent, J. R. (ed.), *The Diaries of Edward Henry Stanley, 15th Earl of Derby, between 1878 and 1893* (London, 1994).

Whelehan, Niall, *The Dynamiters: Irish Nationalism and Political Violence in the Modern World* (Cambridge, 2020).

Whelehan, Niall, *Changing Land: Diaspora Activism and the Irish Land War* (New York, 2021).

Wilson, Trevor (ed.), *Political Diaries of C. P. Scott* (London, 1970).

Wyse Power, Jennie (ed.), *Words of the Dead Chief: Charles Stewart Parnell* (Dublin, 2009; first published 1892), with introduction and notes by Donal McCartney.

Young, G. M., *Victorian England: Portrait of an Age* (Oxford, 1936).

# INDEX

*For the benefit of digital users, terms that are indexed as spanning two pages (e.g., 52–53) may, on occasion, appear on only one of those pages.*

# INDEX